# Unrestrained Killings and the Law

A Comparative Analysis of the
Laws of Provocation and Excessive Self-Defence
in India, England and Australia

STANLEY YEO

DELHI
OXFORD UNIVERSITY PRESS
CALCUTTA  CHENNAI  MUMBAI
1998

*Oxford University Press, Great Clarendon Street, Oxford OX2 6DP*

*Oxford New York*
*Athens Auckland Bangkok Calcutta*
*Cape Town Chennai Dar es Salaam Delhi*
*Florence Hong Kong Istanbul Karachi*
*Kuala Lumpur Madrid Melbourne Mexico City*
*Mumbai Nairobi Paris Singapore*
*Taipei Tokyo Toronto*

and associates in

*Berlin Ibadan*

*ISBN 0 19 564400 X*

Typeset by Wordgraphics, Kalkaji, New Delhi 110 019
Printed at Wadhwa International, New Delhi 110 020
and published by Manzar Khan, Oxford University Press
YMCA Library Building, Jai Singh Road, New Delhi 110 001

For my daughter
Jen-li

# Preface

This work comprises a bringing together of a decade of my research and thinking in relation to the defences of provocation and excessive self-defence. Parts of the discussion have previously appeared in the following articles: 'Lessons on Provocation under the Indian Penal Code', 41 *International and Comparative Law Quarterly* 615 (1992); 'Applying Excuse Theory to Excessive Self-Defence' in S. Yeo (ed.), *Partial Excuses to Murder* (1990, Federation Press); 'Rethinking "Good Faith" in Excessive Private Defence', 30 *Journal of the Indian Law Institute* 443 (1988); and 'The Demise of Excessive Self-Defence in Australia', 37 *International and Comparative Law Quarterly* 348 (1988). I am grateful to the publishers of these articles for their permission to reproduce portions of them here.

The work places the discussions contained in these articles in the wider context of a comparative study of the defences under Indian, English and Australian laws. In so doing, it takes the discussions further and infuses them with new ideas. These, together with the coverage of several features of the defences not previously discussed, culminate in a set of model provisions which make for just and workable laws.

I hope that this study will persuade those Indian lawmakers who still tend to look to the English law for guidance to view the Indian Penal Code as constituting a superior set of laws to the English one. At the same time, I trust that English and Australian lawmakers will be convinced of the great benefit to be gained by studying the Code.

I am grateful to the Law Foundation of New South Wales for covering part of the production cost of this work, and to Robyn Dummermuth for typing assistance and to Shalini Sinha for so patiently bringing the work to its final form.

This work has been written with reference to the laws of India, England and Australia as at November, 1997.

Stanley Yeo
Lismore, 1997

# Contents

Table of Cases                                              xiii
Table of Statues                                            xx

**Chapter 1**
**About this Work**                                          1
1. Unrestrained Killings                                     1
2. Comparativism                                             2
3. Aims and Coverage                                         4
4. Conclusion                                                6

**Chapter 2**
**Provocation**                                              9
1. Introduction                                              9
2. Definitions of Provocation                               10
   A. The English Definition                                11
   B. The Australian Definition                             11
   C. The Indian Definition                                 13
3. Provocative Conduct                                      14
   A. Words Alone as Provocation                            15
   B. Cumulative Provocation                                21
   C. Provocation in the Defendant's Presence               27
   D. Self-Induced Provocation                              32
   E. Lawful Acts as Provocation                            40

4. Actual Loss of Self-Control                                         46

   A. A Subjective Condition                                        46

   B. The Uncertain Nature of Lost Self-Control                    47

   C. The Underlying Emotions of Lost Self-Control                 49

   D. The Requirements of a Sudden Loss of Self-Control           51

5. The Ordinary Person Test                                             56

   A. An Objective Test                                            56

   B. Characteristics of the Ordinary Person                       59

   C. A Comparative Evaluation of the Test                         63

6. The Response to the Provocation                                      93

   A. Rage versus Loss of Self-Control                             94

   B. The Reasonable Relationship Rule                             101

   C. The Modal Rule                                               106

7. Conclusion                                                           113

**Chapter 3**

**Excessive Self-Defence**                                             117

1. Introduction                                                         117

2. Excessive Self-Defence under Indian Law                              119

   A. The Defence and its Role in
Relation to the General Plea of Self-Defence                            119

   B. A Preliminary Difficulty of Interpretation                  123

   C. Resolving the Difficulty                                    126

   D. Poor Adherence to the Requirements of the
Exception                                                              131

3. Excessive Self-Defence under English Law                             134

   A. Previous Judicial Recognition of the Defence               134

   B. Current Judicial Rejection of the Defence                   135

   C. Law Reform Proposals Favouring the Defence                  139

4. Excessive Self-Defence under Australian Law                          141

   A. Previous Judicial Recognition of the Defence               141

B. The Facts of and Decision in *Zecevic*     145

C. The Case for Abolishing Excessive Self-Defence     148

D. The Case for Maintaining Excessive Self-Defence     154

E. Legislation and Law Reform Proposals
Favouring the Defence     160

F. Recognition of Excessive Self-Defence under
Irish Law     165

5. The Place of Excessive Self-Defence in the Law of
Self-Defence and in the Criminal Justice Process     167

A. Justification, Excuse and Self-Defence     167

B. A Partial and Not a Full Defence     170

C. A Partial Defence and Not a Sentencing Factor     171

6. Conclusion     174

**Chapter 4**

**Improving the Law**     **176**

1. Provocation     176

2. Excessive Self-Defence     182

**Appendices**     **186**

I. Indian Provisions on Private Defence     186

II. South Australian Provisions on Defence of
Person and Property     190

III. English Law Commission Provisions on
Public and Private Defence     193

**Bibliography**     **196**

**Index**     **204**

# Table of Cases

Abdul Aziz v Emperor AIR 1933 Pat 508: 126
Abdul Majid v State, 1963 (2) Cr LJ 631: 19, 87, 91, 112
Abdul Majid v State, AIR 1961 All 538: 91
Abdulla v Emperor AIR 1932 Lah 369: 17
A-G for Northern Ireland v Gallagher [1963] AC 349: 33
Ahmed Din v Emperor, AIR 1927 Lah 194: 124
Aktar v State AIR 1964 All 262: 19, 47, 48, 87, 88, 105
Amarjit Singh v State 1970 Cr LJ 835: 19
Ammupujare v Emperor 1942 Cr LJ 753: 129
Appuhamy v R (1952) 53 New LR 313: 96
Atma Ram v State 1967 Cr LJ 1697: 90
Atma Ram v State AIR 1967 Punj 508: 20
Attorney-general (Ceylon) v Perera [1953] AC 200: 9, 10, 96, 155
Bala Saheb v State 1984 Cr LJ 1041: 112
Balasahab v State 1984 Cr LJ 1014: 19
Baljit Singh v State (1976) 4 Scc 590: 132
Beckferd v R [1988] IAC 130: 162, 168
Beddar v DPP [1954] 2 All ER 801: 59, 60
Bennet v Dopke [1973] VR 239: 144
Bhadur v Emperor 1935 Cr LJ 939: 27
Boya Munigadu V R (1881) ILR 3 Mad 33: 25
Chanan Khan v Emperor, 1944 Cr LJ 595: 31
Chhay (1994) 72 A Crim RI: 47, 48, 50, 53
Cook v Cook (1987) 61 ALJR 25: 7, 31
Da Costa v R [1968] 118 CLR 186: 103
Dhanno Khan v State, 1957 Cr LJ 498: 111
Dhira v R (1877) Unrep Cr C122: 48
Dinabandhu Ooriya v Emperor AIR 1930 Cal 199: 85
Dinnah v Emperor AIR 1948 Lah 117: 125
Dohariya v State 1956 Cr LJ 70: 121-2
DPP v Camplin [1978] 2 All ER 168: 36, 59, 61, 63, 64, 67, 68, 70, 71, 75, 86
Edwards v R [1973] AC 648: 34, 37, 38, 40

Emperor v Muzaffar Hussain AIR 1944 Lah 97: 126
Empress v Khogayi ILR (1879) 2 Mad 122: 17, 27
Faid (1983) 2 CC (3d) 513: 154
Falla [1964] VR 78: 10
Gandaram Taria v State 1982 Cr LJ 1229: 90
Ghansham Dass v State 1979 Cr LJ 28: 126
Ghasi Ram v State AIR 1952 Bhopal 25: 125
Ghulam Mustafa Gahno v Emperor AIR 1939 Sind 182: 85, 91
Girdhari Lal v Crown (1940) 42 Pun LR 45: 18
Gohra v Emperor (1890) Pr No 7 of 1890: 32
Halloway's Case Cro Car 131 (1929): 108
Hugget's Case Kel 59 (1666), 84 ER 1082: 42
Holmes v Director of Public Prosecutions [1946] AC 588: 15, 16, 17, 18,
    19, 108, 110, 111, 155
Hussein v Emperor AIR 1939 Lah 471: 20
In re V Padavachi 1972 Cr LJ 1641: 91
In re Barkatulla [1887] PR No 32 of 1887, 65-6: 10
In re Fakirappa, 1971 Cr LJ 951: 87
In re Mala Narayana 1962 (i) Cr LJ 394: 39
In re Murugian (S) AIR 1957 Mad 514: 25
In re Ponthala Narisi Reddi 1914 Cr LJ 447: 129
In re Whittaker 1882, AWN 172: 127
In re Elumalai, 1977 Cri LJ (Notes) 20: 20
Ives [1970] I QB 208: 10
Jabarula v Poore (1989) 68 NTR 26: 83
Jabbar Dar v State, Cr LJ 1179 (1955): 125
Jaipal Kunbi v Emperor, 1922 AIR Nag 141: 124
Jamis v R (1952) 53 New LR 401: 96-7
Jamu Majhi v State, 1989 Cr LJ 753: 87
Johnson v R (1976) 136 CLR 619: 10, 56, 101, 102, 103, 109, 110
Kadir Baksh v Emperor 1910 Cr LJ 699: 54
Kanhaiya Lal v State AIR 1952 Bhopal 21: 39
Kartik Bag v State 1985 Cr LJ 888: 90
Keshoram Bora v State (1978) 2 SCC 407: 133
Khogayi v Emperor ILR (1879) 2 Mad 122: 25
Krishnan Nair v State (1965) Kerala LT 150: 91, 105
Kusta Balsu Kandnekar v State 1936 Cr LJ 662: 39
Lal v Emperor 1946 Cr LJ 809: 128
Latchmi Koeri v State AIR 1960 Pat 62: 129
Laxman v State 1989 Cr LJ 1714: 126
Lee Chun-Chuen v R (1963) AC 220: 10, 102, 155
Lochan v Emperor ILR 8 All 635: 39
Luc Thiet Thuan v R [1996] 2 All ER 1033: 23, 65, 69

Madan Mohan Pandey v State AIR 1991 SC 769: 133
Madhavan v State, AIR 1966 Kerala 258: 87
Madi Adma v State, (1969) 35 Cuttack LT 336: 90
Mahomed Syedol Ariffin v Yeoh Ooi Gark, AIR 1916 PC 242: 130
Mahmood v State, AIR 1961 All 538: 57, 91
Mammum v Emperor AIR 1917 Lah 347: 124
Mancini v Director of Public Prosecutions [1942] AC I: 56, 101, 102, 103
Mani Pradhano v Empress (1882) I Weir 306: 25
Mansa Ram v State 1975 Cr LJ 1772: 19, 90
Martindale [1966] 1 WLR 1564: 9
Masciantonio v R (1995) 69 ALJR. 598: 60, 61, 75, 80, 82, 94, 110, 111
McHale v Watson (1966) 115 CLR 199: 78
McManus (1985) 2 NSWLR 448: 151
Mehra v Emperor AIR 1934 Lah 103: 39
Memon Yakubbhai Janmohmed v State 1989 Cr LJ 1843: 133
Moffa v R (1977) 138 CLR 601: 16, 17, 18, 42, 79
Mohammad Ali v Emperor AIR 1964 Lah 278: 17
Mohinder Pal Jolly v State AIR 1979 SC 577: 126, 133
Morgan v Colman (1981) 27 SASR 334: 151
Munney Khan v State AIR 1971 SC 1491: 128
Nanavati v State AIR 1962 SC 605: 14, 18, 25–6, 30, 40, 47, 51, 54–5, 57,
    85, 89, 105, 112
Narbahadur Darjee v State AIR 1965 Assam and Nagaland 89: 105
Nga Mya Maung v Emperor AIR 1936 Rang 472: 17
Nga Paw Yin v Emperor, AIR 1936 Rang 40: 87, 89
Nga Saw Maung v Emperor AIR Rang 466: 19
Nga Sein Myint v Emperor AIR 1937 Rang 4: 25
Nokul v Emperor 7 WR (Cr) 27: 18
Noukar Mouledino v Emperor, AIR 1937 Sind 212: 90
Nyo Hla Aung v Emperor 1910 Cr LJ 477: 46
Onkornath Singh v State (1973) 3 SCC 276: 133
Padmeshwar Phukan v State 1971 Cr LJ 1595: 121
Palmer v R [1971] AC 814: 135, 136–7, 138, 141, 144, 145, 148, 149, 150
    156, 157, 174
Pancham v Emperor AIR 1947 Oudh 148: 87
Parichatt v State, AIR 1972 SC 535: 125
Parker v R (1963) 111 CLR 610: 24, 37, 43, 48, 53
Parker v R [1964] 111 CLR 665: 10, 24, 25, 77
Pearson's Case (1835) 2 Lew CC 216: 28
Perera v R (1952) 53 NLR 193: 98
Philips v R [1969] 2 AC 130: 48, 102, 109
Po Mye v R, AIR 1940 Rang 129: 126, 130
Potharaju v Emperor, AIR 1932 Madras 25: 20

R (1981) 28 SASR 321: 43, 47

R v Acott [1997] I All ER 706: 16, 36

R v Ahluwalia [1992] 4 All ER 889: 22, 52, 65, 71

R v Alexander (1913) 9 Cr App R 139: 68, 72

R v Ali [1989] Crim LR 736: 69

R v Allwood (1975) 18 A Crim R 120: 36-7

R v Arden [1975] VR 449: 29, 30, 31

R v Asbury (1986) Crim LR 258: 162

R v Bailie [1995] 2 Cr App R 31: 36, 52

R v Biggin [1920] I KB 213: 137

R v Bourne 5 C & P 120 (1831) 172 ER 903: 41, 42

R v Bozikis [1981] VR 587: 144

R v Brown [1972] 2 QB 229: 102

R v Brown Leach 148 (1776): 30

R v Bufalo [158] VR 363: 142

R v Clarke [1991] Crim LR 383: 108

R v Clegg [1995] 2 WLR 80 138, 139, 141

R v Cook, Cro Car 537 (1640), 79 ER 1063: 118, 135, 137

R v Croft (1981) 3A Crim R 307: 48-9

R v Croft [1981] I NSWLR 126: 75

R v Davies [1975] I All ER 890: 22

R v Dincer [1983] VR 460: 75

R v Doughty (1986) 83 Cr App R 319: 41

R v Dryden [1995] 4 All ER 987: 65

R v Duffy [1949] I All ER: 11, 22, 47, 52, 56, 101, 102

R v Dutton [1979] 21 SASR 356: 75, 79

R v Ellor (1920) 15 Cr App R41: 15

R v Enright [1961] VR 663: 57, 142

R v Fennell [1970] 3 WLR 513: 136

R v Fisher 8 C & P 182 (1837): 27, 28, 30, 32

R v Fricker (1986) 23 A Crim R 147: 30

R v Gauthier (1943) 29 Cr App R 113: 102

R v Gillman (1995) 76 A Crim R 553: 160

R v Gladstone Williams (1983) 78 Cr App R 276: 162

R v Haley (1959) 76 WN (NSW) 550: 142

R v Hassin [1963] Crim LR 852: 138

R v Hayward (1833) 6 Car & P 157: 47–8

R v Hill (1980) 3 A Crim R 357: 24, 62, 77

R v Howe (1958) SASR 95: 117, 149, 150, 151, 154

R v Humphreys [1995] 4 All ER 1008: 65

R v Humphries [1995] 4 All ER 1008: 22-3

R v Hutton (1986) 20 Crim R 315: 30

R v Jeffery (1967) VR 467: 24, 25, 47

R v Jimmy Balir (1951-1976) NTJ 633: 83
R v Johnson [1989] Crim LR 738: 36
R v Kelly (1848) 2 Car and Kir 814: 28
R v Kenney [1883] 2 VR 470: 30)
R v Kincaid (1983) 33 SASR 552: 151
R v Kirkham (1837) 8 C & P 115: 85
R v Kontinnen and Runjanjic 1991 53 A Crim R 362: 53
R v Lawson and Forsythe (1986) VR 515: 151
R v Lesbini [1914] 3 KB 116: 68, 72
R v Letenock (1917) 12 Cr App R 221: 30
R v Lord Morley 6 St Tr 769: 15
R v Mason Fost 132, 168 ER 66 (1756): 33
R v Mawgridge J Kel 119 (1707), 84 ER 1107: 15, 41, 42, 108
R v McCarthy [1954] 2 QB 105: 102
R v McCarthy [1992] 2 NZLR 550: 65
R v McDonald (1951–1976) NTJ 186: 83
R v McGregor [1962] NZLR 1068: 64
R v McInnes [1971] I WLR 1600: 137, 141, 148, 150, 153, 174
R v McManua (1985) 2 NSWLR 448: 144
R v Mekay [1957[ VR 560: 118, 142
R v Minehan [1973] I NSWLR 659: 103
R v Morhall [1995] 3 WLR 330: 23, 58, 59, 64, 65, 66, 68
R v Muddarubba (1951–1976) NTJ 317: 83
R v Mungatopi (1919) 57 A Crim R 341: 84
R v Nelson (1951–1976) NTJ 327: 83
R v Newman [1948] VLR 61: 36
R v O'Neill [1982] VR 150: 75
R v Olasiuk (1973) 6 SASR 225: 144
R v Palmer [1913] KB 29: 15
R v Patience 8 C & P 775 (1837), 173 ER 338: 118, 135, 137
R v Patipatu (1951–1976) NTJ 18: 83
R v Peisley (1990) 54 A Crim R 42: 30, 48, 50
R v Punchirala (1924) 25 New LR 458: 26
R v Quartly (1986) II NSWLR 332: 27, 29
R v R [1981] 28 SASR 321: 11–12, 24, 29, 42, 53
R v Radford (1985) 20 A Crim R 388: 37
R v Rowley 12 Cox 145 (1871): 15
R v Scott [1997] Crim LR 597: 22
R v Scriva (No. 2) [1951] VLR 298: 43–4
R v Selten (1871) II Cox CC 674: 33
R v Shannon (1980) 71 Cr App R 192: 163
R v Thornton (1992) I All ER 306: 71
R v Tikos (No. I) [1963] VR 285: 142, 144

R v Trounson [1991] 3 NZLR 690: 79

R v Tsigos (1964) NSWR 1607 [1964]: 103

R v Turner [1962] VR 30: 142

R v Turner [1975] I All ER 70: 52

R v Viro [1978] 141 CLR 88: 142, 144, 145–7, 149-50, 151, 152 154-5, 156, 158-60, 182, 186

R v Voukelatos [1990] VR 1: 37

R v Walker (1969) 53 Cr App R 196: 102

R v Wardrope [1960] Crim LR 770: 30

R v Webb (1977) 16 SASR 309: 43, 79

R v Weston (1879) 14 Cox CC 346: 137

R v Whalley 7 C & P 245 (1835), 173 ER 108: 118, 135, 137

R v Welsh (1869) II Cox CC 336: 85

R v White [1988] I NZLR 122: 31

R v Williams (Gladstone) [1963] 78 Cr App. R 276: 168

R v Wilson [1955] I WLR 493: 136

Ram Lal v Emperor AIR 1928 Oudh 15: 130

Rama Yeshwant Kamat v State 1978 Cr LJ 1843: 125

Raman Raghavan v State 1968 Cr LJ 255: 125

Rafiq v State 1979 AIR SC 1179: 126

Romano (1984) 36 SASR 283: 61, 75

Roshdi v PP [1994] 3 SLR 282: 129

Sabal Singh v State AIR 1978 SC 1538: 124

Sadhu Singh v State (1969) Cr LJ 1183: 87

Sampat Singh v State AIR 1969 SC 956: 133

Saraj Din v Emperor, 1934 Cr LJ 306: 111

Sarju Din v Emperor AIR 1934 Lah 600: 18

Sarwan Singh v State 1954 Cr LJ 1505: 111

Soharab v Emperor AIR 1924 Lah 450: 85

Shyama Charan v State AIR 1969 All 61: 10, 39, 111

Sreckovic v R [1973] WAR 85: 109

State v Bhand Jusub Mamad, 1982 Cr LJ 1691: 87, 105

State v Kamalaksha, 1978 Cr LJ 290: 40, 111

State v Mullan, 1993 Cr LJ 1512, 1514: 20–1

State v Satish Sangma AIR 1954 Ass 56: 121, 125

Stingel v R (1990) 171 CLR 312: 60, 62, 70, 75, 76, 77–8, 80, 82

Sudan Government v Mohamed Adam Onour (1963) SJLR 157: 127, 130

Sundaramurthy v State AIR 1990 SC 2007: 126

Tara Chand v State AIR 1917 SC 1891: 132

Terry [1964] VR 248: 29

The People (A-G) v Dwyer [1972] IR 416: 151, 165–6, 183

Ulla Mahapatra v R AIR 1905 Ori 261: 17, 48

Upendra Mahakud v State, 1985 Cr LJ 1767: 111, 112

Van Den Hoek v R (1986) 161 CLR 158: 50, 53, 154
Yasin Sheikh v Empress, 12 WR (Cr) 68 (1869): 112
Zecevic v DPP (Vic) (1987) 71 ALR 641: 142–3, 145-8, 150–1 152, 153,
    156, 165, 166, 174, 182

# Table of Statutes

## Australia

Criminal Law Consolidation Act (1936) SA: 160–5, 169
Criminal Law Consolidation (Self-Defence) Amendment Act 1997 (SA)
- s 15(1): 161, 190
- s 15(2): 161, 190
- s 15(A)(1): 161, 191
- s 15(A)(2): 161–2, 191–2
- s 15(1)(a): 162, 190
- s 15(2)(a): 162, 190
- s 15A(1)(a): 162–3, 190
- s 15A(2)(a): 162-3, 192
- s 15(1)(b): 163, 190
- s 15A(1)(c): 163, 191
- s 15A(1)(b): 163, 191
- s 15A(2)(b): 163, 192
- s 15A(3): 192
- s 15 (4): 162, 192

## New South Wales

Crimes Act 1900
- s 19A: 171
- s 23: 12, 13, 17, 25, 29, 37, 38, 44, 54, 57, 111, 114, 172, 176, 185
- s 23(2): 25n.58
- s 23(2)(a): 37
- s 23(2)(b): 57
- s 23(3): 104

## Victoria

Crimes Act 1958
- s 3: 171
- s 318: 164n.171

## England

Criminal Law Act 1967
- s 3(1): 138

# India

Indian Penal Code
  s 39: 21
  s 79: 45
  s 96: 186
  s 97(1): 119, 186
  s 97(2): 119, 128
  s 98  : 186
  s 99(1): 187
  s 99(2): 187
  s 99(3): 187
  s 99(4): 120, 187
  s 100: 120, 168, 187–8
  s 101: 188
  s 102: 188
  s 103: 120, 139, 143, 163, 188
  s 103(1): 188
  s 103(2): 188
  s 103(3): 188
  s 103(4): 122, 188
  s 104: 188–9
  s 105: 162, 189
  s 106: 189
  s 300 Exception 1: 13, 18, 25, 39, 45–6, 85, 97, 98, 117
  s 300 Exception 2: 119, 121–2, 123–4, 125, 126–30, 131–4, 143, 163,
     164, 177, 179–80, 184

# New Zealand

Crimes Act
  s 109(2)(a): 79

# Chapter 1

# About this Work

## 1. Unrestrained Killings

A student of criminal law would encounter difficulty identifying a familiar theme from the title of this work, since the expression 'unrestrained killings' is unusual. Nevertheless, it is one that bears out the nature of the two partial defences to murder of provocation and excessive self-defence, which are the subjects of this study. A person who has killed while under a loss of self-control induced by the provocation of the deceased has clearly failed to exercise restraint in her or his reaction to the provocation. The same may be said of a person who, by killing her or his assailant, has applied more force than is reasonable and necessary by way of self-defence.

The law does not tolerate these types of unrestrained killings, as is indicated by its refusal to grant the accused a complete acquittal despite the fact that the deceased was partly at fault in having provoked or attacked the accused in the first place. However, in order to differentiate these cases from one where a person had killed another without any fault whatsoever on the part of the deceased, the law permits the accused to escape liability for the most heinous offence of murder. Instead, the accused is convicted of the still serious but lesser offence of manslaughter (under English and Australian laws) or culpable homicide not amounting to murder (the equivalent of manslaughter under the Indian Penal Code).

Although much has been written about the defence of provocation, there are few studies that have compared the defence and its operation among jurisdictions such as India, England and Australia which share a common legal history and have similar criminal justice systems. As for the defence of excessive self-defence, there is scant literature on the subject, let alone comparative studies. This is primarily because the defence has not been recognized in most jurisdictions with the exception of India and Eire and, for a brief period, by Australian common law. This work seeks to fill the gap in the academic literature on the defence.

## 2. Comparativism

This work comprises a comparative study of the nature, operation and theoretical underpinnings of the partial defences to murder of provocation and excessive self-defence. If an explanation were needed as to the value of a comparative analysis of these defences, the following observation should suffice:

> The primary aim of comparative law, as of all sciences, is knowledge. If one accepts that legal science includes not only the techniques of interpreting the texts, principles, rules and standards of a national system, but also the discovery of models for preventing or resolving social conflicts, then it is clear that the method of comparative law can provide a much richer range of model solutions than a legal science devoted to a single nation, simply because the different systems of the world can offer a greater variety of solutions than could be thought up in a lifetime by even the most imaginative jurist who has been corralled in his [or her own] system. Comparative law is an 'ecole de verite' which extends and enriches the 'supply of solutions' and offers the scholar of critical capacity the opportunity of finding the 'better solution' for his [or her] time and place.[1]

The concluding words of this quotation acknowledge the differing social contexts in which the laws of a particular jurisdiction are devised, interpreted and applied. Clearly, a scholar seeking to compare the laws of various jurisdictions will need to bear this in mind. That said, however, as the main part of the quotation asserts, there is much value in engaging in a formalistic examination of and comparison with the laws of various jurisdictions. The jurisdictions selected for study are India, England and the Australian common law jurisdictions of New South Wales, South Australia and Victoria.[2]

[1] Zweigert, K. and H. Kotz, *Introduction to Comparative Law*, Vol. 1, 2nd edn, p. 15 (1987).
[2] The Irish version of the defence, which is closely similar to the one that used to be part of Australian common law, will be briefly discussed in this work.

With regard to the reasons for this choice of jurisdictions for comparison, generally speaking, the English common law comprises the basis of Australian common law. This explains why I have confined my study of Australian law to the common law jurisdictions of that subcontinent.[3] Although New South Wales has a statutory definition of the defence of provocation, that definition has embodied much of the common law.[4] Furthermore, any improvements contained therein have been largely the result of dissatisfaction with the common law. As for excessive self-defence, the few early English cases supporting its recognition are of dubious standing and the current English judicial thinking is firmly against recognizing the defence. Accordingly, the Australian judges who did recognize the defence did not take their cue from the English common law. Nevertheless, a comparative study of the English and Australian common laws on the matter is both permissible and desirable because the laws on self-defence of these jurisdictions share a common legal history and are the same in many other respects.

As for the Indian law, since both the defences of provocation and excessive self-defence are contained in a criminal code, it may at first sight not be sufficiently suitable for comparison with English and Australian common laws. However, the Indian Penal Code 1860 lends itself particularly well to comparative study as it was a carefully reasoned and crafted effort by leading English jurists of the day as to what the criminal law of England ought to have been. Thus, James Fitzjames Stephen, the celebrated English jurist, was led to remark:

> [The original draft of the Indian Penal Code and revisions made to it] are both imminently creditable to their authors; and the result of their successive efforts has been to reproduce in a concise and even beautiful form the spirit of the law of England; the most technical, the most clumsy, and the most bewildering of all systems of criminal law ... [The] draft gives the substance of the criminal law of England, down to its minute working details, in a compass which by comparison with the original may be regarded as almost absurdly small.[5]

[3]Queensland, Tasmania, Western Australia and the Northern Territory all have Criminal Codes.
[4]See *Crimes Act* 1900 (NSW), Section 23 and reproduced in this work on p. 12.
[5]Trevelyan, G.O., *The Life and Letters of Lord Macaulay*, Vol. I, p. 417 (1920). The original draft was published in 1832 and was followed by several other drafts until the final one was proclaimed in 1860. For a historical survey, see

This work will show that the Indian Penal Code provisions on provocation and excessive self-defence are not perfect. However, Stephen's observation remains true that they were decided advancements of the English law at the time.

In more recent years, the Indian courts have found it necessary to expand upon and clarify certain aspects of the law of provocation as prescribed by the Code. As a result of the shared legal history with English law, the Indian courts have turned to the case authorities of that jurisdiction for instruction. Justice Vivian Bose, of the Supreme Court of India, was thus led to say:

> Because of the tremendous impact the English common law has had on Indian laws, even the codified ones, judges resort freely to English decisions for the elucidation of points that are obscure and many references to English decisions will be found even in the Supreme Court of India. Judges and lawyers here feel and hope that this inter-play of thought will continue for a long time because it is a healthy thing and will prevent stagnation, as codified laws tend to become outworn without the constant stimulus of fresh ideas. As the Secretary-General of the International Commission of Jurists said recently, judges and lawyers in India resort freely to English decisions and would welcome a like recognition by the English courts of their own contributions to legal thought.[6]

Unfortunately, as this work will show, the hope expressed in the concluding part of this comment has yet to be fulfilled. This is to the detriment of the English law on provocation and excessive self-defence because much of the Indian law on these defences has a stronger claim to achieving justice than the English law.

## 3. Aims and Coverage

This work has five interrelated aims:

- to present the existing laws and latest law reform proposals of England, Australia and India on the defences of provocation and excessive self-defence;
- to assess the extent to which these laws and proposals reflect legal principle and notions of justice;
- to confirm the correctness of specific aspects of the defences

---

Patra, A.C., 'An Historical Introduction to the Indian Penal Code', 3 *Journal of the Indian Law Institute* 351 (1961).
[6]'The Migration of the Common Law: India', 76 *Law Quarterly Review* 59, p. 63 (1960).

through the commonality of the laws of England, Australia and India;

- to reject certain aspects of the defences found in the laws of some of the jurisdictions studied through legal argument, comparative analysis and appeal to notions of justice;
- to draw up model provisions which contain all the best features of the defence formulations examined.

The main method used to achieve these aims is comparative analysis of English, Australian and Indian laws. As noted, the laws of these jurisdictions are conducive to comparison because they have the same origins, namely, the English criminal law of the nineteenth century. Indeed, the common law tradition shared by English and Australian jurisdictions remains strong to this day. Indian criminal law is on a different footing because it is embodied in the Indian Penal Code. However, the drafters of the Code took their cue from the common law of England at the time and prescribed a set of laws which they saw as an improvement on English law. It is also noteworthy that for a considerable period of time in both Australia and India, members of the judiciary and the legal profession learnt their law either in England or in locally based institutions which heavily subscribed to the teaching of English law. The result was that the English common law continued for many decades to exert a strong influence in these jurisdictions. The ensuing discussion will show that this was particularly the case when the Indian judges came to interpret the provision on provocation contained in the Code.

It follows that England is the appropriate jurisdiction with which to commence discussion of the law governing the defence of provocation. Due to its continued common links with English law, Australia is the next jurisdiction for study. Indian law is examined last because it is codified and is a good model for legislative prescription of the defence of provocation. Furthermore, having noted various deficiences in English and Australian laws, the reader will be better able to appreciate the ways in which the Indian provision on provocation helps to resolve those deficiencies.

Chapter 2 covers the defence of provocation. Certain aspects of the defence have been selected for careful examination. To facilitate comparison, the same headings and their sequence of appearance will be adopted wherever possible and frequent cross-references will be made to related discussions.

As for the plea of excessive self-defence, the most appropriate jurisdiction to begin my discussion with is India, since it not only has recognized the plea for the longest period of time, but is the only one of the jurisdictions studied to continue doing so. English law will be the next to be examined even though it has given the defence the least support. The reason for choosing to discuss the English law ahead of the Australian law is because the latter grew out of the former. Furthermore, the leading Australian cases which recognized the defence did so out of a conscious and reasoned departure from the English judicial view of the defence. Accordingly, it would serve the reader better to be first presented with the English law, which would enhance her or his appreciation of the Australian law.

Chapter 3 deals with the defence of excessive self-defence. Unlike provocation, which has long been recognized as a defence in all the three jurisdictions studied, excessive self-defence is not part of English law and was recognized by Australian law for only a short period. In contrast, the Indian Penal Code has, ever since its inception, contained a provision on excessive self-defence. Given these very different responses to excessive self-defence, the basic question needs to be tackled as to whether or not it should be a defence. Accordingly, the discussion takes a different thrust to the one on provocation. As explained above, it would be helpful to commence with the Indian law on excessive self-defence, followed by the English law, and to conclude with the Australian law.

The fourth and final chapter of this work contains draft provisions on provocation and excessive self-defence which could serve as models for reform of the laws of India, England and Australia. These model provisions have been drafted to incorporate all the desirable aspects of the defences found in the laws of the jurisdictions studied. At the same time, the provisions have sought to discard those aspects of the defences which have been found to be unjust or contrary to legal principle.

## 4. Conclusion

A major theme which runs through the whole of this work is that the English common law has generally lagged behind the Australian and Indian laws in respect of the two defences. I venture to suggest that an explanation for this is that the English judges have, for many years, been very reluctant to embrace solutions arrived at by foreign courts tackling identical legal problems. This has meant that the English judges have denied themselves the opportunity of tapping freely into the 'supply of solutions' offered by these courts. Fortunately, recent years have seen a gradual softening of this judicial reluctance with the result that significant improvements have been made to the English law.

In contrast, Australian judges have always made the effort to review the English approach to a problem and then to decide on the appropriateness or otherwise of the English position. This stance is evident in the following comment by the High Court of Australia:

> The history of this country and of the common law makes it inevitable and desirable that the courts of this country will continue to obtain assistance and guidance from the learning and reasoning of United Kingdom courts just as Australian courts benefit from the learning and reasoning of other great common law courts. ... [T]he precedents of other legal systems are not binding and are useful only to the degree of the persuasiveness of their reasoning.[7]

As may be expected from such a comparative approach to legal problem-solving, the Australian courts often arrive at decisions which are superior to the English law on the matter or are at least equal to that law.

In the above passage, the High Court of Australia spoke only of obtaining guidance and assistance from the common law courts. This would automatically exclude the Indian courts pronouncing upon the Indian Penal Code. At first glance, such exclusion is entirely understandable. However, on further reflection, the suggestion is made that the Australian courts could have benefited materially from studying Indian decisions on those Code provisions which were improvements upon the English common law. The provisions on provocation and excessive self-defence would fall within this description. Had the Australian courts carried out such a study of Indian decisions in some recent cases, they would have been greatly assisted in arriving at the best solutions (from the viewpoint of justice and practicability) to major legal problems.

While the Indian provisions on provocation and excessive self-defence have certain positive features which Australian courts might learn from, they contain some other aspects which have been found wanting. Indian judges have usually circumvented these defects in

---

[7] *Cook v Cook* (1987) 61 ALJR 25, p. 31.

the Code provisions by clever innovation. However, there have been occasions when a better approach could have been taken by following the line of Australian courts on the same matter. Unfortunately, the tendency of the Indian judges has been to look solely to the English common law for guidance and assistance. In doing so, the Indian courts have found the English law a poor source of sound ideas.

All told, while it would seem that the English law has most to gain from a comparative study such as this, both the Australian and Indian laws also stand to benefit from it. This confirms the concluding words of the quotation cited earlier that comparative law 'offers the scholar of critical capacity the opportunity of finding the "better solution" for his [or her] time and place.'[8]

---

[8]See the quotation in the main text accompanying n. 1 above.

# Chapter 2

# Provocation

## 1. Introduction

It will not be feasible for a work of this nature to conduct a comparative study of the whole breadth of the law of provocation of England, Australia and India. Particular aspects of provocation have been selected because they confirm the hypothesis that the Indian Penal Code is a progressive and innovative instrument containing many legal principles which English and Australian lawmakers have only recently arrived at after a lengthy process of change, deliberation and uncertainty.

Comparing the laws of provocation of England and Australia is especially justified as Australian law has taken its cue directly from English common law. Similarly, but to a far lesser extent, Indian judges have read several English common law principles into the Indian Penal Code provision on provocation. These judges have, however, proceeded to modify these principles to suit local conditions, particularly taking into account the heterogeneous and multicultural communities residing on the Indian subcontinent. It can be readily imagined that this feature of the Indian law will be instructive to England and Australia, which societies have, through the influx of migrants in recent decades, been transformed into increasingly heterogeneous and multicultural societies.

The defence of provocation operates in basically the same way in all three jurisdictions because of its shared roots in English common law. Thus, it has been held in these jurisdictions that the fact that the accused had a murderous intention is not inconsistent with the invocation of the defence.[1] Indeed. the defence needs to

---

[1]For England, see *Martindale* [1966] 1 WLR 1564, p. 1566; *Lee Chen Chuen*

be considered only after a prima facie case of murder has been established against the accused.[2] Likewise, the defence operates in the jurisdictions to reduce a charge of murder to the lesser one of manslaughter (for England and Australia) or culpable homicide not amounting to murder (for India). The common origin of the defence has also resulted in the test for provocation being the same in these jurisdictions. The test is a dual one, requiring the provocative conduct to be such as (1) actually causes in the accused a sudden and temporary loss of self-control as the result of which he or she kills the provoker and (2) might have caused a reasonable (or ordinary) person to suffer such a loss of self-control and, having lost self-control, to act as the accused did.[3] Finally, the underlying rationales for the defence of provocation are the same for all three jurisdictions under consideration. These are the law's limited concession to the accused's human frailty in losing self-control when provoked or alternatively a recognition of the victim's contributory fault in provoking the accused.[4]

## 2. Definitions of Provocation

Before considering selected aspects of provocation it would be useful to present various formulations (both judicial and statutory) of the

---

*v R* [1963] AC 220, p. 227. For Australia, see *Parker v R.* [1964] 111 CLR 665, p. 681; *Falla* [1964] VR 78, p. 80; *Johnson v R* (1976) 136 CLR 619, p. 663. For India, see *In re Barkatulla* (1887) PR No 32 of 1887, 65–6; *A-G of Ceylon v Perera* [1953] AC 200 interpreting the provision on provocation in the Sri Lankan Penal Code, which is identical to the Indian provision.

[2] *Ives* [1970] 1 QB 208, pp. 214–6; *Johnson* (1976) 136 CLR 619, pp. 633, 640; *Shyama Charan v State* 1969 AIR All 61, p. 64.

[3] The first is the subjective condition of the defence, while the second is the objective condition. An alternative description is to call the first the factual question and the second the evaluative question: see Williams, G., *Textbook of Criminal Law*, 2nd edn, p. 527 (1983). The comparative analysis of the law of provocation conducted in this chapter will cover these two questions.

[4] These two rationales of provocation have been frequently discussed in terms of whether the defence should be regarded as an excuse or a justification. For example, see Dressler, J., 'Provocation: Partial Justification or Partial Excuse'? 51 *Modern Law Review* 467 (1988); McAuley, F., 'Provocation: Partial Justification, Not Partial Excuse', in S. Yeo (ed.), *Partial Excuses to Murder*, p. 19 (1991). For a discussion of justifications and excuses, see this work pp. 167–8.

defence from England, Australia and India. These formulations will be frequently referred to in the ensuing comparative study.

## A. *The English Definition*

Beginning with English law, the following definition by Justice Devlin in *R v Duffy* was described by the English Court of Appeal in the same case as a 'classic direction' on the common law defence:

> Provocation is some act, or series of acts, done by the dead man to the accused, which would cause in any reasonable person, and actually causes in the accused, a sudden and temporary loss of self-control, rendering the accused so subject to passion as to make him or her for the moment not master of his mind.[5]

The common law rule was modified under Section 3 of the *Homicide Act* 1957 (UK). The provision reads:

> Where on a charge of murder there is evidence on which the jury can find that the person charged was provoked (whether by things done or by things said or by both together) to lose his self-control, the question whether the provocation was enough to make a reasonable man do as he did shall be left to be determined by the jury; and in determining that question the jury shall take into account everything both done and said according to the effect which, in their opinion, it would have on a reasonable man.

This provision assumes the existence of the defence and amends it in certain respects. But it leaves intact the operation of the common law defence and retains the dual test of provocation contained therein.

## B. *The Australian Definition*

In Australia, the common law defence is found in the States of South Australia and Victoria. The other Australian States and Territories have statutory formulations of the defence. The following definition was given by Chief Justice King in the South Australian Court of Criminal Appeal case of *R v R*:

> The killing of one person by another with intention to kill or do serious bodily harm is murder. Such a killing may, however, be reduced to manslaughter if the killing results from a sudden and temporary loss of self-control on the part of the killer which is brought about by acts or

[5][1949] 1 All ER 932.

words of the deceased amounting in law to provocation. To amount in law to provocation the acts or words must satisfy the following tests: (1) they must be done or said by the deceased to or in the presence of the killer; (2) they must have caused in the killer a sudden and temporary loss of self-control rendering the killer so subject to passion as to make him for the moment not master of his mind; (3) they must be of such a character as might cause an ordinary person to lose his self-control to such an extent as to act as the killer has acted.[6]

Among the Australian statutory formulations of the defence, the one contained in the New South Wales *Crimes Act* 1900 is the most progressive.[7] It embodies many common law principles but differs from the common law in certain respects. Section 23 of the Act provides in part as follows:

23. (1) Where, on the trial of a person for murder, it appears that the act or omission causing death was an act done or omitted under provocation and, but for this subsection and the provocation, the jury would have found the accused guilty of murder, the jury shall acquit the accused of murder and find the accused guilty of manslaughter.

(2) For the purposes of subsection (1), an act or omission causing death is an act done or omitted under provocation where—

(a) the act or omission is the result of a loss of self-control on the part of the accused that was induced by any conduct of the deceased (including grossly insulting words or gestures) towards or affecting the accused; and

(b) that conduct of the deceased was such as could have induced an ordinary person in the position of the accused to have so far lost self-control as to have formed an intent to kill, or to inflict grievous bodily harm upon the deceased, whether that conduct of the deceased occurred immediately before the act or omission causing death or at any previous time.

(3) For the purpose of determining whether an act or omission causing death was an act done or omitted under provocation as provided by subsection (2), there is no rule of law that provocation is negatived if—

[6](1981) 28 SASR 321, pp. 321–2.

[7]The current formulation was drawn up in 1982 and adopted many of the recommendations of a New South Wales Task Force on domestic violence. As we shall see, the changes were aimed at better accommodating the experiences of battered women who kill. For an evaluation of the 1982 formulation, see Weisbrot, D., 'Homicide Law Reform in New South Wales', 6 *Criminal Law Journal* 248 (1982).

(a) there was not a reasonable proportion between the act or omission causing death and the conduct of the deceased that induced the act or omission;

(b) the act or omission causing death was not an act done or omitted suddenly; or

(c) the act or omission causing death was an act done or omitted with any intent to take life or inflict grievous bodily harm.

As with the English legislation, the New South Wales provision keeps basically intact the operation of the common law defence and also the dual test for provocation.

## C. The Indian Definition

Under the Indian law, the defence of provocation appears as Exception 1 to Section 300 of the Indian Penal Code (that is, the provision defining the offence of murder).[8] The Exception reads:

> Culpable homicide is not murder if the offender while deprived of the power of self-control by grave and sudden provocation causes the death of the person who gave the provocation or caused the death of another person by mistake or accident.

The above exception is subject to the following provisos:

(1) that the provocation is not sought or voluntarily provoked by the offender as an excuse for killing or doing harm to any person;

(2) that the provocation is not given by anything done in obedience to the law, or by a public servant in the lawful exercise of the powers of such public servant;

(3) that the provocation is not given by anything done in the lawful exercise of the right of private defence.

*Explanation*: Whether the provocation was grave and sudden enough to prevent the offence from amounting to murder is a question of fact.[9]

---

[8]Exception 1 is one of five exceptions to Section 300, which reduces the offence of murder to culpable homicide not amounting to murder. The other exceptions are excessive self-defence (which will be considered in the next chapter), excessive use of force by public servants in the exercise of their duties, sudden fight (or chance-medley), and consent by a person above the age of eighteen years.

[9]The Exception goes on to state that the defence is unavailable in three instances: in cases of self-induced provocation, where the provocation was given by public servants in the lawful exercise of their powers, and by a person acting in self-defence. There then follow several factual illustrations.

In *Nanavati v State*, the leading Indian case on provocation, the Supreme Court of India read into the Exception the following propositions:

(1) The test of 'grave and sudden' provocation is whether a reasonable man, belonging to the same class of society to which the accused belongs, and placed in the situation in which the accused was placed, would be so provoked as to lose his self-control.

(2) In India, words [or][10] gestures may also, under certain circumstances, cause grave and sudden provocation to an accused so as to bring his act within the first Exception to Section 300 of the Indian Penal Code.

(3) The mental background created by the previous act of the victim may be taken into consideration in ascertaining whether the subsequent act caused grave and sudden provocation for committing the offence.

(4) The fatal blow should be clearly traced to the influence of passion arising from that provocation and not after the passion had cooled down by lapse of time, or otherwise giving room and scope for premeditation and calculation.[11]

Some of the concepts in these propositions were culled from English common law, most notably the reasonable person test, which does not appear on the face of Exception 1 to Section 300. On the other hand, several of these propositions vere not part of the English common law at the time *Nanavati* was decided.

With these definitions in mind, we shall now consider certain selected aspects of the defence.

## 3. Provocative Conduct

This part evaluates the response of English, Australian and Indian lawmakers to the following issues: (a) whether words alone can ever amount to provocation; (b) whether provocation can be cumulative; (c) whether the defendant must have been present when the provocation was made; (d) whether self-induced provocation

---

[10]The original word is 'and' which appears to be an oversight or typographical error. Earlier on in its judgement, the court (at p. 628) posed the issue as being one of 'whether words or gestures unaccompanied by acts can amount to provocation.'

[11]AIR 1962 SC 605, p. 630 per Justice Subba Rao, who delivered the judgement of the court.

can support the defence; and (e) whether the provocative conduct
must comprise unlawful acts.

## A. Words Alone as Provocation

### 1. The English law

The leading case on the matter under English common law is
*Holmes v Director of Public Prosecutions*.[12] Prior to this decision, it
was well established that insults calculated to arouse the hearer's
resentment could not amount to provocation which reduced a
charge of murder to manslaughter.[13] Insults were distinguished from
words used to convey information of a fact, the most common
instance being a confession of adultery by a spouse to the other.
These confessions were recognized as amounting to provocation.[14]
The House of Lords in *Holmes* reaffirmed the view that insults
alone could not amount to provocation.[15] Additionally, the court
rejected the previous case authorities on confessions of adultery,
holding that these confessions without more could not constitute
provocation.[16] If this had been all that was said, *Holmes* would
have stood as clear authority for the proposition that words alone,
whether in the form of insults or confessions of adultery, would
not suffice for the defence of provocation. However, the House
went on to opine that words alone could not amount to provocation
'save in circumstances of a most extreme and exceptional
character'.[17] Another description used by the court for these severe
cases was that the words were of a 'violently provocative character'.[18]
Unfortunately, no example was given of these circumstances and
none is to be found elsewhere in English common law.

---

[12][1946] AC 588.
[13]*R v Lord Morley* 6 St Tr 769, p. 771; *R v Mawgridge,* J Kel 119, 84 ER
1107 (1707); Hale, M., *The History of the Pleas of the Crown,* Vol. I, p. 456
(1736); Hawkins, W., *A Treatise of the Pleas of the Crown,* Vol. I, 8th edn,
ch. 13, s. 33 (1795); East, E.H., *A Treatise of the Pleas of the Crown,* Vol. I,
p. 233 (1803).
[14]The leading case was *R v Rowley* 12 Cox 145 (1871) and applied in *R v
Palmer* [1913] KB 29 and *R v Ellor* (1920) 15 Cr App R 41.
[15][1946] AC 588, p. 599.
[16]Ibid.
[17]Ibid., p. 600.
[18]Ibid.

Section 3 of the *Homicide Act* 1957 (UK) has clarified[19] the common law by stipulating that 'things said' alone may be sufficient provocation if the jury should be of the opinion that they would provoke a reasonable person.[20] Thus, insults and informative words such as a confession of adultery without more can amount to provocation. This legislative modification of the common law recognizes that an absolute rule against words founding a case of provocation is not consonant with the 'benignity of the law' in its concession to 'human infirmity'.[21] Furthermore, such a rule draws 'an arbitrary distinction between words and conduct which is insupportable in logic'.[22]

## 2. The Australian law

With regard to Australian common law, the leading case on the subject is the High Court of Australia decision in *Moffa v R*.[23] A majority of the judges invoked the proposition in *Holmes* that words alone cannot amount to provocation unless they were of a most extreme and exceptional character.[24] As for a confession of adultery without more, no clear majority decision was reached.[25] The position regarding a confession of adultery appears to be as follows: for the confession to suffice, it must be accompanied by insults which

---

[19]Given the allowance in *Holmes* for words of an extreme and exceptional character to amount to provocation, it is not strictly correct to assert that Section 3 abrogated the common rule that words alone can never constitute provocation. Cf. Lanham, D., 'Provocation and the Requirement of Presence', 13 *Criminal Law Journal* 133, p. 141 (1989).

[20]For a recent reconfirmation of this position, see the House of Lords case of *R v Acott* [1997] 1 All ER 706, p. 710.

[21]Foster, M., *Crown Law, Discourse II on Homicide,* 2nd edn, p. 255 (1776).

[22]*Moffa v R* (1977) 138 CLR 601, p. 620 per Justice Mason.

[23](1977) 138 CLR 601.

[24]Ibid., p. 605 per Chief Justice Barwick; p. 616 per Justice Gibbs; p. 619 per Justice Stephen; and p. 620 per Justice Mason. The remaining judge, Justice Murphy, at p. 624 rejected the restriction on words placed by *Holmes*.

[25]Justice Gibbs and Stephen refused to recognize this form of provocation: ibid., at pp. 616 and 619 respectively. Chief Justice Barwick and (by implication) Justice Murphy were prepared to do so: pp. 605, 624. Justice Mason preferred to leave the issue open: p. 620. Cf. Fisse, B., *Howard's Criminal Law,* 5th edn, p. 92 (1990), which read *Moffa* as saying that a mere confession of adultery cannot amount to provocation. By contrast, Lanham, op. cit., n. 19, p. 142, read the case as saying that it could.

combine with the confession to make the provocative words extreme or exceptional in character. For example, in *Moffa*, the court was prepared to leave provocation to the jury because the deceased woman had boasted of wholesale promiscuous sexual conduct with men in the neighbourhood and called the accused (a Southern Italian) a 'black bastard'.

The New South Wales *Crimes Act* stipulates that 'grossly insulting words' alone can amount to provocation.[26] The adjective 'grossly' seems merely to reflect the common law pronouncement in *Holmes* and *Moffa* that the words have to be sufficiently violent or extreme. Hence, it would appear that the provision disallows a mere confession of adultery. This stands in contrast to the English provision which would allow for such a confession to suffice as provocation. It is submitted that the English law is the preferred position. Although there will be many cases where a mere confession of adultery should not permit launching into a homicidal attack, there will be others which could excuse such a response. Take, for instance, the case of D, a member of an ultra-religious and conservative patriachical community, who is suddenly informed by his wife of her infidelity. The affront to his honour and indeed his whole system of values and beliefs could conceivably be so great that the mere confession without more should be permitted to support a plea of provocation.

## 3. The Indian law

Under Indian law, it is well established that words alone, whether in the form of insults or providing information such as a confession of adultery, can amount to provocation. There were some early cases[27] which subscribed to the English common law restriction on words, a course which one Indian commentator has attributed to 'the inexplicable desire to bring Indian law in line with English law'.[28] Fortunately, a preponderance of early Indian case authorities[29] chose to deviate from the English rule, with the Indian

---

[26]Section 23(2)(a).

[27]For example, see *Abdulla v Emperor* AIR 1932 Lah 369; *Empress v Khogayi* ILR (1879) 2 Mad 122; *Mohammad Ali v Emperor* AIR 1946 Lah 278; *Ulla Mahapatra v State* AIR 1950 Ori 261.

[28]Kelkar, R., 'Provocation as a Defence in the Indian Penal Code', 5 *Journal of the Indian Law Institute* 319, p. 338 (1963).

[29]For example, see *Nga Mya Maung v Emperor* AIR 1936 Rang 472; *Sarju*

Supreme Court's proposition in *Nanavati*[30] serving as the final authoritative statement on the matter. The court there declared that words without accompanying conduct of any sort can amount to grave provocation under Exception 1 to Section 300.[31] It arrived at this ruling by examining the notes of the framers accompanying their 1837 draft of the Penal Code. The relevant portion of the notes is as follows:

> His Lordship in Council will remark on one important distinction between the law as we have framed it and some other systems. Neither the English law nor the French Code extends any indulgence to homicide which is the effect of anger, excited by words alone. ...
>
> We greatly doubt whether any good reason can be assigned for this distinction. It is an indisputable fact, that gross insults by word or gesture have as great a tendency to move many persons to violent passion as dangerous or painful bodily injuries; nor does it appear to us that passion as excited by insult is entitled to less indulgence than passion excited by pain. On the contrary, the circumstances that a man resents an insult more than a wound is anything but a proof that he is a man of peculiarly bad heart. It would be a fortunate thing for mankind if every person felt an outrage which left a stain upon his honour more acutely than an outrage which had fractured one of his limbs. If so, why should we treat an offence produced by the blamable excess of a feeling which all wise legislators desire to encourage, more severely than we treat the blamable excess of feelings certainly not more respectable?[32]

The sound reasoning and accord with human reality contained in the above passage would have been among the underlying reasons for the English legislature's eventual resolve to recognize words alone as amounting to provocation. It is noteworthy that this occurred only in 1957, a hundred and twenty years after the views of the code framers were expressed. The comparison with Australian common law yields an even longer time-period, since *Moffa* was decided only in 1977.

An Indian decision contains an interesting discussion of that part of the judgement in *Holmes* where it was held that words

---

*Din v Emperor,* AIR 1934 Lah 600; *Nokul v Emperor,* 7 WR (Cr) 27; *Girdhari Lal v Crown* (1940) 42 Pun LR 45.

[30] AIR 1962 SC 605.

[31] Ibid. p. 630.

[32] Macaulay, T.B., J.M. Macleod, G.W. Anderson and F. Millett, *The Indian Penal Code as originally framed in 1837 with Notes,* Note M, Reprint, p. 144 (1888) and cited by the Supreme Court in *Nanavati* AIR 1962 SC 605, p. 628.

could constitute provocation provided they were of a 'violently provocative character'. In *Aktar v State*, Justice Beg surmised that by postulating a 'violent character', the House of Lords was thinking of 'menacing words holding for the threats of violence, so that the action of the person provoked would be in the nature of defensive action in anticipation of some attack'.[33] This explanation finds some support from *Holmes* itself where the House had expressly excluded 'mere words ... being menace of immediate bodily harm' from the rule that insults could not constitute provocation.[34] In Justice Beg's view, the English judicial reluctance to recognize mere words was due to the common historical development shared in that jurisdiction by provocation and self-defence.[35] This being the case, the Indian courts were entirely correct in refusing to incorporate the English bias against provocative words into Exception 1 as its framers had clearly conducted their drafting exercise without being bound by any historical encumbrances contained in English common law.

It may be helpful to present some incidents where provocative words unaccompanied by conduct have been regarded by the Indian courts as amounting to provocation. In one case, V was an unemployed and drug-addicted father who had demanded money from D, his son, making his demand imperative even if the money had to be raised by prostituting D's mother.[36] In another case, in the course of a quarrel, V had hurled filthy abuses at D including an insinuation that he had once committed an unnatural offence with a pigeon.[37] In a third case, D was very devoted to V, his wife, who was eight months pregnant. During a conversation, D had asked V if she had been cohabitating with a mutual friend and she had answered in the affirmative, whereupon D stabbed her to death with a dagger which he possessed at the time.[38] As a final example, V had gone to D's shop in an aggressive mood and, as the court described it, 'showered virulent abuses' at D.[39] There

---

[33] AIR 1964 All 262, p. 268.

[34] [1946] AC 588, p. 599.

[35] AIR 1964 All 262, pp. 265–7.

[36] *Amarjit Singh v State*, 1970 Cr LJ 835.

[37] *Abdul Majid v State*, 1963 (2) Cr LJ 631.

[38] *Nga Saw Maung v Emperor*, AIR 1937 Rang 466. For another case where a confession of adultery has been recognized, see *Balasaheb v State* 1984 Cr LJ 1014.

[39] *Mansa Ram v State*, 1975 Cr LJ 1772. For other case examples where words

being no evidence that V's verbal abuse had been provoked by D, the court accepted D's plea of provocation and reduced his charge of murder to culpable homicide not amounting to murder. Even without elaborating upon the particular characteristics of the accused which had caused them to regard the words as grave provocation,[40] the brief facts given in these examples should sufficiently suggest to the reader that they were cases deserving of some mitigation.

A case in which words alone were held to be insufficient provocation was the Kerala High Court decision in *State v Mullan*.[41] The facts were that V was in love with a girl whose mother was living in adultery with D. When D questioned V regarding his intentions in respect of the girl, V retorted by stating that if D could have her mother, he could also marry her daughter. D lost his self-control upon hearing this and stabbed V to death. The court rejected the plea of provocation on the ground that:

> the appellant cannot assume such moral indignation or protective attitudes. He who lived in adultery, which the Indian Penal Code makes punishable, cannot adopt a virtuous stance and seek justification for his criminal act of killing one who wanted to marry Janeky's daughter. The posture adopted by the appellant, of moral indignation, approximates to the analogy of the devil quoting the scriptures.[42]

With respect, this reasoning pays little or no attention to the defence's rationale of providing limited concession to human frailty in the face of provocation. As another Indian court has correctly asserted concerning the operation of the defence, 'one cannot supply considerations of social morality to a purely psychological problem'.[43] Indeed, on a differing view of the facts in *Mullan*, since V's retort was directed at a particularly sensitive and personal aspect of D's life, it had the effect of increasing the gravity of the

---

alone have been held to be sufficient provocation, see *In re Elumalai*, 1977 Cri LJ (Notes) 20; *Atma Ram v State*, AIR 1967 Punj 508; *Hussein v Emperor*, AIR 1939 Lah 471.

[40]The relevance of an accused's personal characteristics and circumstances to the gravity of the provocation will be discussed below: see pp. 87–8.

[41](1993) Cr LJ 1512.

[42]Ibid., p. 1514. Adultery remains a crime under Section 497 of the Indian Penal Code.

[43]*Potharaju v Emperor*, AIR 1932 Madras 25. The court in that case ruled that where D had seen a woman in the arms of another man, the fact that she was D's mistress and not his wife did not make any difference for the purposes of the defence of provocation.

provocative words towards D. If it was thought that V's retort should not be regarded as provocation in law, the court could have reached that result by holding that D, by confronting V in the first place about the girl, had voluntarily provoked V as an excuse for doing harm to V. This would take the case outside the purview of the Exception owing to the operation of the first proviso to the Exception.[44]

## B. Cumulative Provocation

### 1. The English law

Since the crux of the defence is a loss of self-control brought about by provocation, the accused must be able to point to a 'triggering' provocative incident which caused the loss. This much is uncontroversial in all the three jurisdictions under consideration. What was contentious under English law until relatively recently was the relevance of previous provocation. On one view, previous provocative incidents merely served as the *setting* for the triggering incident and therefore strictly did not constitute provocation. The opposing view was that these previous incidents amounted to relevant provocative conduct together with the triggering incident. The latter view recognizes that the past provocative incidents can have a cumulative effect on the accused with the last (perhaps trivial) incident being, as it were, 'the straw which broke the camel's back'.

There are case authorities supporting both views under English common law.[45] In favour of the first, Justice Devlin's direction to the jury in *Duffy* contains the following passage:

> Severe nervous exasperation or a long course of conduct causing suffering and anxiety are not by themselves sufficient to constitute provocation in law. Indeed the further removed an incident is from the crime the less it

---

[44]The proviso requires that 'the provocation is not sought or voluntarily provoked by the offender as an excuse for killing or doing harm to any person'. Section 39 of the Code defines 'voluntarily' as follows: 'A person is said to cause an effect "voluntarily" when he causes it by means whereby he intended to cause it, or by means which, at the time of employing those means, he knew or had reason to believe to be likely to cause it.' The proviso is discussed in this work at pp. 39–40.

[45]See Wasik, M., 'Cumulative Provocation and Domestic Killing', *Criminal Law Review* 29 (1982).

counts. A long course of cruel conduct may be more blameworthy than a sudden act provoking retaliation, but you are not concerned with blame here—the blame attaching to the dead man. You are not standing in judgement of him.[46]

Likewise, in *R v Davies,* the Court of Appeal expressed dissatisfaction with part of the trial judge's direction in the following terms:

The judge. ... left the question of provocation to the jury on the footing that they could review the whole course of conduct of W right through that turbulent year of 1972 and decide whether H had been provoked to kill her within Justice Devlin's test. ... [T]hat was really too generous a direction.[47]

The judicial stance taken in *Duffy* and *Davies* is consistent with earlier English law which spelt out a list of provocative conduct, all of which was closely related in point of time to the accused's loss of self-control.[48]

The trend in more recent English decisions, however, has been to embrace the concept of cumulative provocation. The case of *R v Ahluwalia,* in which a battered woman had killed her husband after years of physical violence at his hands, has a good example of a direction which treats past provocative incidents as relevant provocation. The Court of Appeal in that case summarized the effect of the trial judge's direction as follows:

The jury can have been in no doubt that it was necessary for them to consider the history of this marriage, the misconduct and ill-treatment of the appellant by her husband as part of the whole story, culminating in what happened on the [fatal] night.[49]

Another recent example is *R v Humphries,* a case involving D, a girl with a history of cutting her wrists to gain attention, who had been taken in by V to live with him.[50] On the day of the killing, V had returned to the house to find that D had cut her wrists again. He taunted her with the remark that she had not done a very good job of doing so, whereupon D fatally stabbed him. On appeal against her conviction for murder, the Court of Appeal ruled that the trial judge was mistaken in directing the jury to

[46][1949] 1 All ER 932, p. 933 .
[47][1975] 1 All ER 890, p. 897.
[48]Stephen, J.F., *Digest of the Criminal Law,* 3rd edn, Arts 224 and 225(1883).
[49][1992] 4 All ER 889, p. 898.
[50][1995] 4 All ER 1008. See also *R. v Scott* [1997] Crim LR 597.

consider only V's taunt about D's wrist-slashing when deciding whether she had been provoked. The court held that the whole history of their relationship was relevant including past violence and V's taking in another girl.

Recently, the House of Lords in *R v Morhall* affirmed this stance when it said:

> In an appropriate case, it may be necessary to refer to other circumstances affecting the gravity of the provocation to the defendant which do not strictly fall within the description 'characteristics' as for example the defendant's history or the circumstances in which he [or she] is placed at the relevant time.[51]

The Judicial Committee of the Privy Council in *Luc Thiet Thuan v R* was even more explicit when it said that:

> it may be open to a defendant to establish provocation in circumstances in which the act of the deceased, though relatively unprovocative if taken in isolation, was the last of a series of acts which finally provoked the loss of self-control by the defendant and so precipitated his extreme reaction which led to the death of the deceased.[52]

It is submitted that the view accommodating cumulative provocation should be preferred over the one which regards previous provocative incidents as only the setting of the last triggering event. In metaphorical terms, these previous incidents are like wounds which have partially healed but are reopened by the most recent incident. Eventually a time comes when the accused is so worn down by the cumulative effect of the whole series of provocative conduct that he or she suddenly reacts to the latest incident by losing self-control.

Section 3 of the English *Homicide Act* appears to endorse this position. The provision requires the jury to take into account everything both done and said according to the effect which in their opinion it would have on a reasonable person. A jury may well consider that provocative conduct which had occurred over a lengthy time-period would have a cumulative effect on a reasonable person and had such an effect on the accused. It follows that 'everything both done and said' which may in fact have contributed to the accused's loss of self-control is provocative conduct for the purposes of the section.[53]

---

[51][1995] 3 WLR 330, p. 336.
[52][1996] 2 All ER 1033, p. 1047.
[53]Smith, J.C. and B. Hogan, *Criminal Law,* 7th edn, pp. 357–8 (1992).

## 2. The Australian law

The Australian courts have generally been strong subscribers to the concept of cumulative provocation. The High Court of Australia case of *Parker v R* is a good example.[54] D was a farm worker who took his wife and children to work in a sheep station. V was single and over a period of six weeks courted D's wife, eventually persuading her to leave with him. On the day of departure, D had remonstrated with V who responded by laughing at him and making insulting references to his wife and expressing the coarsest intentions towards her. V and D's wife then left and some twenty minutes later D drove in a car after them. D deliberately drove the car into them causing serious injuries. He then bashed and stabbed V to death. The court held that although D's reaction must contain an element of suddenness, the breakdown of self-control may be gradual under the cumulative effect of an unalleviated pressure arising from a series of provocative incidents, as had occurred in this case.[55]

The approach taken in *Parker* is encapsulated in the following remark by Justice Smith in *R v Jeffrey*, a Victorian Court of Criminal Appeal case involving a wife who had killed her husband who had been violent to her over many months:

> Where there has been a sustained course of cruelty which has built up to, and ultimately precipitated, an explosion of passion and loss of self-control, the whole chain of events, and not merely the concluding episode is relevant to the question of adequacy of provocation.[56]

Nevertheless, there are some Australian decisions which appear to confine provocation to the last triggering incident, treating previous provocation as merely a setting for that incident. For example, in *R v R*, a case involving a battered wife who had killed her husband after years of violence at his hands, the South Australian Court of Criminal Appeal said that 'in determining whether the deceased's actions and words on the fatal night could amount to provocation in law, it is necessary to consider them against the background of family and sexual abuse'.[57]

---

[54](1963) 111 CLR 610.
[55]Ibid., p. 630.
[56][1967] VR 467, p. 484.
[57](1981) 28 SASR 321, p. 326. For a similar ruling see *R v Hill* (1980) 3 A Crim R 357, p. 400.

Section 23 of the *Crimes Act* (NSW) adopts the stance taken in cases like *Parker* and *Jeffrey* by stipulating that the provocative conduct may have 'occurred immediately before the act or omission causing death *or at any previous time*'.[58] Being a much clearer pronouncement on cumulative provocation, it is to be preferred over the English provision.

## 3. The Indian law

With regard to Indian law, the courts of that jurisdiction have adopted the concept of cumulative provocation ever since the inception of the Code.[59] This is remarkable given that English law at the time of the Code's promulgation restricted the provocation to the deceased's conduct immediately prior to the killing and refused to take into account previous provocation which might have continued to affect the accused's mental state when the killing occurred.[60] The Supreme Court of India in *Nanavati* was merely reaffirming this long-standing position when it declared that 'the mental background created by the previous act of the victim may be taken into consideration in ascertaining whether the subsequent act caused grave and sudden provocation for committing the offence'.[61]

The Indian courts' willing acceptance of cumulative provocation appears to have been aided by the presence of the requirement of 'sudden provocation' alongside 'grave provocation' in the Exception. The courts could thereby relegate all matters having a time element to the requirement of suddenness, leaving them free to recognize instances of provocation occurring well beyond a limited time-

---

[58]Section 23(2). Emphasis added. This modification to the previous section was made in 1982 in line with the recommendations of a NSW Task Force on domestic violence. The Task Force was set up following huge public outcry over the murder conviction of a battered wife who had killed her alcoholic and violent husband after suffering years of physical and emotional abuse by him: see *Hill*, ibid., especially at p. 397, where there is a passage embracing cumulative provocation.

[59]For example, see *Khogayi* v Emperor ILR (1879) 2 Mad 122; *Boya Munigadu v R* (1881) ILR 3 Mad 33; *Mani Pradhano v Empress* (1882) 1 Weir 306; *Nga Sein Myint v Emperor* AIR 1937 Rang 4; *In re Murugian* (S) AIR 1957 Mad 541; *In re C Narayan* AIR 1958 AP 235.

[60]See Stephen, op. cit., n. 48.

[61]AIR 1962 SC 605, p. 630.

frame under the concept of 'grave provocation'.[62] Thus, considerations such as that the provocation must have been unexpected as opposed to planned in advance by the accused, that the interval between the homicide and the provocation must be brief, and that the accused must have been operating under loss of self-control caused by the provocation are all discussed under the requirement of 'sudden provocation'.[63] But when it comes to deciding on what could count as 'grave provocation', all instances of the deceased's provocative conduct, perhaps extending over weeks, months or even years before the homicidal incident, could constitute provocation.

The above discussion lays the groundwork for a minor criticism of the previously quoted proposition in *Nanavati*. The Supreme Court had stated that the 'mental background created by the previous *act* of the victim'[64] may be considered when determining whether there was grave provocation. It could not have seriously meant to restrict previous provocation to a single occasion. The crux of the matter must surely be whether previous provocation, however numerous the occasions, had an impact on the accused's mental state at the time of the killing. As one court, in seeking to apply the *Nanavati* ruling, has put it:

> [We] think that the particular situation and past experiences of an accused in relation to the deceased may be taken into account in considering the extent to which the accused had been repelled towards the breaking point which is there even in constitutionally normal or average individuals.[65]

The facts of a few cases should amply illustrate the application of cumulative provocation under Indian law. In one case, D had changed their place of residence after he became suspicious that his wife was having an affair with V. On the day of the killing, D

---

[62]This same point was somewhat inelegantly put forward in *Gour's Penal Law of India,* Vol. III, 10th edn, p. 2332 (1983). See also *Nelson's Indian Penal Code* Vol. II, 7th edn, p. 1038 (1983).

[63]These issues are discussed under the heading 'Actual Loss of Self-Control' below, pp. 46–56.

[64]Emphasis added.

[65]*Aktar v State* AIR 1964 All 262, p. 269 per Justice Beg. Similarly, in *R v Punchirala* (1924) 25 New LR 458, p. 462, Chief Justice Bertram said: 'If a man receives comparatively slight provocation at a time when he has been the victim of a series of slights and insults of themselves sufficient to strain his self-control to breaking point, it seems impossible to deny that the court should take this condition of mind into account.'

had returned home to find V present at his hut, whereupon he
lost self-control and caused several injuries to V which proved
fatal.[66] In another case, D had been provoked by V over the course
of many years. V had seduced D's cousin, encroached on his
ancestral ground and cut down trees on his property. Furthermore,
V had persuaded the woman whose land D had cultivated to turn
him out, and had usurped his share in the village. On the fatal
day, V had struck and abused D, which resulted in his losing self-
control and killing V.[67] A third case involved D, who knew that V
was having an affair with his wife for a long time. V would sing,
often in D's presence, songs which virtually declared his intrigue
with D's wife and in the most provocative way. D had managed
to control himself on these occasions when provoked by such songs,
but on the last occasion he lost self-control and shot V.[68] In all
these cases, the accused were held to be entitled to the benefit of
the Exception.

This comparative survey shows that, while cumulative
provocation is now recognized in all three jurisdictions, the Indian
courts were the earliest to adopt it, followed by the Australian
courts with a few exceptions, and only lately by the English courts.
Accordingly, an appraisal of Indian law on the matter by English
and Australian lawmakers might well have persuaded them to sooner
embrace the concept of cumulative provocation.

## C. Provocation in the Defendant's Presence

### 1. The English law

The English law requires conduct (whether in the form of acts or
words) to have occurred in the presence of the accused before it
can be recognized as provocation. Provocation which has occurred
in the accused's absence is sometimes described as 'hearsay
provocation'.[69] An English authority for the rule is *R v Fisher*, in
which V was caught by his landlord sodomizing D's young son.[70]
The landlord duly reported this to D the next day, whereupon D

---

[66]*Babu Lal v State*, 1960 Cr LJ 437.
[67]*Khoyagi v Emperor*, ILR (1879) 2 Mad 122.
[68]*Bahadur v Emperor*, 1935 Cr LJ 939.
[69]See *R v Quartly* (1986) 11 NSWLR 332, p. 338.
[70]8 C & P 182 (1837).

sought V out and, finding him a day later, stabbed him to death. At the trial for murder, the defence conceded that if there had been time for D to regain his self-control, the case would be murder. However, Justice Park rejected the defence of provocation on the ground that D had to have seen the provocative act.[71] The case of *R v Kelly* is to like effect.[72] D, a soldier, killed V, a woman whom he was cohabiting with, when he saw her in the presence of another soldier. He claimed to have been suspicious of some illicit intrigue by V. Rolfe B. directed the jury that such suspicion, however strong, could not support the defence of provocation.[73]

It is uncertain whether section 3 of the English *Homicide Act* has retained the rule requiring presence of the defendant or has abolished it. The restrictive view regards the words 'provoked' and 'provocation' in the section as bearing the meaning they have had at common law, subject only to the expressed changes made by the section. This would mean the retention of the rule expressed in cases like *Fisher* and *Kelly*. The liberal view, and the one which seems to be preferred by the courts, is to give those words their ordinary and natural meaning, unlimited by the technicalities of the common law.[74] It is recalled that the section requires the jury to take into account *everything* both done and said according to the effect which, in their opinion, it would have on a reasonable person. This should be broad enough to include, as happened in the case of *Fisher*, an oral report of a past provocative incident or, as in the case of *Kelly*, any conduct which aroused suspicions of such an incident. It may be that the jury would not give much weight to these forms of provocation. Conversely, as I shall argue, there may be instances when these types of provocation can have as great an effect on a reasonable person (and on the accused) as provocation done in her or his sight or hearing.

## 2. The Australian law

The English cases have been relied on by Australian courts to introduce the rule requiring presence into Australian common law

[71]Ibid., p. 186.

[72](1848) 2 Car and Kir 814.

[73]See also *Pearson's Case* (1835) 2 Lew CC 216. For a critique of *Fisher*, *Kelly* and *Pearson*, see Lanham, op. cit., n. 19, at pp. 137–8.

[74]See Smith and Hogan, op. cit., n. 53, pp. 353–4, for instances of this view as applied to other aspects of the defence.

as well as into the New South Wales provision on provocation. The Victorian Supreme Court case of *R v Arden* is a case in point.[75] D was informed by his de facto wife that V had just raped her, and she showed him her torn underwear. D went to the room where the rape had allegedly taken place and found V asleep. D woke V up and charged him with the rape. V denied the charge, a fight broke out and D killed V. Justice Menhennitt withdrew the defence of provocation from the jury because the rape had not occurred in D's presence. He thought that the rule requiring presence was based on the following rationale:

> Where, however, all that happened is that the accused is told something by a third person, there enters immediately the element of belief, and there is nothing tangible upon which the accused can be said to have acted.[76]

Connected with this rationale was the judge's concern that, without the rule requiring presence, D could avoid a murder conviction even though he may have killed an entirely innocent person. So in *Arden*, had the defence been left to the jury, D may have been convicted only of manslaughter even if his wife had falsely accused V of the rape.

Section 23 of the *Crimes Act* (NSW) has been judicially interpreted as not having altered the common law. In the New South Wales Court of Criminal Appeal case of *R v Quartly*, D, upon being informed by his former girlfriend that V had physically assaulted and raped her, sought V out and killed him.[77] The court rejected the defence argument that the words 'conduct of the deceased ... towards or affecting the accused'[78] were intended by the legislature to include hearsay provocation.[79] The court held instead that the provision left intact the common law rule requiring

---

[75][1975] VR 449. For another example at common law, see *Terry* [1964] VR 248. Similarly, in *R v R* (1981) 28 SASR 321, p. 326, Chief Justice King made the *obiter* remark that 'words or conduct cannot amount to provocation unless they are spoken or done to or in the presence of the killer'. Cf. Lanham, op. cit. n. 19, p. 135 for the suggestion that, since Chief Justice King was prepared to regard the hearsay provocation as part of the background against which the provocation by V to D is to be assessed, the case is more in opposition than in support of the rule requiring presence.

[76]Ibid., p. 452.

[77](1986) 11 NSWLR 332.

[78]Section 23(2)(a).

[79](1986) 11 NSWLR 332, p. 339.

presence, authority for which was to be found in the cases of *Fisher* and *Arden*.[80]

The rule requiring presence has found favour with English and Australian courts because it has certain distinct advantages.[81] It removes weak and unmeritorious cases of provocation from the jury, deters the launching of attacks on people who may have been entirely innocent of any provocative conduct, and reduces the proliferation of killings stemming from passions fuelled by confessions and accusations. However, there are counter-arguments to these advantages. With regard to weak and unmeritorious cases, there may be occasions when the evidence of hearsay provocation may actually be stronger than provocation which had happened in D's presence. Where the provocation is alleged to have occurred in D's presence, the only evidence may be the word of the defendant that it had occurred. In contrast, where a third party had informed the accused of the provocation, there is at least the possibility of that party testifying to the fact of the provocation. Furthermore, while it may generally be true that provocation done in someone's presence is likely to be graver than when done in her or his absence, it need not always be so. For instance, an intensely provocative incident performed in the accused's absence, such as raping or murdering a loved one, may more readily cause a loss of self-control than a moderately provocative incident done in her or his presence, such as an assault or insult. As for the claim that the rule deters attacks on innocent people, it might at the same time operate to protect persons who were in fact guilty of the provocative conduct. Furthermore, the law of provocation has been prepared to extend the defence to the killing of innocent people.[82] As for the argument that the rule prevents widespread killings arising from mere

---

[80] Ibid., p. 338. Cf. *R v Peisley* (1990) 54 A Crim R 42, p. 49, where the New South Wales Court of Criminal Appeal left open the correctness of *Quartly* in this respect: see Yeo, S., Case Comment on *Peisley* 16 *Criminal Law Journal* 197, p. 200 (1992).

[81] Much of the ensuing discussion on the case for and against the rule is gleaned from Lanham, op. cit., n. 19, pp. 147–9.

[82] See *R v Brown*, Leach 148 (1776); *R v Letenock* (1917) 12 Cr App R 221; *R v Wardrope* [1960] Crim LR 770; *R v Kenney* [1983] 2 VR 470; *R v Hutton* (1986) 20 A Crim R 315; *R v Fricker* (1986) 23 A Crim R 147. Admittedly, all these cases involved the killing of an innocent person under a mistake of fact rather than as a result of hearsay provocation.

accusations or confessions, this would be correct if hearsay provocation were to be considered without any qualification. To meet this concern, Professor David Lanham has suggested that hearsay provocation be recognized provided the accused believed on reasonable grounds both that the provocation had occurred and that the deceased perpetrated it. His justification for imposing the requirement of reasonable belief was that:

> The defence of provocation is a compromise between a concession to human frailty and the need to maintain public order. The latter consideration involves certain objective elements in provocation. Where the provocation consists of actions reported to the defendant, it is appropriate to require that the report be one which engenders a reasonable belief.[83]

There is much merit in this approach. It meets many of the concerns about hearsay provocation including the one voiced by Justice Menhennitt in *Arden*[84] and is more rational and just than an arbitrary rule denying the consideration of any hearsay provocation.

## 3. The Indian law

As for Indian law on the matter, there are cases illustrative of Professor Lanham's proposal. In the case of *Chanan Khan v Emperor*, D's father had seen a boy from a lower caste entering the house where his daughter-in-law lived.[85] D was promptly informed by his father and they both proceeded immediately to the house, where they found and killed the couple. The court was prepared to regard the father's information to D as provocation on the ground that:

> information received from a reliable person and believed to be credible as to the existence of a provoking act which was being done in the immediate neighbourhood and the existence of which was instantaneously verified, could within the meaning of [Exception 1] be said to be provocation given by the person committing that act, just as much as if the person provoked had seen it in the first place with his own eyes.[86]

In other words, the reasonableness of D's belief was evidenced by

---

[83]Op. cit., n. 19, p. 149. Lanham went on to discuss the New Zealand Court of Appeal case of *R v White* [1988] 1 NZLR 122, which he construed as having taken his suggested approach.
[84]Quoted in the main text accompanying n. 76.
[85](1944) Cr LJ 595.
[86]Ibid., p. 598.

the reliability of the messenger (D's father), the physical proximity of the place where the alleged provocation happened and the speedy confirmation of the information by D himself.

In *Gohra v Emperor*, the Punjab High Court considered the English case of *Fisher* which involved a father who killed a man whom he heard had sodomized his young son.[87] It held that had the case been tried under the Indian Penal Code the defence of provocation would also have failed but only because the accused had sufficient time to cool. As for the act of sodomy, the court thought that this amounted to provocation as D had heard of it from several people and received confirmation from the person who had actually witnessed the incident. In noting these facts, the court was spelling out the grounds which made D's belief reasonable that the act of sodomy had occurred and had been performed by V.

The Indian judicial recognition of hearsay provocation illustrates once again the progressive and innovative stance taken by Indian judges when interpreting and applying the Code provisions. This approach stands in contrast to that of the English and Australian courts, which have thus far refused to acknowledge that there may be certain circumstances where justice requires hearsay provocation to be recognized.

## D. *Self-Induced Provocation*

The expression 'self-induced' as it applies to provocation describes situations where D has created the circumstances whereby V provokes D and D thereupon loses self-control and kills V. There are actually two broad situations in which this could happen. The first is where D seeks the provocation in the sense of engineering the provocation as an excuse for killing or harming V. The second is where D has merely risked being provoked in the sense of doing something which D knows might provoke V into attacking D but which D has not deliberately done in order to solicit such a response from V.

The rationale for denying the defence to an accused who has sought the provocation is that such a case falls outside the scope

---

[87](1890) PR No 7 of 1890. *Fisher* was presented earlier in this chapter at pp. 27–8.

of the law's policy of providing limited concession to human frailty. In contrast, 'the deliberate exploitation of mental weakness is conscious and outside the scope of the concession'.[88] Put in another way, the law holds D liable for conduct which, when unprovoked, he or she intended to do under provocation.[89] This rationale does not apply to an accused who has merely risked being provoked. As we shall see, not every case of risking the provocation will prevent the operation of the defence. Where the defence is denied, it will be on the premise that D, having created the circumstances which provoked V, should be required to expect and tolerate a certain amount of provocation from V. This point will be elaborated upon below.

## 1. The English law

Under English common law, the defence of provocation is not available to a person who has sought the provocation. Thus, in *R v Mason*, after a fight in a tavern, D left threatening to kill V. He returned with a sword and invited V to hit him with a stick.[90] When V did so, D killed him with the sword. The court held that the crime was murder because there was 'plainly a provocation sought on his part, that he might execute the wicked purpose of his heart, with some colour of excuse'. Many of the early English institutional writers supported such a ruling. For example, Hale gave the illustration of A and B having fallen out. A invited B to take a pin out of A's sleeve, intending thereby to strike B. When B took up the invitation, A killed him. The learned writer opined that there was no provocation because 'it appeared to be a malicious and deliberate artifice thereby to take occasion to kill B'.[91]

The nineteenth century English law reform bodies seeking to codify the criminal law also assumed that such a rule was well

---

[88]Charleton, P., *Offences Against the Person*, p. 149 (1992).
[89]The analogy may be drawn with the case of D who drinks in order to get herself or himself into a homicidal state. Drunkenness is rejected as a defence even though D may have been so intoxicated at the time of killing as to lack the homicidal intent: see the Privy Council case of *A-G for Northern Ireland v Gallagher* [1963] AC 349.
[90]Fost. 132, 168 ER 66 (1756). Cf. the later case of *R v Selten* (1871) 11 Cox CC 674.
[91]Hale, op. cit., n. 13, p. 457. See also East, op. cit., n. 13, p. 239; Hawkins, op. cit., n. 13, c. 31, s. 24.

established under the common law. Thus, Article 46 of the Criminal Law Commissioners' *Digest of the Law of Offences against the Person*, which formed part of their 1839 Report, states:

> The plea of provocation is not available where the offender either seeks the provocation as a pretext for killing or doing great bodily harm, or endeavours to kill or do great bodily harm before provocation is given.[92]

Likewise, Section 176 of the Draft Criminal Code 1879 provides that:

> [N]o one shall be deemed to give provocation to another ... by doing anything which the offender incited him to do in order to provide the offender with an excuse for killing or doing bodily harm to any person.[93]

The above-stated authorities indicate that the English common law has long recognized a rule which denies the defence to one who has sought the provocation. However, the same cannot be said of the law relating to cases where the accused had merely risked being provoked. Indeed, there appears not to have been any authority on the matter until the Privy Council case of *Edwards v R*, which was decided in 1973.[94] D admitted to blackmailing V. He claimed that as a consequence of his act of blackmail, V had verbally abused and attacked him with a knife, whereupon D lost his self-control and killed him. On these facts, D had clearly not sought the provocation as an excuse to kill V, since his intention was solely to blackmail V. The Privy Council held that such a situation could ground the defence notwithstanding that the provocation had been induced by the criminal act of D. Lord Pearson, who delivered the judgement of the court, explained:

> On principle it seems reasonable to say that—
>
> (1) a blackmailer cannot rely upon the predictable results of his own blackmailing conduct as constituting provocation ... and the predictable results may include a considerable degree of hostile reaction by the person sought to be blackmailed, for instance vituperative words or even some hostile action such as blows with a fist;
>
> (2) but if the hostile reaction by the person sought to be blackmailed goes to extreme lengths it might constitute sufficient provocation.[95]

---

[92] Fourth Report, 1839, Parliamentary Papers [168] xix–235.
[93] Royal Commission on the Law Relating to Indictable Offences, 1879 (C. 2345).
[94] [1973] AC 648. *Edwards* was an appeal from Hong Kong.
[95] Ibid., p. 658.

Applying the above explanation to the facts before it, the Privy Council held that V's attack with a knife was an extreme reaction and consequently an unpredictable result of D's blackmail. Accordingly, the attack could amount to conduct constituting sufficient provocation. Lord Pearson's test of predictability appears to be objective in nature: the question is not whether D actually foresaw the possibility of a hostile reaction approximating V's conduct but whether a reasonable (or ordinary) person might have foreseen such a reaction.[96] The basis for excluding V's predictable reaction in cases where D has risked becoming affronted by such a reaction may be explained in part by the partially justificatory nature of the defence. One of the underlying rationales of provocation is that V was partly to blame for V's own death because he or she had contributed to it by provoking D.[97] Hence, the paradigm of provocation involves moral wrongdoing on the part of both V and D.[98] Where V had reacted in a reasonably predictable way to wrongful conduct performed by D, V cannot be regarded as having been morally wrong in so reacting.[99] Such wrongfulness comes about only when V's reaction to D's act was extreme and, consequently, not reasonably predictable.[100]

The preceding discussion presents the English common law on cases of seeking and risking the provocation. However, Section 3 of the English *Homicide Act* 1957 prevents these common law rulings from being treated as fixed rules of law. One of the major changes made by that section to the English law as it then stood was that it abolished the power of the trial judge to withdraw provocation as an issue on the ground that there was no evidence

[96]See Ashworth, A. 'Self-Induced Provocation and the Homicide Act', *Criminal Law Review* 483, pp. 486–7 (1973).

[97]See this work p.10.

[98]See Asworth, op. cit., n. 96, pp. 491–2; Ashworth, A., 'The Doctrine of Provocation', 35 *Cambridge Law Journal* 292, pp. 307–8 (1976).

[99]To the extent that V cannot be said to have brought D's attack upon herself or himself.

[100]Cf. Goode, M., 'On Subjectivity and Objectivity in Denial of Criminal Responsibility: Reflections on Reading *Radford*', 11 *Criminal Law Journal* 131, p. 135 (1987). Goode criticizes the objective nature of the test propounded in *Edwards* on the ground that it ignores the concession to human frailty rationale of the defence. However, the learned author in turn fails to give weight to the alternative rationale of V having been contributorily at fault in provoking D.

on which the jury could find that a reasonable person would have been provoked as the accused was.[101] Henceforth, the jury alone was to decide that question since the section requires the jury to 'take into account *everything* both done and said according to the effect which, *in their opinion*, it would have on a reasonable man'.[102] It was the previous judicial power to withdraw the defence from the jury which had enabled them to devise rules such as that words alone could not amount to provocation in law and, in relation to the present discussion, the rules pertaining to self-induced provocation. This was clearly acknowledged by the English Court of Appeal in *R v Johnson*, a case that involved risking the provocation, with the result that the court refused to follow *Edwards*.[103]

English commentators have criticized the demise of the common law rules concerning provocative conduct, saying that the effect of Section 3 was 'curious'[104] and leaves the jury with the 'unwelcome alternative' of complete discretion to decide, unaided by observations from the judge, whether the case was one of murder or manslaughter.[105] These commentators would prefer to have the section expressly stipulate certain rules which prevent the defence of provocation from going to the jury, such as the common law rule concerning D who had sought the provocation or where D had lost self-control in the face of a reasonably predictable reaction by V to D's own conduct.

## 2. The Australian law

Under Australian common law, the rule is well established that the defence would be denied to a person who had sought the provocation as an excuse to kill or harm the deceased.[106] A good example is the Victorian Court of Criminal Appeal case of *R v Allwood*.[107] D sought out his estranged wife, arming himself with a rifle. He chose the subject matter and controlled the course of

[101]See the House of Lords case of *DPP v Camplin* [1978] 2 All ER 168, p. 173; *R v Acott* [1997] 1 All ER 706, p. 711.
[102]Section 3. Emphasis added.
[103][1989] Crim LR 738. Cf. *R v Baillie* [1995] 2 Cr App R 31.
[104]Williams, op. cit., n. 3, pp. 531, 534–5.
[105]Ashworth, op. cit., n. 96, p. 492.
[106] *R v Newman* [1948] VLR 61, p. 66.
[107](1975) 18 A Crim R 120.

their conversation. He knew the answers that could be expected from her and goaded her into giving them, including a confession of sexual relations. The court held that, in these circumstances, the defence was not available to the accused.

This rule used to be embodied in Section 23 of the *Crimes Act* (NSW) in the form of a proviso that the jury must find that 'such provocation [as is relied upon by the accused] was not intentionally caused by any word or act on the part of the accused'.[108] In the Australian High Court case of *Parker v R*, this proviso was regarded as 'merely a repetition of the old common law rule that a contrived provocation will not suffice'.[109] Unfortunately, this proviso was removed from the present version of Section 23 when it was amended in 1982.[110] Section 23 now requires the accused to have been 'induced' to lose self-control by the conduct of the deceased.[111] Conceivably, where the accused had sought the provocation, the loss of self-control was induced by the conduct of the accused and not by that of the deceased. The meaning of this phrase has yet to be considered judicially. It is submitted that, for the sake of clarity, a proviso such as the one contained in the old Section 23 should have been retained in the present version.

With regard to cases of risking the provocation, the Australian courts have adopted the Privy Council ruling in *Edwards* that the defence is unavailable to a person who had lost self-control in the face of reasonably predictable results of her or his own conduct. For instance, in the South Australian Court of Criminal Appeal case of *R v Radford*, D had gone to the house of V to kidnap his former wife, who was residing with V.[112] The affection between V and D's former wife was the cause of the marital break-up. Since all that V had said to D was 'you leave my friend alone', the court ruled that those words were the reasonably predictable result of D's own conduct in seeking to kidnap his former wife from V's

---

[108]Section 23(2)(a).
[109](1963) 111 CLR 610, p. 658.
[110]By virtue of the *Crimes (Homicide) Amendment Act,* 1982 (NSW), Section 3.
[111]Section 23(2)(a).
[112](1985) 20 A Crim R 388, p. 401. See also *Allwood* (1975) 18 A. Crim R 120, pp. 132–3. Cf. the Victorian Court of Criminal Appeal case of *R v Voukelatos* [1990] VR 1, p. 19, which regarded *Edwards* as a case involving seeking, as opposed to risking, the provocation.

premises. Accordingly, the defence of provocation failed.

Graeme Coss, an Australian expert on the defence of provocation, has drawn up the following possible disqualifying conditions derived from *Edwards,'* case:

(a) The accused provoked the victim with a premeditated intention to kill or to cause grievous bodily harm in response to the victim's expected retaliation.

(b) The accused unreasonably failed to foresee the likelihood of killing the victim in response to the victim's retaliation.

(c) The accused provoked the victim with a premeditated intention to assault the victim in response to the victim's retaliation.

(d) The accused unreasonably failed to foresee the likelihood of assaulting the victim in response to the victim's retaliation.

(e) As in (a)-(d), except that the accused foresaw that the retaliation of the victim was likely to be disproportionate to the provocation initially offered by the accused.

(f) As in (a)-(d), except that the accused unreasonably failed to foresee that the retaliation of the victim was likely to be disproportionate to the provocation initially offered by the accused.[113]

With regard to Section 23 of the *Crimes Act* (NSW), the previous criticism concerning its ambiguity over situations of self-induced provocation applies with even greater force in respect of cases of risking the provocation. The proviso contained in the old Section 23 does not assist since it arguably dealt only with cases of seeking the provocation.[114] In the light of the foregoing discussion of self-induced provocation, the solution would be to rectify the present Section 23[115] by adding the following exclusionary clause:

> For the purposes of subsection (1), any conduct of the deceased which induced the accused to lose self-control cannot be taken into account

---

[113]Fisse, B. (ed.), *The Laws of Australia. The Criminal Law: Homicide*, para. [14] (1992). Unfortunately, the latest edition namely, Fisse, B. and P. Fairall, (eds), *The Laws of Australia. Criminal Offences. Homicide*, Vol. 10.1 (1996) omits reference to this extrapolation of propositions from *Edwards*.

[114]This reading is based on the proviso stating that the provocation must not have been 'intentionally caused' by D's conduct which suggests that D had engineered the provocation as an excuse to kill or injure V.

[115]The section is reproduced in detail on pp.12–13 of this work.

if —

(a) such conduct was sought by the accused as an excuse to kill or cause bodily harm to the deceased or any other person; or

(b) such conduct was a reasonably predictable result of the accused's own conduct.

## 3. The Indian law

Exception 1 to Section 300 of the Indian Penal Code expressly disallows the defence from succeeding in cases where the accused had sought the provocation. The proviso states that the Exception is subject to the following qualifying condition:

> That the provocation is not sought or voluntarily provoked by the offender as an excuse for killing or doing harm to any person.

In the proviso, the Code framers draw a distinction between cases where D had sought the provocation and cases where D had voluntarily (that is, intentionally or by means which D knows to be likely to have the effect[116]) offered provocation. In the former type of case, D goes deliberately in search of the provocation although he or she may not have offered any provocation to V. Examples may be found in cases where an aggrieved husband, upon discovering that his wife is committing adultery, follows her to the place where she meets her paramour and kills him on the spot.[117] In the latter type of case, D provokes V into provoking D in turn. Case examples are where D had himself provoked a quarrel and ensuing fight with V,[118] and where D had uttered highly abusive and sacrilegious remarks to V which prompted V to retort back at him.[119] Arguably, the Code framers may have been unduly pedantic in making this distinction since the notion of seeking the provocation is sufficiently wide to cover cases where D had offered provocation. What appears to be the crucial factor under the proviso for either kind of case is that D must have sought or offered the provocation 'as an excuse for killing or doing harm to any person'.

[116] This definition of the word 'voluntarily' as used in the Code is given in Section 39 which is reproduced in n. 44.

[117] *Lochan v Emperor* ILR 8 All 635; *Mehra Mistak v Emperor* AIR 1934 Lah 103; *Kanhaiya Lal v State* AIR 1952 Bhopal 21.

[118] *Kusta Balsu Kandnekar v State* 1936 Cr LJ 662; *In re Mala Narayana* 1962 (1) Cr LJ 394.

[119] *Shyama Charan v State* AIR 1969 All 61.

This feature of the proviso takes cases of risking the provocation outside its ambit.

It is submitted that the Code would be enhanced were a proviso to be enacted which incorporates the ruling in *Edwards* in relation to risking the provocation. Fortunately, there are cases which show that the Indian courts have not simply waited upon the advent of such legislation but have gone ahead to make decisions which closely parallel the ruling in *Edwards*. In the Karnataka High Court case of *State v Kamalaksha*, D had visited V's wife at her home while V was at work and consequently risked provoking V.[120] Upon discovering this occurrence, V uttered the 'most filthy abuse' at D for two hours and then attacked him with a knife. In these circumstances, the court was prepared to admit the defence of provocation. The similarity of the facts and holding of this case with *Edwards* is obvious, the only major difference being in the type of conduct D had performed which gave rise to the risk of provoking V. There is also the Supreme Court case of *Nanavati*, the facts of which were that D, upon discovering that his wife had committed adultery with V, drove to V's house with a gun, confronted him about the adultery and shot him dead.[121] One of the contentions raised by the defence was that, before the shooting, D had abused V, which provoked an equally abusive reply from V. The court refused to treat V's reply as sufficient provocation.[122] Although the court did not provide a reason for its refusal, the decision may readily be explained in terms of the ruling in *Edwards*, namely, that V's reply was a reasonably predictable result of D's bursting into V's bedroom and hurling abuse at him.

## E. Lawful Acts as Provocation

### 1. The English law

Conventional wisdom dictates that 'the law would be self-contradictory if a lawful act could amount to provocation'.[123] Permitting lawful conduct to constitute provocation would also

---

[120]1978 Cr LJ 290.
[121]AIR 1962 SC 605. For a fuller rendition of the facts, see pp. 54–5 of this work.
[122]Ibid., p. 630.
[123]Fisse, op. cit., n. 25, p. 97.

run counter to the rationale of the defence that the killing was partly the fault of V; that rationale cannot apply in cases where V was acting justifiably in the eyes of the law.[124] The English common law supported this view with a long-standing rule that lawful blows could not be provocation;[125] much less lawful acts not involving blows. While adultery could amount to provocation even though it was not a crime per se under English law, it was construed as illegal in some way, being a matrimonial offence.[126] This common law position was reflected in the Law Commissioners' Digest of 1839 by the requirement that the provocative conduct must be 'a *wrongful* act or insult'.[127] It also appeared in the Draft Criminal Code of 1879, Section 176 of which provides that 'no one shall be deemed to give provocation to another by doing that which he had a legal right to do'.[128]

The advent of Section 3 of the *Homicide Act* 1957 (UK) resulted in the demise of the common law rule against lawful acts constituting provocation. In allowing insults to amount to provocation, the section inevitably altered the common law, since insults uttered in private do not constitute a crime or even a tort. The section does not contain any restriction against lawful acts and, indeed, requires the trial judge to leave the jury to decide whether there was any evidence of provocation on which they could find that a reasonable person would have acted as the accused did. As a vivid example of the effect of the section on the issue of lawful provocation, it has been held that the crying and restlessness of a 17-day-old baby can amount to provocation.[129] The position taken under Section 3 has the support of Professors John Smith and Brian Hogan, who contend that '[i]t is impossible, as a matter of law, to divide acts which [V] is at liberty to do into classes of "good" and "bad".'[130]

The stance taken by the English legislation may be tenable in present-day cases where the provocative conduct is, for the most part, not concerned with clashes between armed men so as to make

[124]Ashworth, op. cit., n. 96, p. 492.
[125]*R v Mawgridge*, J Kel. 119 (1707), 84 ER 1107; *R v Bourne* 5 C & P 120 (1831), 172 ER 903.
[126]Williams, op. cit., n. 3, p. 534. But see Fisse, op. cit., n. 25, pp. 97–8.
[127]Op. cit., n. 92, Art. 41. Emphasis added.
[128]Op. cit., n. 93.
[129]*R v Doughty* (1986) 83 Cr App R 319.
[130]Smith and Hogan, op. cit., n. 53, p. 365.

the unlawfulness of the conduct an important criterion. Instead, modern cases frequently involve provocation in the form of matrimonial infidelity or insulting words and gestures, which conduct is often not unlawful.[131] A strong case may be made for permitting the alternative defence rationale of providing limited concession to human frailty in these cases. However, there remains an area where grave misgivings have been expressed by some commentators.[132] It involves provocation offered by lawful acts performed in obedience to public legal duty, such as the act of a police officer in arresting, a prison officer requiring an inmate to observe prison rules or any other State official requiring a citizen to observe the law.[133] To this may be added cases where the provocation consisted of a lawful act performed in defence of person or property.[134] The vital public policy consideration of maintaining the peace and order in society demands that the law of provocation remove the defence from accused persons who claim to be provoked by a lawful requirement made of them by a person with legal authority to do so. The same public policy consideration dictates that accused persons should be denied the defence where the provocation comprised the lawful exercise of self-defence against the attack of the accused. Presently, however, Section 3 of the English *Homicide Act* prevents the trial judge from directing the jury that these completely lawful acts cannot constitute provocation in law.

## 2. The Australian law

Current Australian common law appears to take a broad view concerning lawful acts amounting to provocation. This approach stems from the judicial recognition of the social reality that 'what

---

[131] *R v R* (1981) 28 SASR 321, p. 327.

[132] Williams, op. cit., n. 3, p. 535; Charleton, op. cit., n. 88, pp. 145–6.

[133] The common law has long recognized that a lawful arrest can never found the defence: see Foster, op. cit., n. 21, pp. 270–7; East, op. cit., n. 13, p 307. The common law also provides that an unlawful arrest may amount to provocation if the illegality is known to the accused: *Hugget's case* Kel 59 (1666), 84 ER 1082; Foster, ibid., pp. 315, 316.

[134] The common law has long recognized that an act of lawful self-defence cannot amount to provocation: see *Mawgridge*, J Kel 119 (1707), 84 ER 1107; *Bourne* 5 C & P 120 (1831), 172 ER 903.

[135] *Moffa* (1977) 138 CLR 601, pp. 616–7. See also the Australian High Court case of *Parker* (1963) 111 CLR 610, p. 654, where Justice Windeyer

might be provocative in one age might be regarded with comparative equanimity in another'.[135] After noting that many modern cases involve provocative conduct that is frequently not unlawful, one judge has gone so far as to express the opinion that 'unlawfulness can no longer be regarded as a separate component of the test of what constitutes provocative conduct'.[136] The judge went on to suggest that if he was wrong and unlawfulness was a legal requirement, then this could be readily satisfied in most cases by regarding the provocative conduct as a breach of the peace.[137] On this view, adultery, while not an offence per se in Australia, is nevertheless an act that may be calculated to provoke a breach of the peace by the injured spouse. Insulting words and gestures could be seen in the same way.

While this relaxation of the common law rule requiring provocative conduct to be unlawful may be tenable at the present time and age, the concern previously expressed when discussing the English law remains, namely, the need for the law to expressly prevent the defence from applying to cases where the provocation constituted the act of someone who was lawfully discharging a legal duty or was lawfully acting in self-defence. The following comment by an Australian judge voices this concern:

> [I]t would be a very serious thing.... [that].... a police officer lawfully arresting an accused person could be killed and the accused pleads provocation arising out of a completely lawful act. ... If we are to hold that lawful acts can ever constitute provocation, then we will be taking away protection from persons in the community such as the police in an area where protection is completely necessary.[138]

Regarding situations where the provocation relied upon constituted a lawful act of self-defence, the Victorian Court of Criminal Appeal case of *R v Scriva (No 2)* suggests that the defence will not be permitted to succeed.[139] The accused killed a person

---

observed that many cases on provocation 'show how different in weight and character are the things that matter in one age from those which matter in another'.

[136]*R* (1961) 28 SASR 321, p. 327 per Chief Justice King. Cf. *R v Webb* (1977) 16 SASR 309, p. 313.

[137]Ibid. See also Fisse, op. cit., n. 25, pp. 97–8.

[138]*R* (1981) 28 SASR 321, p. 339 per Justice Zelling, disagreeing with the view of Chief Justice King. presented above. Justice Zelling did not confine his comment to lawful arrests but to all types of lawful acts.

[139][1951] VLR 298.

who had intervened to restrain him from attacking a motorist who had run down his daughter. The defence was denied on the basis that the accused's conduct was an 'attack [upon] an innocent bystander who was interfering to prevent him completing his attack on [the motorist]'.[140]

From the above discussion, it may be surmised that the Australian common law on the issue of lawful acts as provocation is not without controversy. On the one hand, there is judicial authority in favour of doing away entirely with a rule against lawful provocation, while on the other there are cases which would at least exclude certain kinds of lawful acts from being treated as provocation in law. It would, of course, be preferable for the law on this issue to be made much clearer.

As far as Section 23 of the *Crimes Act* (NSW) is concerned, the section does not incorporate any requirement, expressed or implied, that the provocative conduct be unlawful.[141] This may, generally speaking, be an acceptable position to have in the light of the foregoing discussion. However, the public policy interest of promoting peace and social order requires the section to expressly reject the defence in cases where the provocation involved lawful acts performed in obedience to public legal duty or by way of self-defence.[142] Accordingly, to the previously suggested exclusionary clause[143] should be added the following:

> For the purposes of subsection (1), any conduct of the deceased which induced the accused to lose self-control cannot be taken into account if —
>
> (c) such conduct was performed in the lawful exercise of a public legal duty; or
>
> (d) such conduct was performed in the lawful exercise of defence of person or property.

[140]Ibid., p. 302. The case could alternatively be regarded as one involving an act of lawful restraint.

[141]Throughout, the section describes the provocative conduct simply as 'the conduct of the deceased'.

[142]Lawful arrest as a basis for provocative conduct is expressly excluded under the Criminal Codes of Western Australia and Tasmania: *Criminal Code* 1899 (WA), s. 245; *Criminal Code Act* 1924 (Tas), s. 160(5).

[143]See above, pp. 38–9.

## 3. The Indian law

A reading of Exception 1 to Section 300 reveals that the Code framers arrived at the most appropriate formula on the issue of lawful provocation. The Exception does not have a requirement, expressed or implied, that the provocative conduct must be unlawful. It simply requires the provocation to have been grave and sudden and leaves this question to be determined by the triers of fact.[144] However, the second and third provisos to the Exception specify two types of lawful provocation which are disallowed from supporting the defence. These are the same kinds of lawful provocation which, it was suggested when discussing the English and Australian laws, should be singled out for exclusion. The second proviso stipulates:

> That the provocation is not given by anything done in obedience to the law or by a public servant in the lawful exercise of the powers of such public servant.

There follow two illustrations of the way this proviso operates to prevent the Exception from applying:

> (c) A is lawfully arrested by Z, a bailiff. A is excited to sudden and violent passion by the arrest, and kills Z. This is murder, inasmuch as the provocation was given by a thing done by a public servant in the exercise of his powers.

> (d) A appears as a witness before Z, a Magistrate. Z says that he does not believe a word of A's deposition and that A has perjured himself. A is moved to sudden passion by these words, and kills Z. This is murder.

Although the illustrations are concerned with public servants, the proviso is not limited to these servants exercising their powers but also covers acts done by any person in obedience to law. This latter type of case is covered by the General Exception contained in Section 79 of the Code which provides all persons, and not just public servants, with the justification to perform acts which the law commands or authorizes them to do.[145] Their acts being justified, it follows that resistance is unlawful and that such acts afford no legal basis for provocation. Since the proviso extends the

---

[144]See the Explanation to the Exception.

[145]Section 79 reads: 'Nothing is an offence which is done by any person who is justified by law, or who by reason of a mistake of fact and not by reason of a mistake of law in good faith believes himself to be justified by law in doing it'.

protection of the law only to persons who have lawful authority
and who use that authority in a proper manner, legal acts performed
in an illegal manner will not be covered by the proviso and may
therefore amount to provocation.[146]

The other area where lawful acts are expressly excluded from
amounting to provocation is specified under the third proviso to
the Exception. The proviso states:

> That the provocation is not given by anything done in the lawful exercise
> of the right of private defence.

The following illustration is given for the operation of this proviso:

> (e) A attempts to pull Z's nose. Z, in the exercise of the right of private
> defence, lays hold of A to prevent him from doing so. A is moved
> to sudden and violent passion in consequence, and kills Z. This is
> murder, inasmuch as the provocation was given by a thing done in
> the exercise of the right of private defence.[147]

The General Exceptions contained in the Code define the limits
of the right of private defence and in what cases it extends to
causing death.[148] Since this right is given by law, its lawful exercise
cannot amount to provocation. Here again, the proviso extends
protection of the law only to those who have performed the legal
act of private defence in a lawful manner and not to those who
have done so in an unlawful way.[149]

Overall, on the issue of lawful acts amounting to provocation,
we observe that the Indian Penal Code embodies a superior
arrangement to the present English and Australian laws on the
matter.

## 4. Actual Loss of Self-Control

### A. *A Subjective Condition*

From examining some aspects of provocative conduct, I turn now
to the subjective condition (or factual question) of the defence of
provocation. For the defence to succeed, the provocation must have

---

[146]Morgan, W. and A. MacPherson, *The Indian Penal Code with Notes*, pp.
252–3 (1861).
[147]For a case example, see *Nyo Hla Aung v Emperor* 1910 Cr LJ 477.
[148]See Sections 96–106, which are reproduced in the Appendix to this work.
See also the discussion of some of these provisions in this work pp. 119–21.
[149]Gour, op. cit., n. 62, p. 2345.

caused a sudden loss of self-control during which an accu
committed the homicidal act. Accordingly, the defence is unavail
where a killing contained elements of premeditation or deliberatio
This is not to say that an accused must have lacked a murderous
intent. Indeed, as previously noted, the defence will arise only if a
prima facie case of murder has been made out. What the subjective
condition of the defence requires is that the murderous intent must
not have been formed independently of the provocation. This
subjective condition stands apart from the objective condition (or
evaluative question). If an accused had not in fact lost self-control,
the defence will fail even though a jury may think that a reasonable
or ordinary person in like circumstances could have lost self-control.

All three jurisdictions under consideration make actual loss of
self-control caused by the provocation an essential requirement of
the defence. The following proposition from Justice Devlin's classic
direction in *Duffy* encapsulates this requirement and has been
subscribed to by both Australian and Indian courts:

> Provocation is some act, or series of acts, done by the dead man to the
> accused, which ... actually causes in the accused, a sudden and temporary
> loss of self-control, rendering the accused so subject to passion as to
> make him or her for the moment not master of his mind. ... [A] sudden
> temporary loss of self-control ... is ... the essence of provocation.[150]

## B. *The Uncertain Nature of Lost Self-Control*

While the subjective condition of lost self-control is clearly required,
what is uncertain is the *nature* such a condition. The courts of all
three jurisdictions have yet to define loss of self-control with any
precision. They have resorted instead to metaphor, a good example
of which is found in the English case of *R v Hayward*.[151] There,
Chief Justice Tindal said that the jury were to decide:

> Whether the mortal wound was given by the prisoner while smarting
> under a provocation so recent and so strong that the prisoner might not
> be considered at the moment the master of his own understanding; in
> which case, the law, in compassion to human infirmity, would hold the

---

[150] *Duffy* [1949] 1 All ER 932, p. 932 and approved of in Australia by *Jeffrey*
[1967] VR 467, pp. 479, 488; *R* (1981) 28 SASR 321, p. 336; *Chhay* (1994)
72 A Crim R 1, p. 8. For Indian cases, see *Nanavati* AIR 1962 SC 605, p.
627; *Aktar* AIR 1964 All 262, p. 267.
[151] (1833) 6 Car & P 157.

offence to amount to manslaughter only; or whether there had been time for the blood to cool, and for reason to resume its seat, before the mortal wound was given, in which case the crime would amount to wilful murder.[152]

Australian[153] and Indian[154] judges have invoked the same or similar metaphors to describe the nature of lost self-control for the purposes of the defence. This is an unsatisfactory state of affairs that an Australian judge, Chief Justice Gleeson of the New South Wales Court of Criminal Appeal, described as 'disconcerting'.[155] However, he was reconciled to the use of metaphors because, in his view, 'our understanding of consciousness and mental processes, as compared with our understanding of more readily observable physical phenomena, is so limited that metaphor seems generally to be regarded as essential in the expression of the ideas which guide us in this area of discourse'.[156]

While it may be true that our present comprehension of human consciousness and mental processes is limited, it is nevertheless incumbent on our lawmakers to clarify the *extent* of loss of self-control required for the defence of provocation. Clearly, the law does not require a total deprivation of self-control, for if this were so, the accused would properly have been in a state of automatism, a condition which attracts a complete acquittal.[157] It would be more in line with human reality to say that loss of self-control is not a single mental condition but can vary in intensity over a spectrum. As Lord Diplock suggested in the Privy Council case of *Phillips v R*, there is an 'intermediate stage between icy detachment and going beserk'.[158] This still leaves the extent of lost self-control required for the defence unclear, other than the loss need not be complete. A possible answer may lie in the following comment by Justice O'Brien in the New South Wales case of *R v Croft*:

> It is, of course, obvious that such a history must be taken into account in determining whether the provocative incident was such as could have

[152]Ibid.
[153]For example, see *Parker v R* (1964) 111 CLR 610, p. 679; *Peisley* (1990) 54 A Crim R 42, p. 48; *Chhay* (1994) 72 A Crim R 1, p. 8–9.
[154]For example, see *Dhira v R* (1877) Unrep Cr C 122; *Ulla Mahapatra v R* AIR 1950 Ori 261, p. 264; *Aktar* AIR 1964 All 262, p. 267.
[155]*Chhay* (1994) 72 A Crim R 1, p. 9.
[156]Ibid.
[157]*Chhay* (1994) 72 A Crim R 1, p. 8.
[158][1969] 2 AC 130, p. 137.

caused an ordinary person, placed in all the circumstances in relation to the deceased as the accused then stood, to have so far lost self-control as to have formed an intent to kill or to do grievous bodily harm to the accused *and that the accused did in fact so lose self-control.*[159]

At first reading, this passage seems to be entirely concerned with the relevance of previous provocation to the ordinary person test (that is, the objective condition). But the concluding words, as italicized, throw light upon the extent of actual loss of self-control required for the defence. It comprises the mental state of a person who, as a result of passion, becomes so emotionally charged as to form a murderous intention. Actual loss of self-control is therefore assessed by means of the mental element of murder. However, it is acknowledged that such loss of self-control is an aspect of the defence of provocation. What is normally the mental element of an offence is being used to determine the existence or otherwise of a defence element. Under this approach, the accused must have personally experienced the intense passion which created in her or him the murderous intention leading to the killing of the provoker. The intention must have originated from the accused's highly charged emotional state, which in turn was brought about by the provocation. It follows that a premeditated murderous intention, formulated prior to the provocative incident, would discount a claim of actual loss of self-control. Admittedly, this is a novel suggestion which will require further discussion and, perhaps, fine-tuning. It is offered here as a possible model where none (if Justice O'Brien did not mean to suggest it) currently exists in the three jurisdictions studied.

## C. The Underlying Emotions of Lost Self-Control

Another feature of the subjective condition worth exploring comprises the underlying emotions of a loss of self-control. Jeremy Horder has observed that, from the viewpoint of legal history, anger alone is the underlying emotion.[160] On this premise, he regards other emotions such as fear and panic as irrelevant to the concept of provocation. Present-day English judges seem to have maintained this stance despite the suggestion by Professor Glanville Williams that '[a]nger is the domain of the law of provocation, fear that of

---

[159](1981) 3 A Crim R 307, p. 321. Emphasis added.
[160]Horder, J., *Provocation and Responsibility,* ch. 9 (1992).

the law of private defence—though fear is also capable of amounting to provocation'.[161]

The English judges' reticence over accepting emotions other than anger is to be contrasted with the attitude of their Australian counterparts. In the High Court of Australia case of *Van den Hoek v R*, Justice Mason said:

> Traditionally the onset of sudden passion involving loss of self-control characteristic of provocation has been associated with acts or actions which provoke the accused to uncontrollable anger or resentment ... a notion that may be traced back as far as Aristotle. ... Indeed, the historical concept of provocation as a defence has reflected the ordinary meaning of the word, that is, an act or action that excites anger or resentment. These days, however, judicial discussion of the doctrine places emphasis on the accused's sudden and temporary loss of self-control, without necessarily attributing that loss of self-control to anger or resentment ...
>
> No doubt it is true to say that primarily anger is a feature of provocation and fear a feature of self-defence. But it is too much to say that fear caused by an act of provocation cannot give rise to a defence of provocation.[162]

It is submitted that this is a welcome development. Certainly, anger will be the dominant emotion in many cases where provocation is pleaded, particularly when male defendants are involved. However, other emotions like fear or terror should also be recognized as operating alongside anger, especially in cases involving battered women who kill their spouses after lengthy periods of physical and emotional abuse. In addition to fuelling an accused's loss of self-control, these underlying emotions are valuable in helping to explain an accused's demeanour or behaviour at the time of losing self-control. Thus, anger may give rise to an instantaneous burst of violence and fear may explain why an accused appeared calm and deliberate during and after the killing.[163] Recognizing fear alongside anger is crucial to acknowledging the social reality of battered

[161]Williams, op. cit., n. 3, p. 524.

[162](1986) 161 CLR 158, p. 166–7. See also *Peisley* (1990) 54 A Crim R 42, p. 48; *Chhay* (1994) 72 A Crim R 1, p. 8.

[163]In the latter event, self-defence might be the preferred plea although the law governing that plea tends to be gendered towards masculinity: see Chan, W., 'A Feminist Critique of Self-Defense and Provocation in Battered Women's Cases in England and Wales', 6 *Women and Criminal Justice* 39 (1994). Cf. McColgan, A., 'In Defence of Battered Women Who Kill', *Oxford Journal of Legal Studies* 508 (1993), who argues that the law of self-defence is sufficiently flexible to account for the social reality of battered women who kill.

women who kill. In so doing, the law of provocation reco
that these women are usually targets rather than instigat
violence.[164] I shall shortly continue this discussion of the gender-
specific influences on the law of provocation. For now, the point
may be made that it is incumbent on triers of fact (whether judge
or jury) to consider not only anger but fear where there is evidence
of fear.

As for the Indian law, there does not appear to be any case
authority which has considered emotions other than anger to
underlie the loss of self-control. Arguably, the Supreme Court's
reference in *Nanavati* to the accused's 'mental background' created
by the provocation is sufficiently wide to cover both anger and
fear.[165] An early commentator on the Indian Penal Code, however,
did have the foresight to assert that '[t]error or fear, no less than
anger, may deprive a man of the power of self-control'.[166]

## D. The Requirement of a Sudden Loss of Self-Control

Another feature of the subjective condition worth evaluating here
is the requirement of a 'sudden' loss of self-control. Again, all three
jurisdictions impose this requirement, with the Indian provision
tending to mislead by describing it as 'sudden provocation'. It would
be more correct to attach the descriptor of suddenness to the loss
of self-control than to the provocation.[167] However, the Code is
right insofar as sudden provocation denotes a final triggering
provocative incident which 'unexpectedly' befell the accused.[168]

A useful discussion may be had by placing the issue of sudden
loss of self-control in the context of gender-specific influences on
the law of provocation. The defence of provocation is not gender-
neutral but has been culturally associated with masculinity. This is
well illustrated when two usual types of responses to provocation
are considered—an immediate loss of self-control and a slow
burn reaction culminating eventually in loss of self-control. Either

[164]See Taylor, L., 'Provoked Reason in Men and Women: Heat-Passion
Manslaughter and Imperfect Self-Defence', 33 *UCLA Law Review* 1679, pp.
1715–20 (1986). It is no coincidence that the accused in *Van den Hoek* was
a woman reacting to grave physical provocation by her male abuser.
[165]AIR 1962 SC 605, p. 630.
[166]Morgan and MacPherson, op. cit., n. 146, p. 242.
[167]Smith and Hogan, op. cit., n. 53, p. 355.
[168]Nelson, op. cit., n. 62, p. 1039.

of these responses may be experienced by people, depending on such factors as their personalities, acculturations and the nature of the provocative circumstances. The circumstances in which men kill when provoked tend to foster the immediate loss of self-control type of response. In contrast, the circumstances in which women kill when provoked are more likely to result in a slow burn reaction. Yet the English common law has traditionally only catered for cases involving immediate loss of self-control as manifested in the stipulation of (in the words of Justice Devlin in *Duffy)* a 'sudden and temporary loss of self-control'.[169] For those defendants who have experienced a slow burn reaction, the time-lag between the last provocative event and the homicidal act does not sit well with the requirement of suddenness. The case of *Duffy* itself is a classic example. The accused was a battered woman who had been subjected to severe physical violence by her husband. Some time later, when he was asleep, she killed him with a hatchet and hammer. Her murder conviction was not surprising in the light of the trial judge's direction on suddenness and the jury's (highly likely) lack of understanding of her circumstances as a badly abused wife. This strict application of suddenness continued on after the *Homicide Act* (UK) as the courts held that the requirement of sudden and temporary loss of self-control had not been changed by Section 3 of the Act.[170]

A gradual change has, however, occurred over the past six years. During this time, the English Court of Appeal has cleverly transformed the suddenness requirement from its clear meaning in *Duffy* to a meaning which accommodates the slow burn type of response to provocation.[171] The judges are now prepared to admit

[169]See Edwards, S., 'Battered Women Who Kill', *New Law Journal* 1380 [1990]; Horder, op. cit., n. 160, pp. 69–70.

[170]*R v Turner* [1975] 1 All ER 70.

[171]See *R v Ahluwalia* [1992] 4 All ER 889, pp. 895–6. Some commentators argue that the Court of Appeal still does not go far enough to account for the social reality of battered women who kill: see McColgan, op. cit., n. 163, p. 511–13; Nicolson, D. and R. Sanghvi, 'Battered Women and Provocation: The Implications of *R v Ahluwalia*', *Criminal Law Review* 728 (1993).

In *R v Baillie* [1995] 2 Cr App R 31, the accused was a male. The Court of Appeal applied the ruling in *Ahluwalia* to hold that provocation could be left to the jury even where there had been a great lapse of time between the provocative incident and the killing.

expert evidence of slow burn for the information of jurors who may otherwise not find credible the defendant's evidence as to her emotions at the time of the killing.[172] This is a welcome development which views suddenness as describing the eruption of loss of self-control rather than an instantaneous reaction to provocation. Under this interpretation women who experience slow burn will also have lost their self-control suddenly at the point in time when their emotions erupted or boiled over.

The Australian courts have been much more ready to take the approach only recently adopted by the English judges. For example, in *Parker* (decided in 1963), the facts of which have been previously stated, the Privy Council declared:

> Though there was an interval of time between the moment when the appellant's wife and the deceased went away and the moment when the appellant overtook them and then caused the death of the deceased the jury might well consider and would be entitled to consider that the appellant's whole conduct was such as might 'heat the blood to a proportionate degree of resentment and keep it boiling to the moment of fact'.[173]

This same approach was taken in several Australian cases involving battered women defendants. In *R v R*, the South Australian Court of Criminal Appeal held that the defence of provocation was open to the female defendant even though the victim had been asleep for over twenty minutes before he was killed.[174] In *R v Kontinnen and Runjanjic*, the same court permitted the defence to go to the jury even though there had been a considerable time-lag between the victim's last provocative act and the time he was killed.[175] The New South Wales Court of Criminal Appeal in *R v Chhay* made a similar ruling in a case where a battered wife had killed her sleeping husband several hours after the last provocative incident.[176] Chief Justice Gleeson who delivered the main judgment in *Chhay* accepted that the law of provocation had developed in its practical application as a concession to male frailty. He felt that justice required the law to recognize the research which showed that battered women tend

---

[172] *Ahluwalia*, ibid., p. 896. See generally S. Yeo, 'The Role of Gender in the Law of Provocation', 431 *Anglo-American Law Review* (1997).

[173] (1963) 111 CLR 610, p. 627 citing East, op. cit., n. 13, p. 238. The facts of *Parker* were given above on pp. 24–5.

[174] (1981) 28 SASR 321.

[175] (1991) 53 A Crim R 362.

[176] (1994) 71 A Crim R 1.

to respond to provocation 'by suffering a "slow burn" of fear, despair and anger which eventually erupts into the killing of their batterer, usually when he is asleep, drunk or otherwise indisposed'.[177] He thought that women who reacted in this way were at least as worthy of compassion as men who reacted instantaneously to the provocation.[178]

As may be expected from a provision which was amended pursuant to the recommendations of a Task Force on domestic violence, Section 23 of the New South Wales *Crimes Act* incorporates this liberal approach to loss of self-control. It did so in no uncertain terms by stipulating that 'there is no rule of law that provocation is negatived if the act or omission causing death was not an act done or omitted suddenly'.[179] Hence, the provision expressly envisages that there may be cases where the defence could succeed even where an interval existed between the time when an accused lost self-control and when he or she performed the homicidal act.

The Indian judges have likewise given a liberal interpretation to the requirement of sudden loss of self-control. Thus, it has been stated that the rule would be too narrow if it were held that, in order to entitle the accused to earn the mitigation under the Exception, the homicidal act must immediately follow the provocation.[180] At the same time, there must not be that interval of time which would assuage the first impulse for revenge.[181] This last point is well illustrated in the Supreme Court case of *Nanavati*.[182] D, a sea captain, had momentarily lost his self-control when his wife confessed to having committed adultery with V. D then drove his wife and children to the cinema, left them there and went to his ship, where he performed some business and took and loaded a revolver. After this, he drove to the office of V and, not finding him there, drove to V's flat, where he went straight to the bedroom and shot V dead. The Supreme Court decided that

[177]Ibid., p. 11, citing from an article by Nicolson and Sanghvi, op. cit., n. 171.
[178]Ibid.
[179]Section 23(3)(b). This, together with the provision's recognition of cumulative provocation, effectively accommodates the experiences of battered women who kill.
[180]*Kadir Baksh v Emperor*, 1910 Cr LJ 699.
[181]Gour, op. cit., n. 62, p. 1039.
[182]AIR 1962 SC 605.

D must have regained his self-control during the three hours that had elapsed between his wife's confession of adultery and the fatal shooting. The court applied the following general proposition to the facts of the case:

> The fatal blow should be clearly traced to the influence of passion arising from that provocation and not after the passion had cooled down by lapse of time, or otherwise giving room and scope for premeditation and calculation.[183]

In a similar vein, another Indian court has asserted that the time-interval between the provocation and the homicide should be brief so that if a man is killed within a minute after the provocation it is a case of sudden provocation but if he is killed six hours later, it is not a case of sudden provocation.[184] An example is a case in which D was provoked by witnessing his wife committing adultery with V and had waited for a while until V came out of the room to kill him.[185] In another case, D was informed of a provocative incident by a reliable source and took some time to reach the place where V was. The court held that the provocation could continue to influence D's feelings for a considerable period and, though some time may elapse, it did not necessarily follow that it was sufficient for D to have regained his self-control.[186]

There do not appear to be any reported Indian cases involving battered women who have killed their husbands and who pleaded provocation. It may be that such cases are very rare in India because of the particular social, cultural, religious and gender-specific frameworks within which its inhabitants operate. Or it may be that these defendants have relied on pleas of self-defence instead. Whatever the explanation, should there be a case where a battered woman relied on the defence of provocation, the Australian and English recognition of slow burn reactions of battered women should prove instructive to the Indian courts.[187]

[183]Ibid., p. 630.

[184]*Mahmood v State*, 1961 (2) Cr LJ 591.

[185]*Balku v Emperor*, 1925 Cr LJ 534.

[186]*Chanan Khan v Emperor*, 1944 Cr LJ 595. See also *Abalu Das v Emperor*, ILR 28 Cal 571 (1901), where the accused successfully pleaded the defence even though he had taken the victim some distance away from the venue of the provocative incident before killing him.

[187]Of course, there could well be significant differences in the responses of battered Indian women from those of Western women. Accordingly, scientific research on the reaction of Indian women to violence is vital.

All told, the Australian law appears to be the most enlightened in tackling the various aspects of the subjective condition discussed in this part. This seems in no small measure due to the greater emancipation of Australian women compared to their English and Indian sisters. Australian judges also appear to have shown a greater readiness, compared to their English and Indian counterparts to combat bias in favour of men found in the criminal law.[188]

# 5. The Ordinary Person Test

## A. An Objective Test

In addition to an accused having to lose self-control as a result of provocation, the defence requires that a reasonable (or ordinary) person in the same circumstances could likewise have lost self-control and done what the accused did. This objective condition may be described as the reasonable man (or ordinary person) test. It involves an evaluative question as to whether an accused is deserving of mitigation by measuring her or his reaction to the provocation against that of the hypothetical reasonable or ordinary person.

In England, the direction in *Duffy* embodied the test when it said that provocation comprised conduct 'done by the dead man to the accused which would cause in any reasonable person ... a sudden and temporary loss of self-control'. This common law test was retained in Section 3 of the *Homicide Act* (UK) by the requirement that the jury was to be left with 'the question whether the provocation was enough to make a reasonable man do as he did'.[189]

In Australia, the defence will succeed only if the jury is satisfied among other things that the provocation confronting the accused was 'such as would lead an ordinary man in the accused's circumstances to so lose his self-control as to do an act of the kind and degree as the act in which the accused killed the deceased'.[190]

[188]See Yeo, S., 'Resolving Gender Bias in Criminal Defences', 19 *Monash University Law Review* 104 (1993).
[189]However, the section reversed *Mancini v DPP* [1942] AC1 by removing the judge's power to withdraw the defence from the jury on the ground that there was no evidence on which a jury could find that a reasonable man would be provoked to do as the accused did.
[190](1976) *Johnson v R*, 136 CLR 619, p. 636 per Chief Justice Barwick.

The New South Wales *Crimes Act* leaves the comm
basically intact by stipulating that the provocation '
could have induced an ordinary person in the posi
accused to have so far lost self-control as to have ...
murderous intention.[191]

With regard to Indian law, the wording of the Exception does not expressly specify an ordinary person test but this has not prevented the Indian courts from reading it into the Exception. Thus in *Nanavati*, the Supreme Court declared that 'the test of "grave and sudden" provocation is whether a reasonable man ... placed in the situation in which the accused was placed would be so provoked as to lose his self-control'.[192]

It will be observed that these various expressions of the objective test use either the word 'reasonable' or the word 'ordinary' to describe this hypothetical creature. The preferred term is 'ordinary person' because, as an Australian court has said:

> the 'reasonable man' is not that model of prudence that he tends to become in the law of torts. Here he is, by hypothesis, a person capable of losing his self-control to the extent of intentionally wounding or even killing another, when there is no need to do so for his own protection.[193]

Similarly, an Indian judge expressed the view that:

> there is hardly any point in inquiring whether a reasonable man will kill under a similar provocation, for the simple answer must be that, if he is reasonable, he will not kill under any provocation. A reasonable person ceases to be reasonable when his passions get out of control and he kills a human being; and to make the unreasonable conduct of a reasonable man a standard for the conduct of others is a bit of a paradox.[194]

The House of Lords itself has likewise been alert to the problems created by the expression 'reasonable man'. Thus in *Morhall* it said that:

> In truth the expression 'reasonable man' or 'reasonable person' in this context can lead to misunderstanding. Lord Diplock described it [in *Camplin* (1978) 2 All ER 168] as an 'apparently inapt expression'. This

---

[191] Section 23(2)(b). A significant alteration to the common law is the doing away with the need for the ordinary person to have done what the accused did, that is the mode of killing. This issue is discussed in this work below on pp. 109–111.

[192] AIR 1962 SC 605, p. 630.

[193] [1961] *R v Enright*, VR 663, at 669 per Herring C.J. Smith and Hudson JJ. See also Stingel (1990) 171 CLR 312 at 328.

[194] *Mahmood v State* AIR 1961 All 538, p. 540 per Justice Dhavan.

is because the 'reasonable person test' is concerned not with ratiocination nor with the reasonable man whom we know so well in the law of negligence (where we are concerned with reasonable foresight and reasonable care), nor with reasonable conduct generally. The function of the test is only to introduce, as a matter of policy, a standard of self-control which has to be complied with if provocation is to be established in law.[195]

The reason for the English courts' continuing reference to the 'reasonable man' therefore seems to be entirely due to the use of that expression in Section 3 of the *Homicide Act* (UK). Although it may be contended that an 'ordinary person' is also unlikely to kill upon provocation,[196] this expression at least avoids introducing the concept of reasonableness, which is apt to confuse jurors.

The ordinary person test has, for various reasons, been regarded as being so unsatisfactory by some judges, law reform commissioners and academic commentators that they have called for its total abolition and replacement by a purely subjective test.[197] Among the reasons are the complexity of the test and difficulties in its application, aspects which I shall cover below. The main argument for maintaining the test is that 'the law as to provocation obviously embodies a compromise between a concession to human weakness on the one hand and the necessity on the other hand for society to maintain objective standards of behaviour for the protection of human life'.[198] Hence, it is thought that one outcome of this compromise is the requirement, to some degree at least, of objectivity. Given the continuing strong judicial and legislative recognition of the ordinary person test in England, Australia and

[195][1995] 3 WLR 330, p. 336 per Lord Goff.
[196]See Williams, op. cit., n. 3, pp. 536–67.
[197]The strongest judicial expression against the ordinary person test has been by Justice Murphy in *Johnson* (1976) 136 CLR 619 and *Moffa* (1977) 138 CLR 601. For law reform commissioners taking a similar view, see the Criminal Law and Penal Methods Reform Committee of South Australia, Fourth Report, *The Substantive Criminal Law* (1977) and the Law Reform Commissioner, Victoria, Report No. 12, *Provocation and Diminished Responsibility as Defences to Murder* (1982). For academic commentators, see Brett P., 'The Physiology of Provocation, *Criminal Law Review*' 634 [1970]; Samuels, A., 'Excusable Loss of Self-Control in Homicide', 34 *Modern Law Review* 163 (1971); Gordon, G.H., *The Criminal Law of Scotland* 2nd ed, pp. 782–4 (1978) and Smith, J.C., and B. Hogan, *Criminal Law*, 4th edn, pp. 304–6 (1978).
[198]*Johnson v R* (1976) 136 CLR 619, p. 656 per Justice Gibbs.

India, the criticisms against that test and the consequent enthusiasm over a purely subjective assessment need not concern us here.

## B. Characteristics of the Ordinary Person

While the ordinary person test involves an objective evaluation of an accused's perception of and reaction to the provocation, the test also has a subjective component. The ordinary person is not regarded in a vacuum but is placed in the same circumstances as the particular accused. Furthermore, certain of the accused's personal characteristics are attributed to the ordinary person. This subjectivizing of the test was a relatively recent development which began with the House of Lords case of *Director of Public Prosecutions v Camplin*.[199] Prior to that decision, the test was purely objective, with none of the accused's characteristics attributable to the reasonable man.[200]

In England and Australia, the accused's characteristics are distinguished according to those having an effect on the gravity of the provocation and those which affect the power of self-control expected of an ordinary person. This distinction was drawn by Lord Diplock in *Camplin* in the following terms:

> In my opinion a proper direction to a jury on the question left to their exclusive determination by Section 3 of the [Homicide] Act of 1957 would be on the following lines. The judge should state what the question is using the very terms of the section. He should then explain to them that the reasonable man referred to in the question is a person having the power of self-control to be expected of an ordinary person of the sex and age of the accused, but in other respects sharing such of the accused's characteristics as they think would affect the gravity of the provocation to him....[201]

This distinction has been endorsed by Australian law, as is exemplified by the following passage from *Stingel v R*, the leading High Court of Australia case on provocation:

> While personal characteristics or attributes of the particular accused may be taken into account for the purpose of understanding the implications

[199] [1978] 2 All ER 168.
[200] A good example of the operation of this purely objective test is to be found in the House of Lords case of *Bedder v DPP* [1954] 2 All ER 801.
[201] [1978] 2 All ER 168, p. 175. The passage was expressly approved of by all the other Law Lords in *Camplin* and has recently been reaffirmed by the House of Lords in *R v Morhall* [1995] 3 WLR 330, p. 336.

and assessing the gravity of the wrongful act or insult, the ultimate question posed by the threshold objective test ... relates to the possible effect of the wrongful act or insult, so understood and assessed, upon the power of self-control of a truly hypothetical 'ordinary person'. Subject to a qualification in relation to age ... the extent of the power of self-control of that hypothetical ordinary person is unaffected by the personal characteristics or attributes of the particular accused.[202]

Several criticisms can be made of the distinction adopted by English and Australian laws. First, it runs counter to human reality. Let us take the case of a sexually impotent man who kills a prostitute upon her taunting him about his impotency.[203] Under the current law, the accused's sexual impotence may be attributed to the ordinary person when assessing the gravity of the taunts on him. However, the jury will not be permitted to take into account any personality trait of the accused occasioned by his having grown up with the knowledge of such a physical disability. This is inconsistent with the opinion of behavioural scientists that the accused's personality must be taken as a whole and cannot be dissected into the way he or she would view some provocative conduct on the one hand and the way he or she would respond emotionally to that conduct on the other.[204]

One further example will suffice. Consider the case of a conservative Lebanese woman who is provoked into killing a male relative when he makes sexual advances towards her.[205] Applying the distinction, the trial judge would have to instruct the jury to attribute the accused's ethnic origin to the ordinary person when assessing the gravity of the provocation towards her. However, the jury is not permitted to consider the accused's ethnicity when deciding upon the power of self-control of an ordinary person. In line with our scientific understanding of human behaviour, this approach fails to appreciate that an accused's reaction to the provocation is not solely the result of its being an affront to her traditional or cultural values but is also the result of her emotional and psychological disposition moulded by those values. It is further

---

[202](1990) 171 CLR 312, p. 327 and recently reaffirmed by a majority of the High Court in *Masciantonio v R* (1995) 69 ALJR 598, p. 602.

[203]These were basically the facts in the English case of *Bedder v DPP* [1954] 2 All ER 801.

[204]Brett, op. cit., n. 197, pp. 636–9.

[205]These were basically the facts of the New South Wales case of *R v Saliba* (1986) 10 Crim LJ 420.

submitted that the distinction is too subtle for the jury to appreciate and that there is a natural tendency for jurors to regard the particular characteristic as affecting the whole person of the accused in relation both to the gravity of the provocation and to her or his power of self-control.[206]

A second criticism of the distinction is that it bears no conceivable relationship with the underlying rationales of the defence of provocation (as opposed to the rationale of the ordinary person test itself). The defence has been variously regarded as premised upon the contributory fault of the victim and, alternatively, upon the fact that the accused was not fully in control of her or his behaviour when the homicide was committed.[207] Neither of these premises requires the distinction to be made between characteristics of the accused affecting the gravity of the provocation from those concerned with the power of self-control. Professor Brent Fisse in the latest edition of *Howard's Criminal Law* illustrates this point with the case of D who has recently undergone brain surgery and is taunted mercilessly by V about the unsightly scarring which has resulted from the operation.[208] Furthermore, V is aware that the surgery has left D in an extremely irascible condition. Fisse contends that in such a case, it would not be 'consistent with D's [blameworthiness] and V's contributory fault to deny the defence on the footing that D's extremely irascible condition cannot be attributed to the ordinary person; the fact that this condition affected D's self-control and not the gravity of the provocation offered is of little or no relevance to the merits of

---

[206]These criticisms were acknowledged by Lord Diplock himself in *Camplin* [1978] AC 705, p. 718. See also *Masciantonio* (1995) 69 ALJR 598, p. 606 per Justice McHugh; *Romano* (1984) 36 SASR 283, p. 291. The distinction has also been criticized as being too subtle because characteristics involving mental peculiarities often affect the power of self-control in unpredictable ways: see Horder, J., 'Provocation's Reasonable Man Reassessed', *Law Quarterly Review* 49, pp. 52–3 (1996). For a more general criticism of the difficulties confronting juries when applying the ordinary person test, there is Justice Barry's comment in *Jeffrey* [1967] VR 467, p. 478 that the test 'is unlikely to be applied by a jury, who are more likely to have regard to the limitations of the accused on trial than to the capacity for self-control of a mythical ordinary person'.

[207]See n. 4 and accompanying text.

[208]Op. cit., n. 25, pp. 88–9.

the matter'.[209] Fisse concludes by saying that, short of abolishing the defence of provocation, the difficulty created by the distinction seems avoidable only by abrogating the ordinary person test.

Somewhat paradoxically, this very conclusion constitutes the strongest support for the distinction promulgated by the English and Australian courts. The above discussion suggests that the underlying rationales of the defence of provocation are different from those for the ordinary person test. It is this feature which lends force to the call for completely subjectivizing the defence of provocation. That is, since the underlying rationales of the defence do not require an objective test, such a test can be abolished. However, the objective test does have its own rationales. One which has already been mentioned is that objective standards of behaviour are necessary for the protection of human life. Another and related rationale is the need to adhere to the principle of equality before the law.[210] This principle requires the power of self-control to be shared by all normal or ordinary people in the community. It follows that if an accused's unusual pugnacity or excitable temperament were permitted to be attributed to the ordinary person, whatever equality of treatment the test seeks to achieve would be demolished. For this reason, the High Court in *Stingel* was led to say that:

> No doubt, there are classes or groups within the community whose average powers of self-control may be higher or lower than the community average.... The principle of equality before the law requires, however, that the differences between the different classes or groups be reflected

[209]Ibid, p. 89. The word 'blameworthiness' replaces 'blamelessness' in the quotation which is clearly a typographical error. For another criticism of the distinction based on the underlying rationale of the defence, see Odgers, S., 'Contemporary Provocation Law—Is Substantially Impaired Self-Control Enough?' in Yeo, op. cit., n. 4, pp. 104–5.

[210]See *Stingel* (1990) 171 CLR 312, p. 324 adopting the following comment by Justice Wilson in the Supreme Court of Canada case of *R v Hill* (1986) 25 CCC (3d) 322, p. 345: 'The objective standard, therefore, may be said to exist in order that in the evaluation of the provocation defence there is no fluctuating standard of self-control against which accused are measured. The governing principles are those of equality and individual responsibility, so that all persons are held to the same standard notwithstanding their distinctive personality traits and varying capacities to achieve the standard.' For a comparison between Australian and Canadian law, see Yeo, S., 'Recent Australian Pronouncements on the Ordinary Person Test in Provocation and Automatism' 33 *Criminal Law Quarterly* 280 (1992).

only in the limits within which a particular level of self-control can be characterised as ordinary.[211]

All told, then, the distinction drawn between the power of self-control and the gravity of provocation appears to be a necessary corollary to the ordinary person test in the defence of provocation. The ordinary person's power of self-control must be held constant and unaffected by the accused's particular temperament or personality, save for one or two characteristiscs which will be discussed below.[212] Attributing these peculiar temperaments or personalities to the ordinary person would demolish the objective quality of the test. With this aspect of the test in place, the law is free to follow the dictates of fairness and human reality to permit all characteristics of an accused which have an effect on the gravity of the provocation to be attributed to the ordinary person.

## C. A Comparative Evaluation of the Test

An evaluation of English law will now be conducted under the headings of characteristics affecting the gravity of the provocation and those affecting the power of self-control. This exercise will be repeated for Australian law and then followed for Indian law. In respect of the last, it will be observed that the distinction is not as strictly applied in that jurisdiction, thereby creating the opportunity for a useful reappraisal of the need for and limitations of the distinction.

## 1. The English law

While Lord Diplock in *Camplin* had clearly advocated the distinction between characteristics affecting the gravity of the provocation and those affecting the power of self-control, the distinction and the characteristics on both sides of the divide have had an uncertain and troubled passage through the English courts. The distinction itself has not always been so clearly acknowledged by the courts and commentators. The following statement by Professors John Smith and Brian Hogan in their influential text *Criminal Law* bears this out:

The reasonable man must now be endowed by the jury with the age, sex

---

[211]Ibid., p. 329.
[212]These characteristics include the accused's age and, more contentiously, sex and ethnic or cultural origin.

and other personal characteristics of the accused, whether normal or abnormal. The characteristics may be taken into account by the jury ... both in assessing the gravity of the provocation addressed to the accused and in determining what degree of self-control is to be expected of him.[213]

This statement asserts that all the characteristics of an accused which have a bearing on the gravity of the provocation can also be taken into account in relation to an ordinary person's power of self-control. If this were correct, the distinction propounded by *Camplin* will be extinguished and, with it, the objective test. However, this is an inaccurate statement of the English law. Although not always fully acknowledged by the courts, the distinction has been maintained in the English law and was recently reaffirmed by the House of Lords.[214]

There is some uncertainty under English law over the types of characteristics which may be attributed to the ordinary person. With regard to the gravity of the provocation, unnecessary limitations were imposed by the Court of Appeal before a characteristic could be recognized. Although these limitations have recently been removed by the House of Lords, there remain certain other unresolved issues. With regard to the power of self-control, the English courts have held that an accused's age and sex may be relevant. Why sex should have this function has not been adequately explained. Another question which the courts have not yet answered is why an accused's ethnic origin might not be permitted to affect an ordinary person's power of self-control.

*(i) Characteristics affecting the gravity of the provocation:* The English Court of Appeal, in a series of decisions, unnecessarily restricted the types of characteristics which may have a bearing on the gravity of the provocation.[215] It did so by enthusiastically adopting a test devised by the New Zealand Court of Appeal in *R v McGregor*.[216] In that case, Justice North ruled that a characteristic qualifies for attribution to the ordinary person provided it satisfies three conditions: a sufficient degree of permanence, a sufficient degree of differentiation from the ordinary run of humankind and that the provocation must have targeted the characteristic. It must

---

[213]Op. cit., n. 53, p. 359. Paradoxically, the authors proceed immediately to cite Lord Diplock's direction in *Camplin*, which contains the distinction.
[214]See *R v Morhall* [1995] 3 WLR 330, p. 336 per Lord Goff.
[215]For a fuller discussion of this issue, see Yeo, op. cit., n. 172, pp. 436–41.
[216][1962] NZLR 1068.

be stressed that Justice North had devised his test to determine what characteristics could be permitted to affect the *power of self-control* of an ordinary person.[217] The English Court of Appeal overlooked this important aspect and applied the test to assessing what characteristics were relevant to the gravity of the provocation. For example, in *R v Dryden*, the court was prepared to attribute D's obsessive and eccentric character to the ordinary person for the purpose of determining the gravity of the deceased's provocation only after it was satisfied that the three conditions in the *McGregor* test had been met.[218]

The House of Lords has recently held in *R v Morhall* that the test is to be treated with caution under English law.[219] Save for the requirement that the provocation must have been directed at the characteristic, the House ruled that any characteristic of an accused could be relevant when assessing the effect of the provocation on an ordinary person.[220] In so doing, the House was merely reaffirming the decision in *Camplin* which had imposed restrictions on the types of characteristics affecting the power of self-control (which it confined to age and sex) as opposed to the gravity of the provocation.[221]

[217]See ibid., p. 1081, where he said: 'The offender must be presumed to possess in general the power of self-control of the ordinary man, save in so far as his power of self-control is weakened because of some peculiar characteristic possessed by him. It is not every trait or disposition of the offender that can be invoked to modify the concept of the ordinary man'. He then proceeded to propound his test to determine those traits or dispositions which, while weakening the power of self-control, could be attributed to the ordinary person.
[218][1995] 4 All ER 987. See also *R v Newell* [1980] 71 Cr App R 331; *Ahluwalia* [1992] 4 All ER 889; *R v Morhall* [1993] 4 All ER 888; *R v Humphreys* [1995] 4 All ER 1008.
[219][1995] 3 WLR 330, p. 338, noting that the test has been discredited even in New Zealand in the case of *R v McCarthy* [1992] 2 NZLR 550. See also the Privy Council decision to the same effect in *Luc Thiet Thuan v R* [1996] 2 All ER 1033, p. 1043.
[220]Ibid., pp. 335–8.
[221]An additional reason for excising the *McGregor* test from English law is that Justice North had felt the need to recognize certain characteristics affecting the power of self-control because New Zealand law does not have a defence of diminished responsibility. Since English law recognizes such a plea, defendants with weakened powers of self-control should be pleading diminished responsibility instead of provocation.

While the virtual demise of the *McGregor* test under English law is a salutary development, it is necessary to evaluate whether the House of Lords was correct in holding that *all* characteristics of an accused, without exception, might be relevant to the gravity of the provocation provided the provocation had targeted those characteristics. This issue was neatly raised on the facts in *Morhall*.[222] D, an addict to glue-sniffing, fatally stabbed V after he had chided D throughout the day about his addiction. The Court of Appeal upheld D's murder conviction, holding that the trial judge was correct in not referring the jury to D's glue-sniffing as a characteristic of an ordinary person when evaluating the gravity of the provocation. The court thought that while *Camplin* had decided that the reasonable man should be invested with the accused's characteristics, that decision could not have meant to include characteristics repugnant to the concept of the reasonable man.[223] The court felt that, should D's glue-sniffing be attributed to the reasonable man, similar indulgence should be afforded to an alcoholic or a defendant who had illegally abused heroin to the point of addiction. Similarly, a paedophile, upbraided for molesting children, would be entitled to have his characteristic weighed in his favour on the issue of the gravity of the provocation. Surely, the court concluded, a reasonable man could not be said to possess these addictions or propensities.

When the case came before the House of Lords, it overturned the decision of the Court of Appeal. The House saw no problem with investing the reasonable man with the characteristic of glue-sniffing for the purpose of assessing the effect of V's provocation on the reasonable man, since that provocation had been directed towards D's addiction.[224] The House opined that it would have been prepared to recognize other 'discreditable' characteristics such as being an alcoholic, a drug addict or a sex offender.[225] The court's explanation for its stance was that, while the objective condition in provocation involves considering the issues of the gravity of the provocation and the power of self-control, it is only the latter which has to bear the quality of reasonableness (or ordinariness). In the words of Lord Goff, who delivered the main judgement:

[222][1993] 4 All ER 888 (CA); [1995] 3 WLR 330 (HL) .
[223][1993] 4 All ER 888, p. 893.
[224][1995] 3 WLR 330, pp. 337–8.
[225]Ibid.

the function of the [reasonable man] test is only to introduce, as a matter of policy, a standard of self-control which has to be complied with if provocation is to be established in law.[226]

This comment is entirely consistent with the earlier theoretical discourse on the underlying rationales of the defence and the ordinary person test.

While the House of Lords in *Morhall* was right to overrule the Court of Appeal, its decision should not be read as holding without any qualification that all characteristics of an accused may be attributable to an ordinary person when assessing the gravity of the provocation. It is submitted that the defence of provocation will be denied to members of a cultural sub-group which promotes the use of violence against those who disagree with or are disagreeable to them. Take, for instance, a Nazi who is confronted by a Jew calling for the Nazi Party to be outlawed. Or a black person initiating a conversation with a white racist militant who fervently believes that it is the gravest of insults for coloureds to speak to whites unless spoken to first. Similarly, an ultra-zealous follower of a religion may be deeply committed to acting violently against anyone who he perceives has gravely affronted his faith. In all these cases, should the enraged parties kill their provokers, the law would be countenancing racial and religious intolerance if it permitted the defence of provocation to succeed.[227] It is conceded that the House of Lords in *Morhall* did not expressly make any exception to its ruling on characteristics affecting the gravity of the provocation. However, there is a statement in *Camplin* which suggests that the ordinary person will not be invested with the violent characteristics of these and other racially or religiously intolerant sub-groups. Lord Diplock had said that:

> [a] crucial factor in the defence of provocation from earliest times has been the relationship between the gravity of the provocation and the way in which the accused retaliated, both being *judged by the social standards of the day.*[228]

This comment reminds us that the origins of the defence of

---

[226]Ibid., p. 336.

[227]Horder, op. cit., n. 160, pp. 144–5, has argued that making available the defence in these cases would require the jury to suspend their commitments to fundamental liberal values and to endorse moral agnosticism or cultural relativism.

[228][1978] 2 All ER 168, p. 174. Emphasis added.

provocation under English law was integrally connected with the institution of duelling and the requirements of honour in the face of affronts. Although the English courts had shown some compassion towards duellists in earlier times, they were roundly rejecting the code of honour by the nineteenth century.[229] They did so by refusing to gauge the gravity of the provocation from the view point of members of the duelling subculture. It may be confidently asserted that today's social standards would continue to deny the defence of provocation to members of violent sub-groups who demand that their members protect the group's beliefs and codes of honour with physical violence.

*(ii) Characteristics affecting the power of self-control:* When it comes to characteristics affecting the power of self-control expected of an ordinary person, English law states that the only relevant characteristics are the accused's age and sex. Apart from these, the ordinary person is devoid of any characteristics of the accused which may affect the capacity for self-control. This ruling explains why, for this purpose, characteristics such as a state of intoxication (by alcohol or other drugs),[230] unusual pugnacity or excitability[231] are not attributed to the ordinary person.

By age, the English courts must have meant youthful immaturity. This is evident when we observe that in *Camplin*, Lord Diplock said that the justification for making age a qualification to the ordinary power of self-control requirement was that 'to require old heads upon young shoulders is inconsistent with the law's compassion to human frailty'.[232] The stance taken by the law is based on the generalization that teenagers and young adults are less capable of self-control than older, mature individuals. In this context, youth has no clear boundaries and it is conceivable that the courts will be prepared to recognize older youths of nineteen

---

[229]See Horder, J., 'The Duel and the English Law of Homicide', 12 *Oxford Journal of Legal Studies* 420 (1992).

[230]See *Morhall* [1995] 3 WLR 330, pp. 337–8 where Lord Goff said that because drunkenness 'displayed a lack of ordinary self-control it was excluded as a matter of policy'. His Lordship did, however, observe that, following the *Camplin* distinction, drunkenness would be relevant when assessing the gravity of the provocation should V have taunted D over his condition.

[231]See, for example, *R v Lesbini* [1914] 3 KB 1116; *R v Alexander* (1913) 9 Cr App R 139.

[232][1978] 2 All ER 168, p. 174.

years and beyond, since young adulthood fades gradually into full maturity.[233] Whether logical or not, it seems humane and consistent with the defence's rationale of compassion for human frailty to allow the jury to take youth into account in cases of provocation.[234]

With regard to sex, the English courts have, to date, said very little about its relevance to the power of self-control issue. Apart from expressing sex alongside age as relevant to the power of self-control, there is no clear indication in *Camplin* that their Lordships meant for sex to affect the capacity for self-control. Indeed, the judgements contain statements which suggest the contrary — that men and women are to be held to a *single* standard of self-control. Thus, Lord Diplock decribed the 'reasonable man' as 'an ordinary person of *either* sex ... possessed of such powers of self-control as everyone is entitled to expect that his fellow citizens will exercise'.[235] Likewise, Lord Simon said that '*the* standard of self-control which the law requires before provocation *is* held to reduce murder to manslaughter is still that of the reasonable person'.[236] These judicial pronouncements envisage a single standard of self-control which both sexes should conform to. Complementing these pronouncements is the judgement of Lord Goff in the recent Privy Council case of *Luc Thiet Thuan*.[237] His Lordship cited with approval a passage from a leading High Court of Australia case on provocation which had expressly held that age was the only characteristic which could affect the power of self-control of an ordinary person.[238] Although Lord Goff did not comment further

[233]Cf *R v Ali* [1989] Crim LR 736, where the Court of Appeal held that there was no difference between a reasonable person of twenty years of age and a reasonable person of any other age. The comment on the case in [1989] Crim LR 727 is unhelpful as it confuses the role of age affecting the power of self-control (which was the issue at hand) with that pertaining to the gravity of the provocation to someone of D's age.

[234]Williams, op. cit., n. 3, p. 539.

[235](1976) 2 All ER 168 pp. 173–4. Emphasis added and so noted by the South Australian Court of Criminal Appeal in *Romano* (1964) 36 SASR 283, pp. 288–9.

[236][1978] 2 All ER 168, p. 182. (Emphasis added.) Among the judgements in *Camplin*, Lord Simon's has the most discussion on sex and the law of provocation. However, his statements have mainly to do with the gravity of the provocation, over which there is little controversy.

[237][1996] 2 All ER 1033.

[238]Ibid., p. 1045, citing the High Court of Australia case of *Stingel* (1990) 171 CLR 312, p. 327, which is discussed below.

on the passage, it may be assumed that he had read the whole judgement in which the passage appears and agreed with the High Court of Australia that the characteristic of sex should be taken out of the *Camplin* ruling.

There are sound reasons for interpreting *Camplin* as holding that the capacity for self-control is the same for ordinary men and women. To interpret otherwise would breach the principle of equality before the law which makes it unacceptable to contend that persons of different sex should be held to different standards of self-control. Equality is achieved among persons having different levels of self-control when the minimum level expected of ordinary people is applied to everyone. Thus, assuming that it can be scientifically proven that women on average possess a higher power of self-control than men, a female accused will not receive unequal treatment because the law requires her to be assessed according to the lowest level of self-control regarded as 'ordinary' by the community. This would be the average power of self-control of ordinary men in the community. This was the approach taken by the High Court of Australia in *Stingel*, where the court said:

> [I]t may be that the average power of self-control of the members of one sex is higher or lower than the average power of self-control of members of the other sex. The principle of equality before the law requires, however, that the differences between different classes or groups be reflected only in the limits within which a particular level of self-control can be characterised as ordinary. The lowest level of self-control which falls within those limits or that range is required of all members of the community.[239]

The result of this approach has been that Australian law, while accepting the *Camplin* distinction, has expressly rejected sex as affecting the power of self-control, leaving age as the only relevant exception.

Another reason for excluding sex is that differentiating the capacity for self-control according to sex promotes the contentious stereotypes which depict women as the gentler sex and normally passive and submissive in the face of provocation while men are normally active and aggressive. Such stereotyping perpetuates the image of women who kill as being either aberrational and evil monsters or excessively pathological.[240] Women are viewed in the

---

[239](1990) 171 CLR 312, p. 329.
[240]Nicolson, D., 'Telling Tales: Gender Discrimination, Gender Construction and Battered Women Who Kill', 3 *Feminist Legal Studies* 185, pp. 201–5 (1995).

first way if they have acted like men, that is, rejected their femininity by having the lower level of self-control accredited to normal men. They are viewed as pathologically mad if they are accorded all aspects of passive femininity for then their killing would have been so contrary to the behaviour expected of a 'normal' woman that it must be the act of a sick or mentally abnormal mind.[241] The social reality of the matter is that female homicides might be exceptional because they are rare but they are the actions of ordinary women who have been pushed to an extreme. Courts should therefore desist from the practice of casting women killers as 'either passive and irrational or abnormally active and rational but never active and rational'.[242] The law's insistence on a single standard of self-control for both sexes will assist considerably with this exercise. Hence, the sooner sex is left out of the *Camplin* equation pertaining to the power of self-control, the better.[243]

One other characteristic will be raised here because it has received considerable attention in the Australian and Indian courts. It is the ethnic origin of an accused. The contention is that there may be ethnic communities whose members possess a lower capacity for self-control than members belonging to other ethnic groups. Justice and fairness may dictate that in such cases an accused's ethnicity should be attributed to the ordinary person when assessing the power of self-control. At this juncture, it may be asked why an accused's sex should be excluded but her or his ethnicity should be included.[244] The reason is that we are here concerned with those ethnic groups which have a *lower* capacity for self-control. In this respect, they are in the same position as youths. In contrast, when dealing with sex, we were concerned with the *higher* capacity for self-control expected of ordinary women. Thus, what is involved is the consideration of whether characteristics like youthful immaturity

---

[241]In his illuminating article, Nicolson, ibid., uses *R v Thornton* [1992] 1 All ER 306 to illustrate how legal discourse might present a woman killer as doubly bad and *R v Ahluwalia* [1992] 4 All ER 889 to present the pathologically mad woman killer.

[242]Ibid., p. 204.

[243]For the proposal that reference to sex in the *Camplin* direction covers the gender-specific response patterns of accused persons rather than the power of self-control, see Yeo, S., 'Sex, Ethnicity, Power of Self-Control and Provocation Revisited', 18 *Sydney Law Review* 304 (1996).

[244]See Leader-Elliott, I., 'Sex, Race and Provocation: In Defence of *Stingel*', 20 *Criminal Law Journal* 72, p. 92 (1996).

and the relatively lower tolerance levels of certain ethnic groups should be attributed to the ordinary person as an exercise in mitigation. This is to be contrasted with an exercise in penalizing defendants, as would occur should the standard of self-control be raised whenever female defendants were involved.

The English courts have not really dealt with the characteristic of ethnicity in this manner. The little there is by way of case authority indicates that this characteristic will not be recognized. There is, of course, Lord Diplock's direction in *Camplin*, which mentioned age and sex as the only characteristics which may be relevant to the issue of power of self-control. There is also the following statement by Lord Simon in the same case, which is directly on the point:

> In my judgement the reference to 'a reasonable man' at the end of [Section 3 of the *Homicide Act* (UK)] means 'a man of ordinary self-control'. If this is so the meaning satisfies what I have ventured to suggest as the reasons for importing into this branch of the law the concept of the reasonable man, namely, to avoid the injustice of a man being entitled to rely on his exceptional excitability (whether idiosyncratic or by cultural environment or *ethnic origin*) or pugnacity.[245]

The problem with this passage is that it describes as exceptionally excitable the emotional state that may traditionally be ascribed to members of an ethnic group. In the same vein, it compares such an emotional state with pugnacity. Thus, in Lord Simon's view, all members of an ethnic community whose indigenous temperamental dispositions prompt them into reacting more quickly than the 'ordinary person' (who is, in England, presumably still the phlegmatic Anglo-Celtic/Saxon) are to be described as unusually excitable or pugnacious. This view, it is submitted, extends the characteristic of unusual excitability or pugnacity well beyond what was contemplated in cases such as *R v Lesbini*.[246] That case, as well as the earlier case of *R v Alexander*,[247] involved accused persons who were afflicted with some recognizable mental defect. Furthermore, these cases were pronouncements on the mental deficiencies of individuals and not whole communities. It is contended that had persons such as Lesbini or Alexander been

---

[245][1978] 2 All ER 168, p.182. (Emphasis added.) See also the comment on this passage by Williams, op. cit., n. 3, p. 541.
[246][1914] 3 KB 1116.
[247](1913) 9 Cr App R 139.

measured by the standards of ethnic communities with traditionally more volatile temperaments than the Anglo-Celtic/Saxons, they would still have been regarded as exceptionally excitable or pugnacious. In an increasingly heterogeneous society like the one in England, the description of a person as being unusually excitable or pugnacious should be measured not by what a segment of that society regards as acceptable behaviour but by what that mixed society as a whole would commonly expect as acceptable behaviour. I shall defer my conclusions on whether ethnicity should be recognized as affecting the power of self-control of an ordinary person till after I have discussed the Australian and Indian laws on the subject.

*(iii) Law reform proposals:* At this juncture, I might usefully digress a little to examine the latest English law reform proposals on the ordinary person test. The English Criminal Law Revision Committee in its report on *Offences Against the Person* proposed that:

> The test of provocation should be reformulated so that provocation is a defence to a charge of murder if, on the facts as they appeared to the defendant, it can reasonably be regarded as a sufficient ground for the loss of self-control leading the defendant to react against the victim with a murderous intent.

> The defendant should be judged with due regard to all the circumstances, including any disability, physical or mental, from which he suffered.[248]

These proposals replace the ordinary person test with a more liberal objective measurement, namely, the 'reasonableness' of the provocation in causing loss of self-control. Furthermore, the proposals require that account be taken of an individual's 'mental disability', which may be quite abhorrent to the community to which he or she belongs.[249] It is therefore obvious that the Committee sought to do away with the ordinary person test and the *Camplin* distinction as to characteristics. Given the clear intention of the Committee, it is surprising that the English Law Commission on codification of the criminal law advocated the

---

[248]14th Report (1980), Cmnd 7844, recommendations 9 and 10.
[249]That the Committee was contemplating an accused's characteristics involving capacity for self-control is further instanced by its acknowledgement that its proposal would bring the defence of provocation closer to that of diminished responsibility: see ibid., at para. 83.

*Camplin* distinction while claiming to be merely summing up the Committee's proposals.[250] The Commission's purported summing-up is as follows:

> [T]he provocation is, in all the circumstances (including any of his personal characteristics that affect its gravity) sufficient ground for the loss of self-control.[251]

The Commission gave the illustration of a sexually impotent person who had killed upon being subjected to assault with intent to rob. In the Commission's view, the characteristic of sexual impotence would not affect the gravity of the assault. Such a characteristic would, however, be highly relevant if the provocation consisted of taunts of sexual impotence. But what if the accused's sexual impotence had left him with an extremely iracible personality? Certainly under the proposals of the Criminal Law Revision Committee, this would have to be accounted for. In this respect, it cannot be said that the Commission's definition of provocation in its Criminal Code Bill accurately reflects the recommendations of the Committee.

Should the present law be changed in the ways suggested by the Criminal Law Revision Committee? Doubtless, the complexity of the ordinary person test is bound to perplex juries. By comparison, the Committee's proposal is simple and therefore an attractive alternative. However, the proposal still suffers from requiring the jury to imagine how a particular accused with her or his various characteristics (including physical and mental defects) might have viewed the provocation. Even if the jury could imagine this, it would then be required to decide whether the provocation could reasonably have led the accused to react against the provoker with murderous intent. These are evaluative questions which involve moral judgements over whether the law should exercise mitigation for a killing induced by provocation. The Committee's proposal leaves insufficient guidelines for the jury to carry out its tasks. The current English law, with its detailed rules, provides this much-needed guidance. As one supporter of the ordinary person test has so persuasively argued, the common law has created:

> an imaginary being — a near double for the accused — who was subjected to the same stresses as the accused, to provide a measure of the degree of

---

[250]The English Law Commission, No. 177, *A Criminal Code for England and Wales*, Vol. 2, para. 14.18 (1989).
[251]Draft Criminal Code, cl. 58(b).

wrongdoing when provocation induces fatal violence. Like court cards in the Tarot pack, the ordinary individuals generated by current provocation doctrine give body and substance to the moral imagination and provide a vehicle for the exercise of intuitive judgement. Though provocation doctrine is complex, jury instructions can draw on the concept of an ordinary person to illuminate, rather than obscure, that exercise of judgement.[252]

## 2. The Australian law

Australian courts have long followed *Camplin* in categorizing characteristics into those going to the gravity of the provocation and those affecting the power of self-control.[253] The distinction was recently reaffirmed by the High Court of Australia in *Stingel*[254] and in *Masciantonio*. [255]

*(i) Characteristics affecting the gravity of the provocation:* Australian law recognizes all characteristics of an accused as possibly affecting the gravity of the provocation, provided the provocation was directed at the characteristic. The position is accordingly identical to the current English law as clarified recently by the House of Lords in *Morhall*. There are some Australian decisions which followed the English Court of Appeal in restricting the types of characteristics according to the *McGregor* test.[256] However, this trend has been reversed by more recent decisions which have seen the error of applying the test to Australian law.[257] For instance, Chief Justice King in the South Australian case of *Romano* criticized the test by first noting the statement in *McGregor* which said that 'the offender must be presumed to possess in general the power of self-control of the ordinary man, save insofar as his power of

[252]Leader-Elliott, op. cit., n. 244, p. 96.
[253]Although *Camplin* was a case interpreting an English statutory provision, it has been regarded by Australian courts as representing the common law on the ordinary person test in provocation: see *R v O'Neill* [1982] VR 150; *R v Croft* [1981] 1 NSWLR 126; *R v Dutton* [1979] 21 SASR 356.
[254](1990) 171 CLR 312.
[255](1995) 69 ALJR 598.
[256]For example, see *R v Dincer* [1983] VR 460; *R v Croft* [1981] 1 NSWLR 126.
[257]This is clearly evident in the recent decisions of the High Court of Australia of *Stingel* and *Masciantonio* where a detailed examination of the law of provocation was conducted without any reference whatsoever to the *McGregor* test.

self-control is weakened because of some peculiar characteristic possessed by him'.[258] The judge then pointedly rejected the test on the following ground:

> To speak of the power of self-control of an ordinary person save insofar as his power of self-control is weakened by his own characteristics, is to deprive the test of its objective content except to the extent that transient states are to be disregarded. Unusual excitability and pugnacity would be relevant if they resulted from the individual's permanent temperament, or mental condition, as distinct from a transient condition. This would be contrary to long established authority: *R v Lesbini*; *DPP v Camplin*. ... This Court is bound by the authority of the High Court to apply the objective test: *Moffa*. ... This Court is not at liberty to adopt a view which would substantially subvert the objective character of the test.[259]

Had the English Court of Appeal conducted a similarly careful scrutiny of *McGregor* the test propounded in that case would not have been permitted to gain the recognition that it did under English law.

The following statement of the High Court of Australia in *Stingel* is declaratory of the law on the types of characteristics which may affect the gravity of the provocation to the ordinary person:

> [A]ny one or more of the accused's age, sex, race, physical features, personal attributes, personal relationships and past history may be relevant to an objective assessment of the gravity of a particular wrongful act or insult.[260]

The High Court seems to have made no exceptions to the types of characteristics which might possibly be taken into account in this way. However, it is contended that, if pressed with the point, the court would not go so far as to recognize the characteristic of certain cultural sub-groups whose codes of conduct demanded that their members act in violence against anyone who disagreed with or were disagreeable to them.[261] We have previously suggested that this would be the stance taken by the English courts in respect of people such as Nazis, militant racists and members of fanatical religious groups.[262] One could readily contend that such groups

---

[258][1984] 36 SASR 283, p. 290.

[259]Ibid., pp. 290–1. The decision in *Romano* was recently reaffirmed by the South Australian Court of Criminal Appeal in *R v Georgatsoulis* (1994) 62 SASR 351.

[260](1990) 171 CLR 312, p. 326.

[261]See Leader-Elliott, op. cit., n. 244, pp. 78–9.

[262]See above p. 67.

are the present-day equivalents of the duelling subculture which
the law afforded a measure of indulgence in earlier times but was
completely frowned upon by the nineteenth century. There are
expressions by the High Court which suggest the occurrence of a
similar development under Australian law. For example, in *Stingel*,
the court observed the role which 'contemporary conditions and
attitudes' play in determining the capacities for self-control of the
ordinary person.[263] And in *Parker*, the court noted the many rulings
in provocation cases which 'show how different in weight and
character are the things that matter in one age from those which
matter in another'.[264]

***(ii) Characteristics affecting the power of self-control:*** The Australian
courts have followed their English counterparts in recognizing age
(in the sense of youthful immaturity) as affecting the power of
self-control expected of an ordinary person. Besides the need to
exercise compassion towards the young, the courts have provided a
further reason in support of this qualification to the power of self-
control aspect of the objective test. In explaining its recognition of
youth, the High Court in *Stingel* said:

> But the approach may be justified on grounds other than compassion,
> since the process of development from childhood to maturity is something
> which, being common to us all, is an aspect of ordinariness.[265]

These ideas of a continuum of development and ordinariness are
linked to the principle of equality underpinning the ordinary person
test. This is well expressed by Justice Wilson in *R v Hill*, a decision
of the Supreme Court of Canada, which was heavily relied on by
the High Court in *Stingel*. Her Honour said:

> The incorporation of the accused's age into the objective 'ordinary person'
> standard is an attempt to reflect the extent of the legal rights and
> responsibilities of children in the legal system. The law treats all persons
> as equal members of society and holds them responsible on an equal

---

[263](1990) 171 CLR 312, p. 327. Admittedly, the statement refers to the
power of self-control aspect of the ordinary person test rather than the gravity
of the provocation. However, the statement is equally applicable to the gravity
aspect of the test given the wider context in which it was made.
[264](1963) 111 CLR 610, p. 654 per Justice Windeyer and cited by the High
Court in *Stingel*, ibid., p. 326. Likewise, in *Moffa* (1977) 138 CLR 601, pp.
616–7, Justice Gibbs said that 'what might be provocative in one age might
be regarded with comparative equanimity in another'.
[265](1990) 171 CLR 312, p. 330.

basis for their actions except to the extent that they are in a development stage en route to achieving full adulthood and full legal rights and duties.[266]

A brief comment may be made concerning senility, which is at the opposite end of the age continuum from youth. The High Court in *Stingel* refused to recognize this characteristic as affecting the issue of power of self-control.[267] The reasons for this are unclear. The relevance of senility is that people of great age may manifest a decline in their capacity for self-control, as is sometimes indicated by the expression 'undergoing a second childhood'. While it may be true that old people rarely act in violence especially to the extent of killing, we should not rule out the possibility of cases of provocation involving aggressive septuagenarians. Clearly, the reason of compassion with which the law has recognized youthful immaturity applies with equal force to immaturity brought about by senility. To modify Lord Diplock's assertion in *Camplin*, requiring senile heads on young adult shoulders is inconsistent with the law's compassion to human frailty. The reason based on ordinariness applies to both youth and senility: just as it is 'ordinary' for all of us to have been young at some stage of our lives, it is ordinary for all of us to grow old. Then there is the reason given by Justice Wilson in *Hill* for treating youth as an exception to the principle of equality. While it is true that a person's youth is given special preference in many areas of the law, this alone should not prevent senility from being recognized as a further qualification to the ordinary person test. If youth is regarded as a development stage en route to achieving full adulthood, senility can be seen as a development stage en route to full degeneration. Since both stages of youth and senility are commonly experienced by us all, it is difficult to appreciate why the law should recognize the immaturity

---

[266](1986) 25 CCC (3d) 322, p. 351 and comparing this to a similar development in the law of negligence, citing the High Court of Australia case of *McHale v Watson* (1966) 115 CLR 199. The court in *Stingel* also relied on this passage in *McHale v Watson*: see (1990) 171 CLR 312, p. 330.

[267]Ibid., p. 300. The rejection is implied rather than expressly stated. Of course, if by 'senility' the High Court meant mental disorders experienced by a small handful of the aged, such a characteristic would be excluded. However, the court's discussion of senility alongside sex (an ordinary characteristic) suggests that it was considering cases of mental deterioration commonly experienced by the aged.

of one stage but not that of the other.[268] It is therefore submitted that age as a qualification to the ordinary person's power of self-control should cover the emotional immaturity of people both in their youth and in their senility.[269]

With regard to sex as a characteristic affecting the power of self-control, reference has already been made to the High Court's rejection of this and its reasons for doing so.[270] To reiterate, the court held that the principle of equality requires accused persons not to be differentiated by their sex but to be measured by the same standard of self-control to be expected of ordinary people. This is accomplished by gauging men and women against the lowest (or minimum) level of self-control within the range of levels which can be categorized as ordinary. In this regard, it is submitted that the Australian law is to be preferred to the English one insofar as the former has declared in no uncertain terms that the accused's sex does not affect the power of self-control expected of an ordinary person.

Turning now to the characteristic of ethnicity, the usual type of case envisaged here is of a migrant who has spent her or his formative years in a foreign culture and may perhaps continue to live in a cultural enclave in Australia. There is a line of case authorities prior to *Stingel* which recognized this as possibly affecting the power of self-control of an ordinary person.[271] The High Court's omission to comment on these authorities was unfortunate. Nevertheless, there can be no denying the pronouncement in *Stingel*

---

[268]The assumption here is that senility brings about a lowering of the power of self-control. Cf. Leader-Elliott, op. cit., n. 244, pp. 88–9 who appears to have overlooked this assumption. Whether senile persons have the physical strength to commit homicidal acts is a separate matter.

[269]This is the position in New Zealand where the Court of Appeal in *R v Trounson* [1991] 3 NZLR 690 held that there may be little room for age to be admitted as a 'characteristic' under Section 169(2)(a) of the New Zealand *Crimes Act* (the provision on provocation) except perhaps at the extremes of senility or obvious youthful immaturity.

[270]See section 5C1 (ii) above.

[271]See *Moffa* (1977) 138 CLR 601, p. 606; *R v Webb* (1977) 16 SASR 309, p. 314; *R v Dutton* (1979) 21 SASR 356, p. 377. However, there were other case authorities around the same time which refused to recognize ethnicity in this way. For a discussion of the two conflicting lines of authorities, see Yeo, S., 'Ethnicity and the Objective Test in Provocation', 16 *Melbourne University Law Review* 67 (1987).

that age alone is to be attributable to the ordinary person when assessing her or his power of self-control and, by implication, ethnicity is relevant only in so far as it affects the gravity of the provocation. This has since been confirmed by a majority of the High Court in *Masciantonio*. There, four of the five judges[272] reaffirmed that age alone was relevant with the dissenting judge, Justice McHugh, holding that ethnicity was another characteristic which should be permitted to affect the power of self-control of an ordinary person.[273]

There are several reasons why ethnicity has a strong claim to being recognized, alongside age, as a qualification to the power of self-control aspect of the ordinary person test. The various justifications, canvassed earlier, for making age a qualification are equally supportive of ethnicity. First, as regards the justification based on compassion to human infirmity, it could be argued that the law should account for the comparative lack of exposure on the part of the migrant to the various socializing institutions of the host country, such as the family and school, when compared to one who has been raised there since early childhood.

Second, in relation to the claim of ordinariness which age is said to have, it could be asserted that ethnicity can similarly be regarded as being an ordinary characteristic. The crux of the matter lies in what is meant by 'ordinary'. If the term involves the concept of universality, it may be conceded that the diverse spread of ethnic cultures lacks such a quality when these cultures are compared with one another. But if by 'ordinary' is meant normal, unexceptional and generally acceptable, it could be argued that every one of the cultures which make up Australia's heterogeneous society satisfies that quality. This contention may be more clearly evidenced if we spoke in terms of the power of self-control influenced by one's ethnic background. To borrow the words of the High Court in *Stingel*, 'no doubt, there are classes or groups within the community whose average powers of self-control may be higher or lower than the community average'.[274] The High Court did not then proceed to discount those groups with lower powers of self-control as failing the test of ordinariness. Instead, it spoke

---

[272](1995) 69 ALJR 598, p. 602   per Justices Brennan, Deane, Dawson and Gaudron.
[273]Ibid., p. 607.
[274](1990) 171 CLR 312, p. 329.

of 'limits' or a 'range' within which the level of self-control could be regarded as ordinary.[275] Hence, while one ethnic group may have a lower threshold of self-control than another in the same community, that lower level would still be regarded as 'ordinary' if it fell within the limits or range acceptable by the community as a whole. Under this scheme, there could be individuals whose pugnacious and excitable temperaments might be so pronounced as to be deemed extraordinary by every ethnic group in the community.[276] Such unusual and unacceptable levels of self-control would then certainly not be attributed to the ordinary person. In this way, the societal protection rationale underlying the ordinary person test remains intact.

The third reason for recognizing age as a qualification is what Justice Wilson in *Hill* described as youthfulness being 'in a development stage en route to achieving full adulthood and full rights and duties'.[277] As a result, Justice Wilson was prepared to withold the principle of equality normally required by the ordinary person test. This justification can also be applied to ethnicity. An analogy may be drawn with a migrant who needs time to assimilate into her or his host community. When applying the ordinary person test in provocation, the migrant may be viewed as being in a development stage en route to achieving full socialization in the ways, values and expectations of her or his host community. The rider to this is that the level of self-control exercised by the migrant during this development stage must be within the limits or range regarded as 'ordinary' by society.

For those who remain unpersuaded by the third reason and who insist on adherence to the principle of equality for ethnicity, there is a further argument. This argument challenges the traditional way in which equality is seen to be accomplished. In the Australian (and indeed, English) context, we have a host of residents originating from diverse cultural backgrounds who intermingle with one another in both work and recreational settings. Consequently, to insist that all these different ethnic groups conform to the one standard of

[275]Ibid. Consistent with this approach, the High Court later (at pp. 331–2) stressed that the law was concerned with an ordinary person with powers of self-control within the range or limits of what is 'ordinary' rather than the precisely identifiable powers of self-control found in the 'average' person.

[276]This argument was made earlier in this work on pp. 72–3.

[277]*Hill* (1986) 25 CCC (3d) 322, p. 351.

behaviour set by the group having the greatest numbers (or holding the political reins of power) would create gross inequality. Equality among the various ethnic groups is achieved only when each group recognizes the others' right to be different and when the majority does not penalize the minority groups for being different.[278]

A fourth reason concerns the inter-relatedness of human perception and reaction. Behavioural science would regard an individual's assessment of the gravity of provocative conduct as being integrally tied together with her or his personal make-up.[279] Taking age again as an example, it is readily conceivable that an adolescent might be much more greatly affronted by some provocative conduct than would a mature adult. The law currently takes cognizance of this scientific fact by attributing an accused's age to the ordinary person both as to the gravity issue and as to the power of self-control. If age is so recognized, it is difficult to appreciate why the law does not extend the same recognition to an accused's ethnicity. Surely, one's personality can often be powerfully influenced by culture, as is well illustrated by the case mentioned earlier of the conservative Lebanese woman who kills a male relative making sexual advances towards her.[280] The deceased's conduct was undeniably provocative to the accused in view of her cultural background and the law does presently take cognizance of this. But what of her emotional and psychological make-up, which were likewise strongly moulded by her culture and which led to her being so deprived of her power of self-control as to kill?[281]

These reasons were sufficiently compelling for Justice McHugh in the High Court of Australia case of *Masciantonio* to revise his earlier decision in *Stingel*[282] so as to recognize ethnicity when gauging the ordinary person's power of self-control.[283] The learned judge's concluding remarks on this issue are worth citing in full:

[278]See the Editorial Note entitled 'The Cultural Defense in the Criminal Law' 99 *Harvard Law Review* 1293 (1986).

[279]Brett, op. cit., n. 197.

[280]See above p. 60. There, the example of the sexually impotent man was given alongside this case. However, the same concession afforded to the Lebanese woman will not be extended to the sexually impotent man because his peculiar characteristic fails the test of ordinariness.

[281]See further, Yeo, op. cit., n. 271, pp. 79–81.

[282]In *Stingel*, Justice McHugh was party to a single joint judgement of the High Court which held that age alone was relevant to the power of self-control aspect of the ordinary person test.

[U]nless the ethnic or cultural background of the accused is attributed to the ordinary person, the objective test of self-control results in inequality before the law. Real equality before the law cannot exist when ethnic or cultural minorities are convicted or acquitted of murder according to a standard that reflects the values of the dominant class but does not reflect the values of those minorities.

If it is objected that this will result in one law of provocation for one class, I would answer that that must be the natural consequence of true equality before the law in a multicultural society when the criterion of criminal liability is made to depend upon objective standards of personhood. Moreover, to a large extent a regime of different laws already exists because the personal characteristics of the accused including attributes of race and culture are already taken into account in determining the effect of the provocative conduct of the deceased on the ordinary person. In any event, it would be much better to abolish the objective test of self-control in the law of provocation than to perpetuate the injustice of an 'ordinary person' test that did not take into account the ethnic or cultural background of the accused.[284]

I shall leave my final submissions as to whether these reasons are sufficiently compelling for ethnicity to be recognized as a qualification until after my analysis of the Indian law.

At this juncture, mention should briefly be made of the special position of members of Aboriginal enclaves located in isolated regions of Australia. Prior to the decision in *Stingel*, there existed a long line of Northern Territory cases involving Aboriginal defendants who had resided in these enclaves.[285] The Northern Territory Supreme Court ruled in these cases that Aboriginality was significant for the purpose of assessing the gravity of the provocation as well as the capacity for self-control. For example, in *Jabarula v Poore*, Justice Kearney held that an accused of that ethnic background is expected to possess 'such powers of self-control as everyone is entitled to expect an ordinary person of that culture and environment to have'.[286] That ruling seems to have continued

---

[283](1995) 69 ALJR 598, p. 607. His Honour expressly referred to this author's article in which the various justifications mentioned were presented: see Yeo, S., 'Power of Self-Control in Provocation and Automatism', 14 *Sydney Law Review* 3, pp. 11–3 (1992).

[284]Ibid.

[285]For example, see *R v Patipatu* (1951–1976) NTJ 18; *R v McDonald* (1951–1976) NTJ 186; *R v Muddarubba* (1951–1976) NTJ 317; *R v Jimmy Balir* (1951–1976) NTJ 633; *R v Nelson* (1951–1976) NTJ 327.

[286](1989) 68 NTR 26, p. 34; (1989) 42 A Crim R 479, p. 488.

with the decision in *R v Mungatopi*, a case which came after *Stingel*.[287] This approach is arguably confined to cases occurring within Aboriginal enclaves and does not cover cases involving migrants from a foreign culture settling in Australia. The concession to Aborigines may be justified on the ground that they were (and unfortunately still remain) political nonentities while migrants, who are usually persons of enterprise and pertinacity, are not.[288] The host country can therefore only confer upon these new migrants equal (but not more) social rights and opportunities with those who are already enjoying full rights of citizenship. Another justification is that, whereas Aborigines and Australians of Anglo-Celtic/Saxon origin can be easily differentiated because they generally live apart from one another, the same cannot be said of migrants who join a community having a strange and altogether different background from their own. In the case of migrants, the law would be over-complicated if the triers of fact had to enquire whether, at the time of killing, the migrants were more under the influence of their original homeland than of their new host country.

*(iii) Law Reform proposals:* By way of Australian efforts to reform the ordinary person test by legislative fiat, there is the proposal by the Law Reform Commission of Victoria in its *Homicide* reference.[289] The proposal is very similar to the one suggested by the English Criminal Law Revision Committee.[290] The Commission recommended that a person suffering loss of self-control as a result of provocation who intentionally kills another is not guilty of murder but guilty of manslaughter 'if, in all the circumstances, including any of the defendant's personal characteristics, there is a sufficient reason to reduce the offence from murder to manslaughter'.[291] As with the Criminal Law Revision Committee's proposal, it is immediately apparent that this formula provides few clues to the jury to guide them in their determination whether to convict of murder or manslaughter. In this respect, the detailed

---

[287](1991) 57 A Crim R 341. The court found that *Stingel* did not govern the provision on provocation contained in the *Criminal Code* 1983 (NT).

[288]Brown, B., 'The Ordinary Man in Provocation: Anglo-Saxon Attitudes and Unreasonable Non-Englishmen', 13 *International and Comparative Law Quarterly* 203, pp. 226–7 (1964).

[289]Report No. 40, *Homicide* (1991).

[290]Discussed above on pp. 73–4.

[291]Op. cit., n. 289, para. 191.

rules devised by the common law, although complex, afford much-needed guidance to juries.

## 3. The Indian law

In *Nanavati*, the Supreme Court read the ordinary person test into the wording of Exception 1 to Section 300 of the Indian Penal Code by ruling that:

> The test of 'grave and sudden' provocation is whether a reasonable man, belonging to the same class of society as the accused, placed in the situation in which the accused was placed would be so provoked as to lose his self-control.[292]

The court was not breaking new ground, as there already existed several Indian decisions which had proposed such a test.[293] It will suffice now to observe that the concept of a reasonable person losing self-control was not contemplated by the framers of the Code since it grew in popularity under English law only after the promulgation of the Code.[294] Certainly, the Exception contains neither the expression 'reasonable man' nor some variation of it, thereby strongly suggesting that the framers had in mind a quite different test for grave provocation than the English version. In any event, it is clear from the judgements of the Indian courts which have prescribed the concept that they had derived it from English authorities rather than from a strict reading of the Exception itself. I shall leave discussing the test proposed by the Code framers to the next part.[295]

When the Indian courts first considered embracing the English reasonable man test to assess grave provocation, the test was a purely objective one. Hence, any characteristics personal to the accused could not be attributed to the English reasonable man. As previously noted, this position continued until 1978, when it was partially

---

[292]AIR 1962 SC 605, p. 630.

[293]For example, see *Soharab v Emperor* AIR 1924 Lah 450; *Dinabandhu Ooriya v Emperor* AIR 1930 Cal 199; *Ghulam Mustafa Gahno v Emperor* AIR 1939 Sind 182.

[294]Although this concept was first accorded recognition under English law in *R v Kirkham* (1837) 8 C & P 115, judges continued to pose the question of provocation in subjective terms to the jury until *R v Welsh* (1869) 11 Cox CC 336. The Code became law in India in 1862. This point is considered again below on p. 95.

[295]See pp. 94–101 below.

subjectivized by the House of Lords in *Camplin*. Right from the outset, however, the Indian courts were very clear that a purely objective test would create injustice if applied to a multi-cultural, multi-religious and multi-class structured society like the one in India. They were assisted in reaching this viewpoint by referring to the Code framers themselves:

> A person who should offer a gross insult to the Mahomedan religion in the presence of a zealous professor of that religion; who should deprive some high-born rajpoot of his caste; who should rudely thrust his head into the covered palanquin of a woman of rank, would probably move those he insulted to more violent anger than if he had caused them some severe bodily hurt. That on these subjects our [English] notions and usages differ from theirs is nothing to the purpose. We are legislating for them, and though we may wish that their opinions and feelings may undergo a considerable change, it is our duty, while their opinions and feelings remain unchanged, to pay as much respect to those opinions and feelings as if we partook of them.[296]

The proposition of the Supreme Court in *Nanavati* cited at the beginning of the discussion on this aspect of the Indian law is a good example of the way the Indian courts have modified the purely objective test contained in the English law of the time. By placing the ordinary person in the 'same class of society as the accused' and in the 'situation in which the accused was placed', the court was obviously contemplating certain of the accused's personal characteristics and circumstances to have a bearing on the ordinary person test. As with English and Australian laws, these characteristics can be categorized into those affecting the gravity of the provocation and those affecting the power of self-control of an ordinary person.

*(i) Characteristics affecting the gravity of the provocation:* As a general proposition, it appears that the Indian law is prepared to recognize all characteristics as relevant to the gravity of the provocation provided the provocation was directed at the characteristic. This stems from the Explanation to Exception 1, which states that the question whether the provocation was grave and sudden enough to prevent the offence from amounting to

---

[296]Macaulay, McLeod, Anderson and Millett, op. cit., n. 32, Note M, p. 145. The passage also expresses the Code framers' view that words or gestures could amount to provocation under Indian law although they could not under the English law of the time.

murder is a question of fact. Hence, the Code framers had deliberately left the question to be decided by the jury in every case, finding it futile to lay down a universal standard for measuring the gravity of the provocation.[297] This is a sensible approach, given the infinite variety of accused's characteristics and circumstances which, when attributed to the ordinary person, might persuade the jury to decide that such a person could be provoked into losing self-control. The Indian courts have recognized a host of characteristics and circumstances including age,[298] sex,[299] religious beliefs and values,[300] mental and physical disabilities,[301] drunkenness,[302] criminal conduct,[303] ethnicity,[304] cultural and social environment[305] and past experiences.[306] We can see from the inclusion of some of the characteristics on this list that the Indian courts have managed to avoid subscribing to the *McGregor* test. They have also avoided the pitfall of excluding 'discreditable' characteristics from affecting the gravity of the provocation to the ordinary person.[307]

It was suggested in the English and Australian discussion on the gravity of the provocation that the law should not recognize a

---

[297] *Abdul Majid v State*, 1963 (2) Cr LJ 631, pp. 633.

[298] *State v Bhand Jusub Mamad*, 1982 Cr LJ 1691.

[299] *Abdul Majid v State*, 1963 (2) Cr LJ 631.

[300] For example, in *Madhavan v State*, AIR 1966 Kerala 258, V threatened to leave D, her husband, at the same time removing her 'Thali' (a string signifying her marital tie with D) and throwing it at his face. The court held that V's conduct was sufficient provocation to warrant the application of the Exception. See also *Pancham v Emperor*, AIR 1947 Oudh 148.

[301] *Aktar v State*, AIR 1964 All 262.

[302] *Sadhu Singh v State* (1969) Cr LJ 1183.

[303] *Nga Paw Yin v Emperor*, AIR 1936 Rang 40.

[304] *Jamu Majhi v State* (1989) Cr LJ 753.

[305] *Nanavati v State*, AIR 1962 SC 605. In the Mysore High Court case of *In re Fakirappa*, 1971 Cr LJ 951, D had killed his cousin's daughter on finding that she had illicit intimacy with strangers. The court held that he could not claim that he had killed her under provocation when she was not under his protection and guidance. The court was effectively taking cognizance of the cultural and social environment of D and V, which regarded the familial relationship between them as being too distant to permit regarding the provocation as sufficiently grave.

[306] *Aktar v State*, AIR 1964 All 262.

[307] These mistakes were made by the English Court of Appeal and were discussed in this work at pp. 64–66.

specific type of anti-social characteristic. This concerns a cultural sub-group whose codes of honour and conduct encourage its members to act in violence against people who disagree with them or they find disagreeable. Although there do not seem to be any reported Indian cases on the matter, there are judicial statements which suggest that the Indian courts will take this line in an appropriate case. One such statement is that the jury must decide, on the particular facts of a case, whether 'the provocation was grave and sudden enough to permit an indulgent view of the crime committed by the accused'. Presumably, a jury would not be indulgent towards, say, a leader of the Thugees, a subcultural criminal group, who had killed a subordinate for being disrespectful to him in breach of the group's code of conduct. The jury would rather conclude that an ordinary person does not assume the defendant's identity as a Thugee leader. Another statement appears in the Allahabad High Court case of *Akhtar v State* where Justice Beg said:

> [W]hat is put forward as ... provocation ... must ... be capable of being considered grave, according to the norms or standards which govern the accused. These norms or standards represent ideas and sentiments about what is right and wrong. They may be the result of the membership of a particular social group such as a nation, a community, or, even a family —or of the peculiar history and circumstances of the accused, determining the accused's reactions towards the victim at a particular time.[308]

Thus far, Justice Beg seems to be prepared to recognize all of the accused's characteristics and circumstances, without any exception, when assessing the gravity of the provocation. However, he went on to impose the following important rider at the end of this passage:

> In every case, the test applied is an objective one in the sense that it must be capable of acceptance by reasonable men.[309]

Applying this rider to the example of the Thugee leader, there is little doubt that the jury as a collective group of reasonable people would not accept his plea of provocation to mitigate his charge of murder.

***(ii) Characteristics affecting the power of self-control:*** Like their English and Australian counterparts, the Indian courts have insisted

[308]AIR 1964 All 262, p. 269.
[309]Ibid.

that the ordinary person be held to a single standard of self-control save for a few limited exceptions. As with the law in these other jurisdictions, the Indian courts have recognized youthful immaturity as capable of affecting the power of self-control of an ordinary person.[310] With regard to sex, there are no Indian cases directly on the point. This tentatively suggests that the Indian courts do not differentiate the capacity for self-control according to the accused's sex. For the reasons given earlier for the need for equality before the law and to minimize the dangers of stereotyping, it is submitted that this is a sound position for the courts to have taken.[311]

The Indian courts have gone further to recognize that an accused's ethnic, cultural or social background can also have a bearing on the power of self-control of an ordinary person. The Supreme Court in *Nanavati* put it this way:

> Is there any standard of a reasonable man for the application of the doctrine of 'grave and sudden' provocation? No abstract standard of reasonableness can be laid down. What a reasonable man will do in certain circumstances depends upon the customs, manners, way of life, traditional values etc.; in short, the cultural, social and *emotional background* of the society to which the accused belongs. In our vast country there are social groups ranging from the lowest to the highest state of civilization. It is neither possible nor desirable to lay down any standard with precision: it is for the court to decide in each case, having regard to the relevant circumstances.[312]

By 'emotional background' the court was clearly discussing the normal level of self-control present in the particular ethnic, cultural or social group to which the accused belonged.

Some case examples can usefully be presented here. In *Jamu Majhi v State*, the Orissa High Court cited the above passage from *Nanavati* as authority for recognizing the accused's ethnic background for the purpose of assessing the power of self-control of an ordinary person of the same background. The court then noted that the accused belonged to the 'Adivasis', who 'are a class, comparatively more volatile and more prone to lose their self-control on slightest provocation'.[313] There are also cases where the ethnic, cultural or social background of the accused is relevant to both the

---

[310] *Nga Paw Yin v Emperor*, AIR 1936 Rang 40; *State v Bhand Jusub Mamad*, 1982 Cr LJ 1691.
[311] See pp. 70–1 above.
[312] AIR 1962 SC 605, pp. 629–30 per Justice Subba Rao. Emphasis added.
[313] Ibid., p. 755 per Justice Patnaik.

issues of gravity of provocation and power of self-control of the ordinary person. This occurred in *Atma Ram v State,* where an accused had killed his wife after she had denied his request for sexual intercourse and had used foul language on him.[314] The Allahabad High Court was prepared to take into account the fact that the accused was a villager in a remote part of the country and observed:

> It is important to emphasise that the impact of provocation on human frailty is to be judged in the context of the social position and environments of the person concerned. The restraint which is generally shown by sophisticated persons used to modern living is hardly to be expected in the case of a villager who still regards a wife as his personal property and chattel amenable at all times to his desire for sexual intercourse.[315]

The accused's characteristic of being a villager was accordingly relevant in relation to both the seriousness of the wife's affront and the power of self-control expected of an ordinary person from his village. The result was that the accused was given the benefit of the Exception. This may be compared with the case of *Madi Adma v State,* where the accused, an Aborigine, had killed his wife after she had retorted that it was none of his concern why she had gone out during the night.[316] The Orissa High Court recognized that the accused belonged to an ethnic group whose members are 'easily inflammable'. While this worked in favour of applying the Exception, it was eventually denied to the accused because the court found that women in the group were 'very free' to move about, unlike the customary restrictions on women of higher classes. Consequently, the court concluded that the wife's retort was not sufficiently grave to attract the Exception.[317]

It is observed that the Indian courts recognize only the level of self-control of a *whole class of ordinary* people of a particular ethnic, cultural or social group. This envisages that there may be individuals whose powers of self-control are regarded as abnormal within their

---

[314]1967 Cr LJ 1697 and cited with approval in *Gandaram Taria v State* 1982 Cr LJ 1229.

[315]Ibid., p. 1698.

[316](1969) 35 Cuttack LT 336.

[317]Ibid., pp. 340–1 per Justice Misra. For other cases where classes with lower levels of self-control have been recognized, see *Kartik Bag v State,* 1985 Cr LJ 888; *Mansa Ram v State,* 1975 Cr LJ 1772; *Noukar Mouledino v Emperor,* AIR 1937 Sind 212; *Nga Paw Yin v Emperor,* AIR 1936 Rang 40.

own class or group. In such cases, their peculiar temperaments will be precluded from affecting the power of self-control aspect of the ordinary person test.[318] Accordingly, while the ordinary person test under Indian law permits a greater amount of subjectivity than under English and Australian laws, it still retains the quality of objectivity by requiring the characteristic in question to be commonly shared by a whole group of ordinary people. The following comment by an Indian judge clearly makes the point:

> Although the social setting and psychological factors, determined by the circumstances and history of the particular offender ... appear to be intended to be taken into account to a much greater extent in this country, with its greater diversities of norm and standard, than it is possible or necessary to do so in England, yet, individual traits of the offender's character, such as his peculiar pugnacity or exceptional sensitiveness to insults or temperamental instability or an aberrant outlook, are not considered as grounds for any preferential treatment of the offender either in this country or in England.[319]

The Indian approach is preferable to the one under English and Australian laws, since it is much more in accord with human reality. Unlike these other laws, the Indian approach fully appreciates that an accused's reaction to the provocation is not solely the result of its being an affront to her or his traditional or cultural values but is also the result of her or his emotional and psychological disposition moulded by those values.

The various reasons supporting the recognition of ethnicity have been presented earlier.[320] These reasons, coupled with its successful application by the Indian courts, lead to the conclusion that, if possible, the laws of England and Australia should follow suit. However, there appear to be significant practical difficulties in the application of ethnicity in these jurisdictions. Unlike the characteristic of age, which every trier of fact has personally experienced or observed, the ethnicity of a particular accused and

---

[318]See *In re V Padavachi*, 1972 Cr LJ 1641, p. 1642; *Krishnan Nair v State*, Kerala LT 150, p. 158 (1965); *Abdul Majid v State*, 1963 (2) Cr LJ 631, p. 633; *Mahmood v State*, AIR 1961 All 538, p. 540; *Ghulam Mustapa Gahno v Emperor*, AIR 1939 Sind 182, pp. 183–4.

[319]*Akhtar v State*, AIR 1964 All 262, pp. 268–9 per Justice Beg . The judge's implication that England has a homogeneous society must, of course, now be qualified with the considerable influx of migrants from non-Anglo-Celtic/Saxon countries in recent years.

[320]See above, on pp. 80–3

the way it may affect her or his capacity for self-control may be far removed from their experiences. Consequently, expert witnesses would be required to inform the trier of fact on this issue, and these experts can, at best, only make generalizations about racial or cultural variations in the capacity for self-control.[321]

Furthermore, the evidence of these experts has a hope of having some measure of accuracy provided they are studying an essentially homogeneous ethnic group living in relative isolation from other ethnic groups. This is where the societies found in India differ significantly from those of England and Australia. There reside on the Indian sub-continent a multitude of communities which continue to be rigidly separated from one another by caste, race, religion and socio-economic considerations. In this regard, they are similar to the Australian Aboriginal communities living in geographical isolation. It is contended that expert evidence on the behavioural responses of members of these types of groups is feasible. The same, however, cannot be said of recent migrants from a foreign culture to England or Australia. Even if they were to reside in cultural enclaves, some process of assimilation into their host country is inevitable. It would then be practically impossible for experts to indicate, other than in the most speculative manner, the capacity for self-control of these migrants who have been subjected partly to the influences of their country of origin and partly to those of their new homeland. This is because there would be different degrees of assimilation experienced by each member of the ethnic group with the result that strict cultural homogeneity would be lacking. I would therefore submit that the Indian approach with regard to ethnicity should continue in that jurisdiction and, though it would be ideal for it to be invoked in England and Australia, problems of a practical nature do not make this feasible.

*(iii) Law reform proposals:* The Law Commission of India evaluated the operation of all the provisions of the Indian Penal Code and delivered its report in 1971.[322] With regard to the Exceptions to Section 300, the Commission said:

In substance, these Exceptions appear to us to have been carefully thought

---

[321]See Leader-Elliott, op. cit., n. 244, p. 89.
[322]Law Commission of India, 42nd Report, *Indian Penal Code* (1971).

out and they have stood the test of practical application over the years. We have only a few minor and formal amendments to suggest.[323]

The only amendment proposed by the Commission in respect of -he Exception on provocation was that the Explanation accompanying it was no longer required after the abolition of jury trials.[324] The Explanation, it is recalled, stipulates that whether the provocation was sufficiently grave and sudden to satisfy the Exception is a question of fact.

Although the Commission may have been correct to say that the defence of provocation has been operating in a reasonably satisfactorily way, my discussion has shown that this has largely been due to the work of the courts in clarifying and elaborating upon the wording of the Exception. Accordingly, the Commission should have taken the opportunity to incorporate these judicial pronouncements into the Exception.

By way of summary of this part, the first submission is that the distinction between characteristics affecting the gravity of provocation and those affecting the power of self-control is ideologically defensible and practical. All characteristics relevant to the gravity of the provocation should be attributable to the ordinary person save for those of certain violent cultural sub-groups. With regard to characteristics affecting the power of self-control, only the accused's age (in terms of youthful immaturity and senility) should be relevant in England and Australia. For India, however, in addition to age, the retention of cultural homogeneity by its many ethnic communities makes ethnicity another characteristic which should be permitted to affect an ordinary person's power of self-control. The same may be said of cases involving Australian Aboriginal accused persons residing in isolated communities.

## 6. The Response to the Provocation

For the defence to succeed, the provocation of the deceased must have induced the accused to lose her or his self-control. I have suggested earlier that the accused must have lost self-control to the extent of forming a murderous intention.[325] Besides this subjective

---

[323]Ibid., para. 16.7.
[324]Ibid.
[325]See above, pp. 48–9.

response, the law also requires a particular response from an ordinary person placed in the same circumstances and sharing certain characteristics with the accused. The laws of England, Australia and India require the ordinary person to have lost self-control and to have done what the accused did. The notion of 'doing what the accused did' includes a mental state accompanying some physical action. Here, the mental state of the ordinary person would logically be the same as that experienced by the accused, namely, the formation of a murderous intent against the provoker.[326] It must then be shown that, with this mental state, an ordinary person could have performed the homicidal act committed by the accused.

Until recently, the law in some of the jurisdictions under consideration required this homicidal act to bear a reasonable relationship to the provocation. This requirement sought to ensure that only very serious provocation could be relied on to explain the homicidal response of the accused. Another legal requirement is that the mode of killing must be morally acceptable. Here, the concern of the law is to deny any mitigation to the accused should her or his homicidal act have been assessed by the jury to be unacceptably brutal. The focus of this rule therefore differs from the reasonable relationship rule in that it considers whether the particular mode of killing falls within the types of modes which society is prepared to tolerate. In contrast, the focus of the reasonable relationship rule is on the degree of seriousness of the provocation. The treatment of these two rules by the courts of England, Australia and India will be examined below. But first, I shall present and evaluate the type of objective response to provocation which the framers of the Indian Penal Code had in mind.

## A. *Rage versus Loss of Self-Control*

Thus far, we have examined the Indian judicial contribution to the law of provocation in formulating a modified version of the English ordinary person test. The hypothesis is now raised that although the Indian judicial modifications invoke a more progressive posture than the English test, the Code framers had in mind a

[326]See *Masciantonio v R* (1995) ALJR 598, p. 604.

quite different and possibly superior test for grave provocation under Exception 1 to Section 300.

To appreciate that there was a different test intended by the Code framers, we need to return to 1860, when the Penal Code was first promulgated. There is first the claim by the framers that 'the system of law which we propose is not a digest of any existing system, and that no existing system has furnished us with even a groundwork'.[327] Here then was an express disclaimer of any subscription to English law from which the ordinary person test owes its origin. Even if this claim was not entirely accurate and the framers did rely on English legal principles, the ordinary person test had barely emerged under English common law during this period so it cannot be properly asserted that the framers had it in mind when they drafted the Exception.[328] What then was the test contemplated under the Indian Penal Code? The fact that the framers did not feel the need to spell it out strongly suggests that they saw the test as an uncomplicated one which could be confidently left to the jury to arrive at in a given case. Indeed, this is precisely what the framers did in enacting the Explanation to Exception 1, which makes it a question of fact whether provocation was sufficiently grave and sudden. Viewed in this light, the highly complex ordinary person test (even in its modified form devised by the Indian courts) cannot have been the one envisaged by them.

It is contended that the test envisaged by the Code framers would have been as follows. To be grave under the Exception, the provocation must be capable of inciting rage in an ordinary person of the class of society to which the accused belongs. Rage here denotes intense anger but not necessarily of the intensity which deprives a normal person of her or his power of self-control to the extent of forming a murderous intent. In a spectrum of emotional ferocity, rage features at the opposite end from going completely berserk, with loss of self-control coming after rage and increasing in degrees until it culminates in total deprivation of self-control.[329] Hence, rage would be a more common occurrence than loss of

---

[327]Macaulay, Mcleod, Anderson and Millett, op. cit., n. 32, p. viii.

[328]Brown, op. cit., n. 288, pp. 204–5.

[329]That part of the spectrum covered by loss of self-control was recognized by Lord Diplock in the Privy Council case of *Phillips v R* [1969] 1 AC 130, pp. 137–8. His Lordship regarded loss of self-control as a matter of degree ranging from icy detachment to going berserk.

self-control and in this respect, the Code framers would classify more instances of provocation as being grave than the Indian courts would be prepared to do.

A case which arrived at precisely the above test was the Court of Criminal Appeal of Ceylon (now Sri Lanka) decision in *Appuhamy v R*.[330] This case appears to have been virtually forgotten as a result of being overruled very shortly after it was decided.[331] A reading of the cases will show that, while the court in *Appuhamy* strove to discover the test for grave provocation from the wording of Exception 1 and from the commentaries of its framers, the judges who overruled *Appuhamy* were content to rely on English law. Consequently, for the purposes of the present discussion, *Appuhamy* must be regarded as more accurately reflecting the intentions of the Code framers.

Nagalingam SPJ, who delivered the main judgement of the court in *Appuhamy*, defined 'grave provocation' in the following terms:

> provocation may be said to be grave when it arouses violent anger or violent passion. Here 'violent anger' or 'violent passion' which is the equivalent of 'rage' merely describes a state of mind, and not ... that the person subject to such anger or passion should act violently or use physical violence. In fact the term 'violent' in these expressions means nothing more than intense or very strong.[332]

The judge found support for this definition from the Code framers themselves, who said:

> We agree with the great mass of mankind and with the majority of jurists ancient and modern in thinking that homicide committed *in the sudden heat of passion* on great provocation is to be punished but that in

---

[330] (1952) 53 New LR 313. Exception 1 to Section 294 of the Sri Lankan Penal Code is identical to Exception 1 to Section 300 of the Indian Penal Code.

[331] It was rejected by a majority of the Full Bench of the Court of Criminal Appeal of Ceylon in *Jamis v R* (1952) 53 New LR 401. Readers would be more familiar with the case of *A-G for Ceylon v Perera* [1953] AC 200, decided a year after *Jamis*. The Privy Council there read the reasonable retaliation rule into Exception 1 to Section 294 of the Sri Lankan Penal Code with scant regard for the wording of Exception 1. This issue will be discussed below.

[332] (1952) 53 New LJ 313, p. 316. Compare this comment with the one by the House of Lords in *Holmes* [1946] AC 588, p. 600 that, for words alone to amount to provocation, they had to be of a violently provocative character. See above, p. 15

general it ought not to be punished so severely as murder....

In general, however, we would not visit homicide committed *in violent passion* which had been suddenly provoked with the highest penalties of the law.[333]

After quoting these passages, Nagalingam SPJ asserted that the meaning of 'grave provocation' could be gleaned from the italicized phrases.[334] He regarded these phrases as describing states of mind such as rage as opposed to physical acts of violence. Hence the difference between this definition and the English ordinary person test is evident: it is only the latter test which required the provocation to have resulted in acts of physical violence.

The judge then turned to the prosecution's contention that grave provocation should be measured by the deprivation of an ordinary person's power of self-control. This contention has some accord with the view of the Code framers, since loss of self-control is a state of mind only, involving a greater intensity of anger than rage. However, it was rejected by Nagalingam SPJ after a careful examination of the wording of Exception 1. He found that the express wording of the Exception did not support the argument, since there was no connection between the expression 'grave provocation' (which was concerned with an ordinary person being enraged) and the notion of 'loss of self-control' (which had to be suffered by the particular accused). In the judge's opinion:

> A perusal of the language of the Exception would clearly reveal that loss of self-control is not set out as a standard to be applied in determining the gravity of the provocation. The Exception does not say that there should be *such* grave provocation *as* would result in a deprivation of the power of self-control. Nor does it say that loss of self-control should always be the result of grave provocation. For a proper appreciation, however, of what the Exception does imply, one must give full purport to the adverb 'whilst' and the meaning would then be clear that only in such cases where [a prisoner has actually been deprived] of the power of self-control as a result of grave and sudden provocation can the benefit of the Exception be claimed by a prisoner.[335]

[333]Macaulay, Mcleod, Anderson and Millett, op. cit., n. 32, Note M, p. 144. Emphases added by the court in *Appuhamy*. For another passage to like effect, see Cameron, C.H. and D. Eliott, *First and Second Reports on the Indian Penal Code as originally framed in 1837* (1888), para. 271. These reports were delivered in July 1846 and June 1847 respectively.
[334](1952) 53 New LR 313, pp. 316–7.
[335]Ibid., at 315 (judge's emphasis).

Nagalingam SPJ concluded his analysis of the Exception by quoting from his earlier judgement in the Court of Criminal Appeal of Ceylon case of *Perera v R*:

> It has to be stressed that the Exception itself expressly refers to the offender being deprived of his power of self-control, and in view of this express reference to the offender, it would be altogether unwarrantable to hold, as contended for by the learned Solicitor-General, that one must first determine in this instance too whether the average man under contemplation would himself have been deprived of his power of self-control as a result of the provocation given before determining whether the offender himself did in fact lose his power of self-control. We are of opinion that once the conclusion is reached that the provocation, taking the case of the average man, was grave and sudden, the next question that need receive the attention of the Jury is whether the prisoner himself, as a result of the provocation received did lose his self-control, it being immaterial whether the average man would or would not have lost his power of self-control.[336]

To summarize the preceding passages from *Appuhamy* and *Perera*, the determination of grave provocation and its effect on a particular accused should proceed on the following two-step analysis:

(1)  The court should first consider whether the provocation was grave by asking whether it was such as to incite rage (or intense anger or passion) in the mind of an ordinary person belonging to the same class of society as the accused.

(2)  Once the conclusion has been reached that the provocation was grave as outlined in (1), the court should then consider whether, as a result of the provocation, the particular accused did actually lose her or his power of self-control. It is unnecessary to enquire further as to whether an ordinary person could or could not have lost her or his power of self-control.

This analysis fully reflects the scheme intended by the Code framers.

From a practical perspective, the Code framers' test for grave provocation is certainly much simpler to understand and to apply than the English ordinary person test with its reliance on self-control as the determinative measurement. This sits well with the declared objectives of the framers to express the law in simple,

---

[336](1952) 53 NLR 193 pp. 203–4. This ruling was subsequently overturned by the Privy Council in *A-G for Ceylon v Perera* [1953] AC 200. However, the Privy Council did so by adopting the English common law, with scant regard for the wording of the Exception.

precise and certain terms,[337] objectives which continue to be much sought after by present-day lawmakers. Under the Code framers' test, the triers of fact have only to determine whether the provocation was a sufficiently serious affront to an ordinary person of the accused's social class. In cases involving accused persons from unfamiliar ethnic, cultural or social backgrounds, the jury may require the assistance of expert witnesses. The experts would be asked whether normal individuals from the accused's community could perceive the provocation as being so grave as to enrage them. This is a matter susceptible of proof by the experts. In contrast, they would have to engage in generalizations and speculation if the question was whether the provocation would have caused these individuals to have lost their self-control to the extent of forming a murderous intent and carrying out that intention by performing a homicidal act. This is because the responses of people after losing self-control is unpredictable.[338]

The relative ease of application of the Code framers' test extends to the trier of fact. The test avoids the need for the trier of fact to carry out such highly problematic tasks as appreciating just what the power of self-control of an ordinary person is[339] and surmising what effect a particular form of provocation could have on the self-control of an ordinary person. The ease of application of the framers' test compared to the English ordinary person test is borne out clearly in the following case. X, who belongs to an ethnic minority group, kills Y, another member of the group, after the latter had gestured towards X in a particular fashion. The trier of

---

[337]Macaulay, McLeod, Anderson and Millett, op. cit., n. 32, pp. xiv–xvi.

[338]Leader-Elliott, op. cit., n. 244, p. 93 has criticized the Code framers' test by saying that rage is a highly variable quality and the fact that provocation could enrage an ordinary person to utter a sharp rebuke or even commit a minor assault seems insufficient to attract a finding of manslaughter. This criticism could be equally mounted against an objective test based on loss of self-control, which Leader-Elliott advocates. Apart from this observation, my reply to his criticism is as follows: it may well be that an ordinary person who was enraged by provocation may have reacted less violently than killing. On the other hand, he or she might be so enraged as to kill. Rather than speculate upon what the physical reaction of an enraged person might be, the Code framers' test simply requires a finding that an ordinary person could be enraged without more.

[339]The issue is complicated by the heterogeneous nature of English, Australian and Indian societies. As noted previously, while Indian law has tackled the

fact should not have too much difficulty in determining whether the deceased's gesture was highly contemptuous and consequently caused members of the particular ethnic group to become enraged. This is what the Code framers envisaged for grave provocation. Under the English ordinary person test, the trier of fact would have to decide whether the gesture could have moved an ordinary person of X's ethnic background to lose self-control to the extent of killing. The trier of fact would experience considerable difficulty with such a determination because it involves aspects of human psychology which cannot be easily reduced into answers of the kind demanded by the English test.

The Code framers' test is attractive for effecting a compromise between advocates of the current ordinary person test and those who want to see its demise on the ground that it is complex and unworkable. The notion of an ordinary person being enraged is simple enough to comprehend and to apply compared to the notion of lost self-control. Although an easier test to satisfy than the current one, it nevertheless affords some measure of societal protection by remaining an objective test. Since trivial provocation would not cause ordinary people to enter into a state of rage, the defence would be denied to individuals who do so. By the same token, the defence would be denied to unusually bad-tempered persons if an ordinary person might not have been enraged by the provocation. If it be thought that a test based on rage enables the defence to be satisfied too readily, we should remind ourselves that a person who kills under the influence of grave provocation is in a different position to that of a person who kills without such provocation and it is this difference which the law of provocation seeks to recognize.

---

problem by recognizing the effect of ethnicity on the power of self-control, English and Australian laws have continued to insist on a single level of self-control. Of course, the problem may be answered by prescribing the level of self-control expected of a member of the majority ethnic group to all persons. However, this would be subject to charges of inequality and a failure to acknowledge human reality. The Australian solution is an interesting one: to set the power of self-control at the lowest level found among the different classes or groups of ordinary members of the community (see above, p. 70). While theoretically attractive, this solution has obvious practical difficulties. It assumes that the trier of fact has the ability to account for the levels of self-control of all the various groups in society regarded as ordinary, and to then decide upon the lowest level of self-control present.

All told, the test for grave provocation envisaged by the Code framers has much to commend itself. It is regrettable that it has not been permitted to take root in those jurisdictions which have the Indian Penal Code, and has been eclipsed by the English ordinary person test in the one case which recognized it. Such a test would also be readily comprehensible and practicable in England and Australia. Accordingly, in the model provision for the defence of provocation drawn up in chapter 4, this test of grave provocation is adopted.

## B. *The Reasonable Relationship Rule*

There have been occasions when judges have held that the law of provocation imposes a separate legal test requiring the accused's retaliatory conduct to be proportionate to the provocation offered. The origin of such a rule has frequently been traced to Viscount Simon LC's statement in *Mancini v Director of Public Prosecutions* that 'the mode of resentment must bear a reasonable relationship to the provocation if the offence is to be reduced to manslaughter'.[340] By way of illustration, 'fists might be answered with fists but not with a deadly weapon'.[341] However, the rule has been criticized for being inconsistent with the loss of self-control feature of the defence of provocation. An accused who has been provoked into a murderous frenzy cannot then be expected to have retained the capacity to measure the number of blows he or she inflicts on the deceased.[342] Requiring the degree of retaliation to be commensurate with the degree of provocation in this way undermines the 'compassion to human frailty' rationale of the defence. As one judge has said, 'The law of provocation is not concerned with reasonable retaliation, but with unreasonable retaliation.'[343] At most, a reasonable relationship between the provocation and the retaliation is *evidence* as to whether the accused had killed the victim while deprived of self-control or had merely taken the opportunity of the provocative incident to kill her or him. Thus, one would not expect some trivial provocation to excite gross and savage violence

[340][1942] AC 1, p. 9.
[341]*Duffy* [1949] 1 All ER 932 per Justice Devlin.
[342]See Williams, op. cit., n. 3, p. 543; Ashworth, 'The Doctrine of Provocation' op. cit., n. 98, p. 305, n. 70.
[343]*Johnson* (1976) CLR 619, p. 670 per Justice Murphy.

which kills the provoker.[344] What follows is an examination of the way this so-called rule has been regarded in England, Australia and India.

## 1. The English law

There was a period when the English courts treated Viscount Simon's statement in *Mancini* as a rule of law.[345] Fortunately, this is no longer the case. The relationship between provocation and retaliation is now regarded as merely a consideration which a jury may take into account when deciding whether the provocation was enough to cause an ordinary person to do what the accused did.[346] In *Phillips v R*, the Privy Council took the occasion to consider Viscount Simon's statement in the light of Section 3 of the *Homicide Act* (UK).[347] This case was an appeal from Jamaica, which has an identical provision to the English one. Lord Diplock, who delivered the judgement of the court, had this to say:

> Since the passing of the legislation, it may be prudent to avoid the use of the precise words of Viscount Simon in *Mancini* ... 'the mode of resentment must bear a reasonable relationship to the provocation' unless they are used in a context which makes it clear to the jury that this is not a rule of law which they are bound to follow, but merely a consideration which may or may not commend itself to them.[348]

Despite this clear judicial rejection of a rule of reasonable relationship, concern has continued to be expressed that the rule remains. The source of this concern lies in the phrase 'make a reasonable man do as he did' appearing in Section 3 of the *Homicide Act* (UK). This has made Professors John Smith and Brian Hogan opine that 'in a sense, the reasonable relationship rule still is a rule of law because the defence is made out only if the provocation was enough to make the reasonable man "do as he did"'.[349] Likewise,

---

[344] *R v Walker* (1969) 53 Cr App R 196, p. 202 per Fenton Atkinson; *Johnson* (1976) 136 CLR 619, p. 656 per Justice Gibbs.

[345] For example, see *R v Gauthier* (1943) 29 Cr App R 113; *R v Duffy* [1949] 1 All ER 932; *R v McCarthy* [1954] 2 QB 105; *Lee Chun-Chuen v R* [1963] AC 220.

[346] *R v Brown* [1972] 2 QB 229, p. 235.

[347] [1969] 2 AC 130.

[348] Ibid., p. 138 and cited with approval by the English Court of Appeal in *Brown* [1972] 2 QB 229, p. 233–4.

[349] Op. cit., n. 53, p. 362.

the Criminal Law Revision Committee said that the phrase might be thought to restate the reasonable relationship rule in different words.[350] In order to remove the rule altogether from the law, the Committee omitted any reference to the nature of the retaliation. Under its proposal, all that is required is for the provocation to have induced the defendant to react against the victim with a murderous intent.[351] It will be contended below that, while this proposal achieves its intended purpose, it has the unfortunate effect of also doing away with the rule relating to the mode of killing, which is distinct from the reasonable relationship rule.

## 2. The Australian law

As with English law, there was a period when the Australian courts accepted Viscount Simon's decision in *Mancini* as laying down a separate legal requirement of reasonable relationship between the provocation and the retaliation.[352] However, this changed with the High Court of Australia case of *Johnson v R*, where a majority relegated the requirement to a factor which the jury may consider when answering the question whether an ordinary person could have so lost self-control as to have done what the accused did. In the words of Chief Justice Barwick:

> the proportion of the fatal act to the provocation is part of the material on which the jury should consider whether the provocation offered the accused was such as would have caused an ordinary man, placed in all the circumstances in which the accused stood, to have lost his self-control to the point of doing an act of the kind and degree as that by which the accused killed the deceased. That proportion is not, in my opinion, a separate matter to be considered after it has been decided that an ordinary man would have lost self-control in the circumstances.[353]

Justice Murphy delivered a dissenting judgement in *Johnson*. He held that the concept of reasonable relationship should not be

[350]Op. cit., n. 248, para. 78.

[351]Ibid., para. 81.

[352]For example, see *Parker* (1963) 111 CLR 610, p. 627; *R v Tsigos* [1964] NSWR 1607; *Da Costa v R* [1968] 118 CLR 186, pp. 214–5; *R v Minehan* [1973] 1 NSWLR 659.

[353](1976) 136 CLR 619, p. 636. See also Justice Gibbs at p. 656 (with Justices Jacobs and Mason concurring). Although the case was strictly concerned with the provision on provocation under the *Crimes Act* (NSW), the judges said that they were also pronouncing upon the common law.

given any weight whatsoever in the law of provocation for the following reason:

> Contrary to some opinions, it would be open to a jury to find that a disproportionate response was strong evidence of loss of self-control, and that a proportionate response tended to disprove loss of self-control.[354]

His Honour was thereby subscribing to the view that it was more consistent with human experience for persons provoked into a frenzy not to be able to measure their responses.[355]

Section 23(3) of the New South Wales *Crimes Act* expressly rejects the reasonable relationship rule by providing that:

> there is no rule of law that provocation is negatived if ... there was not a reasonable proportion between the act or omission causing death and the conduct of the deceased that induced the act or omission.

The provision further omits all references to the nature of the retaliation in its formulation of the ordinary person test. This is achieved under Section 23(2)(b), which requires the jury to consider whether the conduct of the deceased 'could have induced an ordinary person in the position of the accused to have so far lost self-control as to have formed an intent to kill, or to inflict grievous bodily harm upon, the deceased'. In this respect, the provision is closely similar to the English Criminal Law Revision Committee's proposal.[356] It will be contended later that this stance taken by the New South Wales provision, like the Committee's proposal, has the regrettable consequence of also doing away with the rule governing the mode of killing.

## 3. The Indian law

Unlike their English and Australian counterparts, the Indian courts have had the wisdom to avoid adopting the reasonable relationship rule. They have done so by desisting from going beyond requiring the provocation to have caused an ordinary person lose self-control. The leading Indian case on provocation does just that. In *Nanavati*,

---

[354]Ibid., p. 670.
[355]Justice Murphy's view is analogous to the doctrine of excessive force in self-defence which was part of Australian common law until 1987 and remains part of the Indian law. This topic is covered in chapter 3. The doctrine, like provocation, reduces a charge of murder to manslaughter in cases where the law recognizes that some retaliation is excusable but that the accused's retaliation was excessive in the circumstances.
[356]Discussed above at p. 103.

the Supreme Court expressed the position as follows:

> The test of 'grave and sudden' provocation is whether a reasonable man, belonging to the same class of society as the accused, placed in the same situation in which the accused was placed would be so provoked as to lose self-control.[357]

A subsequent Indian decision by the Allahabad High Court interpreted the above ruling in this way:

> In determining whether an accused person was overwhelmed by a grave and sudden provocation, the Courts in this country do and must investigate whether the offender acted reasonably or normally or properly, as an average person in the position and circumstances of the offender may be expected to do, until the point in time at which the offender is actually deprived of his power of self-control. But, once his power of self-control has been lost, it would be futile to expect him to retain such a degree of control over himself as to exercise choice over the weapon used by him for the attack or to show that his 'mode of resentment' bore 'a reasonable relationship to the provocation' which operated upon him.[358]

The approach taken by these Indian decisions denies any foothold to the reasonable relationship rule and thereby brings the law into accord with human reality. As Justice Beg in *Akhtar* asserts, it is futile to apply any yardstick of reasonableness to an accused's behaviour performed while he or she was deprived of self-control. Thus, the Indian courts have held that the large number of blows inflicted does not prevent the defence from succeeding; to the contrary, it may be evidence showing that self-control was lost.[359] Whether an ordinary person could have killed under similar provocation as the accused is surely a matter of pure conjecture. After all, the human reality is that while ordinary people may frequently lose their self-control, they very rarely kill, and if this fact were to be strictly accounted for by the courts, the defence of provocation would almost never succeed.[360] The role of the ordinary person's power of self-control should therefore be confined to the

---

[357] AIR 1962 SC 605 at 630 per Justice Subba Rao.

[358] *Akhtar v State* AIR 1964 All 262, p. 266 per Justice Beg, and approved in *Krishnan Nair v State* (1965) Kerala LT 150, p. 158.

[359] *State v Bhand Jusub Mamad* 1982 Cr LJ 1691; *Narbahadur Darjee v State* AIR 1965 Assam and Nagaland 89. This was also the view of Justice Murphy in *Johnson* (1976) 136 CLR 619, p. 670: see main text accompanying n. 354.

[360] See Williams, op. cit., n. 3, at p. 537, who, after citing criminal statistics showing the dearth of homicides on confessions of adultery, asserts that 'to

point in time prior to the accused's loss of self-control, without more. The law would be crossing over to the point in time after the accused had lost self-control if it enquired further into the degree of retaliation expected from an ordinary person reacting to the same provocation as the accused.

Lest it be thought otherwise, the Indian courts do share the same concern as their Western counterparts against permitting trivial provocation to reduce a charge of murder to culpable homicide not amounting to murder. Thus, under the Indian approach, the gravity of the provocation is to be assessed by reference to an ordinary person of the same ethnic, cultural or social background to which the particular accused belongs. Only provocative conduct which could cause loss of self-control (which, it should be emphasized, is a highly charged emotional state) in such an ordinary person will constitute grave provocation, thereby preventing cases of trivial affronts from becoming the basis of a successful defence.

## C. The Modal Rule

The hypothesis presented here is that there are two related but distinct issues contained in the concept of provoking an ordinary person to lose self-control and to react as the accused did. The first issue measures the degree of provocation against the degree of retaliation, the objective being to ensure that a trivial provocation does not warrant a retaliatory act of killing. The reasonable relationship rule, when it was part of the law, dealt with this matter. The second issue evaluates the mode of the killing, that is, the manner in which the victim was killed. The enquiry here has passed on from the one of whether the provocation was sufficiently grave to cause an ordinary person to lose her or his self-control, to determining whether the mode of killing was morally acceptable. This may be described as the modal rule.[361] Hence, although both the reasonable relationship rule and the modal rule are concerned with the retaliatory response to the provocation, they differ in that only the former compares the provocation with the retaliation.

---

say that the ordinary man or woman kills for adultery in England is a grotesque untruth, and has been so for centuries'.

[361]See Williams, op. cit., n. 3, p. 543. Unfortunately, Professor Williams' discussion is confusing because he merges this rule into the one of reasonable relationship by calling it the 'modal reasonable relationship rule'.

Another difference between the two rules lies in their functions. While the reasonable relationship rule is concerned with the degree of provocation needed to support a successful plea of provocation, the modal rule is concerned to ensure against affording mitigation to a person who has killed through acts of unjustifiable cruelty.[362] Unfortunately, these differences have been overlooked by some commentators[363] and, it seems, by current English judges,[364] with the result that the modal rule has been overshadowed by the reasonable relationship rule. As the immediately preceding part has indicated, one unfortunate consequence of this has been that efforts to remove the reasonable relationship rule from the law of provocation have also resulted in the debunking of the modal rule.[365] It is contended that the function served by the modal rule is sufficiently distinct and important to warrant its retention as a separate legal requirement.

The rationale for the modal rule in the law of provocation was ably put by James Stephen:

> The moral character of homicide must be judged of principally by the extent to which the circumstances of the case show, on the one hand, brutal ferocity, whether called into actions suddenly or otherwise, or on the other, inability to control natural anger excited by serious cause.[366]

The modal rule therefore serves to deny a concession to human frailty when circumstances of the killing evince a 'brutal ferocity' rather than a 'natural anger excited by serious cause'. In the same vein, in *East's Pleas of the Crown*, we find the proposition that where the retaliation is:

> outrageous in its nature, either in the manner or the continuance of it, and beyond all proportion to the offence, it is rather to be considered as the effect of a brutal and diabolical malignity than human frailty.[367]

---

[362]See Horder, op. cit., n. 160, pp. 145–6 for a similar recognition of these differences.

[363]See Williams, op. cit., n. 3, p. 543; Smith and Hogan, op. cit., n. 53, pp. 362–3; Criminal Law Revision Committee, op. cit., n. 248, para. 86.

[364]This remark is made on the premise that the English judges have not, of late, devoted any separate treatment to the modal rule.

[365]See above, pp. 103–4.

[366]*History of the Criminal Law of England* Vol. III, p. 171 (1883).

[367]Op. cit., n. 13, p. 234. Also, East at p. 252 states that 'malice ... rather than ... human frailty ... will be presumed ... if the instrument or manner of retaliation be greatly inadequate to the offence given, and cruel and dangerous in its nature'.

## 1. The English law

These comments by Stephen and East find their modern expression in the House of Lords case of *Holmes*.[368] There, Viscount Simon said that:

> [a jury must] form the view that a reasonable person so provoked could be driven, through transport of passion and loss of self-control, to the degree and method and continuance of violence which produces death.[369]

It is observed that the enquiry is solely concerned with evaluating the manner or mode of killing and is unlike the reasonable retaliation rule which requires a comparison to be made between the provocation and the retaliation.

Examples from English cases where the modal rule has been applied to deny the defence include a parent who was provoked by his child into trampling it to death,[370] tying a provoker to a horse and making the horse gallop away so as to cause mortal injuries to the provoker,[371] and placing live electric wires into the provoker's mouth, fatally electrocuting her.[372] The reason why a jury is unlikely to mitigate these forms of homicidal acts is that they are not characteristically (in cultural and moral terms) acceptable responses to grave provocation in the way some more familiar forms of retaliation are, such as hitting, stabbing or strangling. As one commentator has put it, these reactions may count against the defendant 'because the unjustifiable cruelty inherent in the nature of the action colours or counters the spontaneity, the "warmth and hastiness" of the over-reaction that

---

[368][1946] AC 588.

[369]Ibid., p. 597. Although Lord Diplock in *Camplin* [1978] 2 All ER 168, p. 175 had held that the decision in *Holmes* was no longer to be treated as an authority on the law of provocation, it is contended that he did not mean to abolish the modal rule expressed in *Holmes*. Rather, his Lordship was saying that *Holmes* was incorrect insofar as it empowered the judge to withdraw the defence from the jury on the ground that there was no evidence on which the jury could find that a reasonable man would have been provoked to do as the accused did. By virtue of Section 3 of the *Homicide Act* (UK), the judge must now leave this issue to be determined by the jury.

[370]*R v Mawgridge*, J Kel 119 (1707), 84 ER 1107 and discussed by Horder, op. cit. n. 160, p. 146.

[371]*Halloway's Case*, Cro Car 131 (1629).

[372]*R v Clarke* [1991] Crim LR 383. For a criticism of various aspects of the decision in this case, see Horder, op. cit., n. 160, pp. 147–50.

is part of the rationale for excusing its excessive degree'.[373]

Revisiting the 'do as he did' expression found in English common law and embodied in Section 3 of the *Homicide Act* (UK), it is contended that this covers the modal rule rather than the reasonable relationship rule. The expression should therefore be retained. Accordingly, the Criminal Law Revision Committee's proposal to remove the phrase so as to abolish the reasonable retaliation rule is somewhat misplaced and should not be followed. Lord Diplock's interpretation in *Phillips* of this expression confirms this position.[374] He said:

> [the expression in Section 3 of the *Homicide Act* (UK)] explicitly recognises that what the jury have to consider ... is not merely whether in their opinion the provocation would have made a reasonable man lose his self-control but whether, having lost his self-control, he would have retaliated in the same way as the person charged in fact did.[375]

Lord Diplock was here assigning what was once the reasonable relationship rule (and clarified by him in another part of his judgement as being merely an evidentiary consideration) to the earlier part of his comment, that is, whether the provocation would have caused a reasonable person to lose self-control. His Lordship then proceeded in the later part of the comment to regard the manner of killing as a legal rule.

## 2. The Australian law

As far as Australian law is concerned, we have noted previously that the courts have abrogated the reasonable relationship rule. However, they have kept the modal rule as a separate legal requirement by adopting Viscount Simon's ruling in *Holmes*.[376] In the High Court of Australia case of *Johnson v R*, Chief Justice

---

[373]Horder, ibid., p. 153.
[374][1969] 2 AC 130.
[375]Ibid., p. 137.
[376]Quoted in the main text accompanying n. 369. This ruling has been cited with approval by the Australian courts in numerous occasions. For example, see *Stingel*, (1990) 171 CLR 312, p. 325; *Sreckovic v R* WAR 1973 85, p. 91. In the High Court case of *Moffa* (1977) 138 CLR 601, p. 613, Justice Gibbs quoted the passage in *Holmes* in which the statement appears and said that it 'has been cited with approval again and again, in England and in Australia, and is supported by the views expressed recently in this Court in *Johnson v R*'.

Barwick was alive to the need for a moral evaluation of the manner of killing when he said:

> If the extremity of the resentment [that is, the accused's reaction] is due to the idiosyncrasy of the accused [rather] than to the reactions of an ordinary man in the circumstances, then the provocation cannot be relevantly effective.[377]

Unfortunately, the latest High Court pronouncement on the matter has thrown confusion over the modal rule. In *Masciantonio*, the majority had this to say:

> It is the nature and extent—the kind and degree—of the reaction which could be caused in an ordinary person by the provocation which is significant, rather than the duration of the reaction or the precise physical form which that reaction might take. And in considering that matter, the question whether an ordinary person could form an intention to kill or do grievous bodily harm is of greater significance than the question whether an ordinary person could adopt the means by the accused to carry out the intention.[378]

With respect, the distinction sought to be drawn by the majority between the nature and extent (or kind and degree) of the reaction and the precise physical form the reaction might take is too subtle to make any real sense of. If their Honours had meant to stress the need for the loss of self-control to have been of such a degree as to create an intention to kill or to do grievous bodily harm to an ordinary person, they could have done it without downplaying the ruling in *Holmes*. The majority had relied on a statement by Chief Justice Barwick in *Johnson* for placing a premium on the murderous intent aspect of loss of self-control.[379] The learned Chief Justice had said that 'it is the induced intent to kill rather than the induced fatal act which is the critical consideration'.[380] However, examination of the part of his Honour's judgement leading up to this statement reveals that he did not mean for the mode of retaliation to be irrelevant. While Chief Justice Barwick objected to there being a rule of law requiring the retaliatory conduct to be proportionate to the provocation, he did accept that it was necessary:

> to take into account the mode and extent of retaliation when determining

[377](1976) 136 CLR 619, p. 639.
[378](1995) 69 ALJR 598, p. 604. Justice McHugh alone (at p. 611) gave unqualified support to the *Holmes* ruling.
[379]Ibid., p. 603.
[380](1976) 136 CLR 619, p. 639.

whether an ordinary man, subjected to the like acts of provocation in all the circumstances in which the accused then stood, would have lost self control to the point of doing something akin to what the accused had done.[381]

Ultimately, the point to note here is that the majority in *Masciantonio* did not abrogate the *Holmes* ruling on the manner of the accused's response to the provocation. That response may, in the majority's view, be of lesser significance than the need for an ordinary person to have formed a murderous intent, but the majority still gave it significance.[382]

Mention should be made that Section 23 of the New South Wales *Crimes Act* has removed entirely the moral relevance of the manner of the accused's physical response to the provocation. All that matters is whether the provocation was sufficient to induce an ordinary person to have so far lost self-control as to have formed a murderous intent.[383] Hence, the parent who tramples his child to death would be treated in exactly the same way as one who had hit or strangled the child in response to the same provocation. It is submitted that the modal evaluation of the accused's mode of killing forms a natural and inevitable backdrop to a jury's determination of whether an ordinary person might likewise have reacted when deprived of self-control and the legislative abrogation of this evaluation unduly diminishes the moral underpinnings of the defence.

## 3. The Indian law

With regard to Indian law, we have previously noted that the courts of that jurisdiction have not adopted the reasonable relationship rule. However, they have recognized a modal rule by requiring a court 'to consider whether a reasonable person placed in the same position as the accused was, would have reacted under that provocation in the manner in which the accused did'.[384] Some

[381]Ibid.

[382]This clearly appears in the last sentence of the passage of the majority's judgement reproduced in the main text accompanying n. 378.

[383]Section 23(2)(b). The provision makes no reference whatsoever to the physical reaction of the defendant nor of the reaction of the ordinary person.

[384]*Shyama Charan v State*, AIR 1969 All 61, p. 64 per Justice Chandra. See also *Upendra Mahakud v State*, 1985 Cr LJ 1767; *State v Kamalaksha*, 1978 Cr LJ 290; *Dhanno Khan v State*, 1957 Cr LJ 498; *Sarwan Singh v State*, 1954 Cr LJ 1505; *Saraj Din v Emperor*, 1934 Cr LJ 306.

Indian cases have also expressly approved of the ruling in *Holmes*.[385] Indeed, the Indian law's recognition of and justification for a modal rule goes as far back as the inception of the Code, as is clear from the following comment by an early text writer:

> Bearing in mind that the Exception is founded upon a principle of indulgence shown by the law to human frailty but not to human ferocity, it may be safely laid down that the provocation which is allowed to extenuate, must be something which a man is conscious of, and which he feels keenly, and resents, at the instant the act which he would extenuate is committed. A permanent subjection to a wicked and cruel disposition does not mitigate or excuse an offence. So, if the act can be traced to a previous brutal malignity, and not merely to the influence of passion arising from provocation, however grave and sudden the provocation, it will not extenuate.[386]

Making the same point, although less elegantly, is the recent judicial comment that '[t]he law does not take into account the abnormal creatures reacting abnormally and contemplates the acting of normal beings in given situations'.[387] An example of a case where the defence failed because of the 'abnormal reaction' of the accused is *Balasaheb v State*.[388] The accused had killed his unfaithful wife while deprived of his power of self-control. However, he was denied the defence of provocation because of the mode of his killing, which was to use the broken end of a bottle to inflict numerous injuries on the victim's face and neck, to twist her neck so as to fracture the vertebra, and to bang her face repeatedly on the floor. In another case, the accused failed in his plea of provocation because he had beaten his provoker severely and then severed his head.[389] In these cases, the Indian courts were not prepared to exercise compassion towards the accused because of the brutal malignity shown in the manner of killing their victims.

My proposals regarding the reasonable relationship and modal rules can be summarized by using a case study. D is gravely provoked when he unexpectedly finds V in the act of sexual intercourse with D's wife. D loses his self-control and kills V.

---

[385]For example, see *Abdul Majid v State*, 1963 (2) Cr LJ 631, p. 633. The Supreme Court in *Nanavati* AIR 1962 SC 605, p. 620 cited the ruling without any adverse comment.

[386]Morgan and MacPherson, op. cit., n. 146, p. 243.

[387]*Upendra Mahakud*, 1985 Cr LJ 1767, p. 1770 per Justice Behera.

[388]1984 Cr LJ 1014.

[389]*Yasin Sheikh v Empress*, 12 WR (Cr) 68 (1869); 4 Beng LR (A Cr J) 6.

Whether D should receive mitigation through the plea of provocation will depend on the response of an ordinary person to the same provocation. D may still have the benefit of the defence if, in a state of frenzy, he inflicts multiple stab wounds on V. As long as the provocation was grave enough to cause an ordinary person to lose self-control so as to form a murderous intent, the law will not go on to compare the number of stab wounds which D inflicted on V with the degree of provocation received from V. However, the law will evaluate the particular mode or manner of killing to see if it is characteristically a reaction which could be expected from an ordinary person who has lost self-control. For instance, the defence would probably be denied to D if he had cut off V's genitals and let him bleed to death. This is a normative judgement for the jury to decide and, it is submitted, is a judgement sufficiently important to be made a separate legal rule. Accordingly, any reform which removes the modal rule should be vigorously resisted. As Jeremy Horder has argued:

> our actions ... are most certainly our responsibility, and are shaped by cultural and moral norms that bear on the manner ... of our (re)action. These norms form a natural and inevitable backdrop to the jury's decision as to whether a reasonable person might likewise have acted in anger, and reform which seeks to weaken their influence unacceptably debases the moral currency of the provocation defence.[390]

## 7. Conclusion

This comparative analysis of the defence of provocation reveals that the Indian law has been an advancement of the English law in many significant respects. Although the Indian law of provocation may have originated from English common law, the Indian courts have modified the defence in ways which better reflect the human and social realities of the parties to provoked killings. Thus, in respect of provocative conduct, Indian law has long recognized that words alone can in certain circumstances amount to provocative conduct, that the effect of the provocation on the accused can be cumulative and that the provocation need not have occurred in the accused's presence. Furthermore, the Indian Code has been progressive for its time in not limiting provocative conduct to

[390]Horder, op. cit., n. 206, p. 155.

unlawful acts alone. However, the Code does adhere to the important public policy consideration of maintaining peace and social order by expressly disallowing provocative conduct in certain specified instances. These are provocative conduct that was sought by the accused as an excuse to harm a person, and conduct which comprised lawful acts performed in obedience to a legal duty or in the exercise of private defence. As for the subjective condition of actual loss of self-control, the Indian courts were well ahead of their English counterparts in recognizing that a person could still be deprived of self-control even with a time interval between the last provocative incident and the homicidal act.

This progressive stance of the Indian courts has continued into the objective condition with the courts prepared from the outset to attribute the accused's characteristics to the ordinary person when assessing both the gravity of the provocation and the power of self-control of an ordinary person. The advanced thinking of the Indian judges is also evident in the treatment of the retaliatory response to the provocation. While these judges have refused to recognize a reasonable relationship rule, they have insisted that the mode of killing must not be morally repugnant. For every one of these issues, the English courts have been slow to arrive at these positions and many of the changes have come about only recently. Indeed, there are a couple of matters which have still to be altered by the English courts.[391]

The Australian courts have generally taken an enlightened approach, arriving at the Indian prescriptions earlier than the English courts and without the aid of legislation such as Section 3 of the English *Homicide Act* (UK). Although references have been made to Section 23 of the New South Wales *Crimes Act* we have seen that many of its requirements merely confirmed the Australian common law or else brought to fruition more quickly an emerging common law development. Another admirable feature of the Australian judges is their willingness to accommodate the experiences of battered women who kill under provocation. In this regard, English and Indian judges could learn much from them. Certainly, there may be features of the Indian law of provocation

---

[391]One is the rule against hearsay provocation. Another is the uncertainty, of late, of viewing the modal rule separately from the reasonable relationship rule.

which might work well in that jurisdiction only because of the peculiar racial, social, cultural and religious conditions of Indian society. An example discussed in this chapter is the attribution of an accused's ethnicity to the power of self-control expected of an ordinary person. I have argued that, while this feature of the Indian law is ideologically sound, it should not be introduced into English and Australian laws because the societies in these jurisdictions are not sufficiently fragmented into distinct cultural groups to permit proper scientific enquiry.[392] In numerous other respects, however, the Indian law of provocation does readily suit English and Australian social conditions. It is surmised that, had the English and Australian lawmakers made a practice of studying the Indian law, many of the progressive changes which have only recently come to light could have been implemented sooner.

There is one matter which my discussion has shown would have improved the Indian law considerably. This is the test of grave provocation devised by the Code framers. The test measures the gravity of the provocation by whether it could have enraged an ordinary person. This is a more comprehensible and practicable test than the one applied by the Indian judges (and adopted from the English law) of whether the provocation could have induced an ordinary person to lose self-control. The incorporation of the Code framers' test into Exception 1 to Section 300 is therefore recommended.

While there certainly are some aspects of the defence that could be improved upon, it is contended that the present law of provocation in the three jurisdictions under consideration is in a reasonably satisfactory state. This is only to be expected since the best judicial minds have, for decades, diligently worked at reaching the most appropriate legal response to killings under provocation. Recent law reform proposals to radically alter the law should therefore be treated with caution. For example, the English Criminal Law Revision Committee's proposal to replace the ordinary person test with a test of 'reasonably sufficient ground' for loss of self-control has its own problems. One of these is that juries are not given as much guidance as under the present law when deciding whether an accused is deserving of mitigation. This same problem

---

[392]The only exception may be in respect of Australian Aboriginal accused persons residing in geographically isolated enclaves.

undermines the version of the defence proposed by the Law Reform Commission of Victoria. Aside from these law reform proposals, there is much to be said for bringing together all the best features devised by the judges of the jurisdictions studied under a model provision. This will be done in the final chapter of this work.

# Chapter 3

# Excessive Self-Defence

## 1. Introduction

The doctrine of excessive self-defence, sometimes described as excessive force in self-defence, is popularly regarded as a creation of Australian common law. The leading authority is *R v Howe*, where, at the South Australian Court of Criminal Appeal level, it was held that:

> A person who is subjected to a violent and felonious attack and who, in endeavouring, by way of self-defence, to prevent the consummation of that attack by force exercises more force than a reasonable man would consider necessary in the circumstances, but no more than what he honestly believed to be necessary in the circumstances, is guilty of manslaughter and not of murder.[1]

This description of the doctrine clearly indicates that it establishes a form of voluntary manslaughter. An accused who would otherwise be convicted of murder may have her or his charge reduced to manslaughter on account of the extenuating circumstance of having honestly believed that the force applied was necessary by way of self-defence.

However, Australian common law was not the first to recognize the doctrine. Indeed, the doctrine found expression in the Indian Penal Code 1860 nearly a hundred years before it made its first appearance in Australian common law.[2] That was in 1957 in the

---

[1] (1958) SASR 95, pp. 121–2 per Justice Mayo.
[2] The doctrine actually found expression back in 1837 when the Code framers delivered their first report to Lord Auckland, the Governor-General of India in Council: see Macaulay, T.B., J.M. Macleod, G.W. Anderson and F. Millett, *The Indian Penal Code as Originally Framed in 1837 with Notes*, Note M, pp. 146–8 (1888). The doctrine appears as Exception 2 to Section 300 of the Code and is reproduced below at p. 119.

Victorian case of *R v McKay*.[3] The Australian recognition of excessive self-defence seems to have come quite independently of the provision in the Indian Penal Code, at least insofar as no judicial reference was made to the existence of the provision. It is possible that a study of the Code by Australian judges might have prompted them to introduce this form of manslaughter sooner into Australia.

As far as English judges are concerned, they appear to have played an obstructionist rather than a contributory role in the recognition of excessive self-defence under both English and Australian laws. We shall see later that the current Australian law no longer recognizes the doctrine, a development which was in no small way due to the views of English judges who had rejected it. That said, there were some nineteenth century English decisions[4] which had lent support to the doctrine and it has been suggested that they may have influenced the framers of the Indian Penal Code when they put together their first draft.[5] Apart from these early cases, however, the English common law has made no positive contribution to the recognition and development of excessive self-defence.

This chapter begins with a discussion of the Indian law due to its long-standing and continued recognition of the defence, followed by a discussion of the English and Australian laws. The part on Indian law will critically analyse the wording of the Code provision embodying excessive self-defence and the various interpretations given to it by the Indian courts. It will be seen that one of these interpretations is inconsistent with the doctrine, and a way will be suggested to circumvent the inconsistency. The part on English law will be necessarily brief because the English courts have given scant reasons for their rejection of excessive self-defence. This stands in contrast to the part on Australian law which examines at some length the recognition of the doctrine by the Australian courts and their reasons for doing so, followed by the courts' more recent abrogation of the doctrine in recent years and their reasons for

[3][1957] VR 560.
[4]Notably *R v Whalley,* 7 C & P 245 (1835), 173 ER 108; *R v Patience,* 8 C & P 775 (1837), 173 ER 338; *R v Cook,* Cro Car 537 (1640), 79 ER 1063. These cases will be discussed below.
[5]Kaye, J.M., 'Early History of Murder and Manslaughter', 83 *Law Quarterly Review* 569, p. 574 (1967); Sornarajah, M., 'Excessive Self-defençe in Commonwealth Law', 21 *International and Comparative Law Quarterly* 758, p. 761, n. 15 (1972).

this change. In the final part of the chapter, I examine the relationship between excessive self-defence and the general plea of self-defence, and  consider whether excessive self-defence has been correctly regarded as a partial defence to murder rather than a mitigating factor in sentencing.

# 2. Excessive Self-Defence under Indian Law

## A. The Defence and its Role in Relation to the General Plea of Self-Defence

A plea of excessive self-defence has been part of the Indian Penal Code since its inception. It appears as one of several Exceptions to Section 300, which defines the offence of murder.[6] A successful reliance upon any of these Exceptions results in a conviction of the lesser offence of culpable homicide not amounting to murder. Excessive self-defence is defined in Exception 2 as follows:

> Culpable homicide is not murder if the offender, in the exercise in good faith of the right of private defence of person or property, exceeds the power given to him by law, and causes the death of the person against whom he is exercising such right of defence, without premeditation and without any intention of doing more harm than is necessary for the purpose of such defence.

Before examining the Exception in detail, it is pertinent to place its role within the context of the general plea of self-defence recognized by the Code.[7] Every person has a right to defend her or his person or that of another against any offence affecting the human body: Section 97(1). This right extends to defending one's own property or that of another against theft, robbery, mischief, criminal trespass or attempts to commit these offences: Section 97(2). The Code stipulates both a general and a specific limitation in respect of the force permitted by way of defence of person or property. The general limitation is that the accused must not have inflicted 'more harm than it is necessary to inflict for the purpose

---

[6]We have considered one of these exceptions, namely, provocation, in chapter 2. The other exceptions are excessive force by a public servant in the exercise of her or his duty, sudden fight and consent by a person above the age of eighteen years.

[7]The main provisions in the Indian Penal Code on the right of private defence are reproduced in the Appendix to this work.

of defence': Section 99(4).[8] This involves an objective assessment of the necessity of the particular action taken by the accused in the given circumstances. The specific limitation comprises the existence of certain threats before a person is permitted to kill her or his assailant. These threat occasions vary according to whether the accused was protecting her or his person or whether it was property that was being protected. With regard to protection of the person, a killing is justified only when it was necessary to repel an attack causing a reasonable apprehension of death, grievous hurt, rape, gratification of unnatural lust, abduction or kidnapping: Section 100.[9] In respect of protection of property, a killing is justified only when it was necessary to repel a robbery, housebreaking by night, mischief by fire committed on a human dwelling, or theft, mischief or house-trespass in circumstances which caused reasonable apprehension that death or grievous hurt would be the consequence if the right of defence were not exercised: Section 103.[10] It is observed that these listed offences are not solely

[8]The sub-section reads: 'The right of private defence in no case extends to the inflicting of more harm than it is necessary to inflict for the purpose of defence.'

[9]The relevant part of Section 100 reads: 'The right of private defence to the body extends ... to the voluntary causing of death or of any other harm to the assailant, if the offence which occasions the exercise of the right be of any of the descriptions hereinafter enumerated, namely: (1) Such an assault as may reasonably cause the apprehension that death will otherwise be the consequence of such an assault; (2) Such an assault as may reasonably cause the apprehension that grievous hurt will otherwise be the consequence of such an assault; (3) An assault with the intention of committing rape; (4) An assault with the intention of gratifying unnatural lust; (5) An assault with the intention of kidnapping or abducting; (6) An assault with the intention of wrongfully confining a person, under circumstances which may reasonably cause him to apprehend that he will be unable to have recourse to the public authorities for his release.'

[10]The relevant part of Section 103 reads: 'The right of private defence of property extends ... to the voluntary causing of death or of any other harm to the wrongdoer, if the offence, the committing of which, or the attempting to commit which, occasions the exercise of the right, is an offence of any of the following descriptions: (1) robbery; (2) housebreaking by night; (3) mischief by fire committed on any building, tent, or vessel, which building, tent, or vessel is used as a human dwelling, or as a place for the custody of property; (4) theft, mischief, or house-trespass, under such circumstances as may reasonably cause apprehension that death or grievous hurt will be the consequence, if such right of private defence is not exercised.' The Joint

against property but contain an element of personal violence or a threat of such violence. The serious consequences to the defender brought about by these combined attacks upon property and person justify the defender's repelling such attacks with fatal force provided, of course, that such force was reasonably necessary in the circumstances.

The joint operation of these general and specific limitations is that in cases involving unlawful homicide, the court initially determines whether the killing was in order to repel any of the kinds of threats mentioned in Section 100 or 103. If none of these threats are present, the killing is excessive and the general plea of self-defence fails. Even if one of these kinds of threats was present, the court must go on to decide whether the killing was reasonably necessary in the circumstances. Should the killing be found to have been reasonably necessary, the accused has not committed any offence whatsoever, not even culpable homicide not amounting to murder, and no question arises as to the application of Exception 2 to Section 300.[11] If the killing was found not to be reasonably necessary, it is excessive and the general plea of self-defence is not made out.

In the event of the accused's act of killing being assessed as excessive (either because none of the specified threats were present or the killing was not reasonably necessary), the court proceeds to enquire whether Exception 2 to Section 300 operates to reduce the charge against the accused from murder to culpable homicide not amounting to murder. The charge will be so reduced if the conditions of the Exception are met, namely, that the accused had killed without premeditation and without any intention of doing more harm than was necessary for the purpose of defence. A case example will help to illustrate the interplay between the general plea of self-defence and the partial plea under Exception 2. In the Madhya Bharat High Court case of *Dohariya v State*, the relationship between D and V was very strained.[12] On the fatal

Committee of the Parliament of India, in its 1976 report on the Indian Penal Code (Amendment) Bill 1972, recommended certain additions to this list such as mischief by explosive substance, hijacking of aircraft and sabotage. Even if these additions were to become law, they retain the feature of being property offences containing an element of personal violence.

[11] *State v Satish Sangma* (1954) AIR Ass 56; *Padmeshwar Phukan v State* [1971] Cr LJ 1595.

[12] 1956 Cr LJ 70.

day, V had entered D's house and threatened to beat D and his mother with the handle of the axe V was carrying. While the mother fled, D wrestled the axe from V and struck him in the face with its sharp edge, killing him. The court found that D was exercising his right of defence against V, who was the aggressor. This right extended to the killing of V by virtue of Section 103(4) since V had committed house-trespass under circumstances which reasonably caused apprehension to D that V was about to cause grievous hurt to D and his mother. However, the court found that, contrary to Section 99(4), the killing amounted to more harm than it was necessary to inflict for the purpose of defence. Consequently, D was denied the operation of the general plea of self-defence. The court then turned its attention to Exception 2 to Section 300 and found on the evidence that D had caused V's death without premeditation and without any intention of doing more harm than was necessary for the purpose of his defence. Accordingly, he was entitled to have his murder charge reduced to culpable homicide not amounting to murder.

The Code framers expressed their justification for recognizing in Exception 2 this half-way house between a murder conviction and a complete acquittal in the following terms:

> That portion of the law of homicide which we are now considering is closely connected with the law of private defence and must necessarily partake of the imperfections of the law of private defence. But, wherever the limits of the right of private defence may be placed, and with whatever accuracy they may be marked, we are inclined to think that it will always be expedient to make a separation between murder and what we have designated as culpable homicide in defence.[13]

With regard to cases of killing in excessive defence of the person, the Code framers provided the following explanation for the need to partially exculpate the accused:

> ...[T]hat a man should be merely exercising a right by fracturing the skull and knocking out the eye of an assailant, and should be guilty of

---

[13]Macaulay, Macleod, Anderson and Millett, op. cit., n. 2, Note M, p. 147. The need to distinguish between the two cases does not depend entirely on the form of punishment for murder (in this passage, the death penalty). Indeed, the justification propounded by the Code framers is equally relevant in jurisdictions where murder attracts a discretionary sentence, for example, New South Wales and Victoria. It should also be noted that the Indian Penal Code provides a limited sentencing discretion in murder cases, namely, the imposition of the death penalty or life imprisonment: Section 302.

the highest crime in the code if he kills the same assailant, that there should be only a single step between perfect innocence and murder, between perfect impunity and liability of capital punishment, seems unreasonable. In a case in which the law itself empowers an individual to inflict any harm short of death, it ought hardly we think, to visit him with the highest punishment if he inflicts death.[14]

As for the same need in respect to killing in excessive defence of property, the Code framers had this to say:

It is to be considered also that the line between those aggressions which it is lawful to repel by killing and those which it is not lawful so to repel, is in our Code, and must be in every Code, to a great extent an arbitrary line, and that many individual cases will fall on one side of that line which, if we had framed the law with a view to those cases alone, we should place on the other. Thus, we allow [under Section 103(3)] a man to kill if he has no other means of preventing an incendiary from burning his house; and we do not allow him to kill for the purpose of preventing the comission of a simple theft. But a house may be a wretched heap of mats and thatch, propped by a few bamboos, and not worth altogether twenty rupees. A simple theft may deprive a man of a pocket-book which contains bills to a great amount, the saving of a long and laborious life, the sole dependence of a large family. That in these cases the man who kills the incendiary should be pronounced guiltless of any offence, and that the man who kills the thief should be sentenced to the gallows ... would be generally condemned as a shocking injustice. We are, therefore, of the opinion that the offence which we have designated as voluntary culpable homicide in defence ought to be distinguished from murder in such a manner that the Courts may have it in their power to inflict a slight or a merely nominal punishment on acts which, though not within the letter of the law which authorises killing in self-defence, are yet within the reason of the law.[15]

These explanations emphasize the moral distinction between murder and killings done in excessive self-defence and declare that a person who has killed as a result of applying excessive force in defence of the person or of property is morally less culpable than one who has killed in circumstances which provide no extenuating circumstances whatsoever.

## B. A Preliminary Difficulty of Interpretation

The expression 'in good faith' contained in Exception 2 raises a difficulty which needs to be canvassed in some detail. The Code

[14]Ibid.
[15]Ibid., p. 148.

uses that expression to connote the doing of or believing in something with 'due care and attention'.[16] The courts have generally regarded the clause 'in the exercise in good faith of the right of private defence' in the Exception as affecting, among other things, the infliction of harm by the accused.[17] Under this view, for excessive self-defence to succeed, the accused's belief that the harm inflicted by her or him was necessary must have been honest or genuinely arrived at after due care and attention (that is, the belief must have been reasonable).[18]

This stance of linking 'in good faith' with the defensive action taken by the accused can be criticized on several counts. First, it requires a distinction to be made between what a reasonable person would regard as necessary harm (that is, the Section 99(4) requirement) and what the accused reasonably believed to be necessary harm (that is, the element of 'good faith' under the Exception). This distinction is too fine. It is difficult to envisage a case where the harm which was reasonably believed by the accused to be necessary was not considered excessive by the hypothetical reasonable person and *vice versa*.[19] This is especially so given the relaxing of the objective standard in Section 99(4) by the Indian courts. There is a line of authority which holds that 'in the excitement and confusion of the moment it is not to be expected that an average man would weigh the means that he intends to adopt in golden scales'.[20] Indeed, one court after reviewing the cases went so far as to make the following observation:

[16]See Section 52, which reads: 'Nothing is said to be done or believed in "good faith" which is done or believed without due care and attention'.

[17]For two examples of cases in which judgements clearly attach 'in good faith' to the infliction of harm, see *Mammum v Emperor* AIR 1917 Lah 347 and *Jaipal Kunbi v Emperor* (1922) AIR Nag 141.

[18]Another suggested way of stating this is that the accused must not have been reckless in the force applied in self-defence: see *Sabal Singh v State* AIR 1978 SC 1538, p. 1541. While the concept of recklessness affords a possible interpretation of 'good faith' under the Exception, its obvious difficulty is that it is an English legal concept and nowhere is it used or defined in the Code: see Koh, K.L., C. Clarkson and N. Morgan, *Criminal Law in Singapore and Malaysia: Text and Materials*, pp. 455–6 (1989).

[19]This criticism and the remaining discussion in this and the next section were previously canvassed in Yeo, S., 'Rethinking Good Faith in Excessive Private Defence', 30 *Journal of the Indian Law Institute* 443 (1988). See also Charleton, P., *Offences Against the Person*, p. 154 (1992).

[20]*Ahmed Din V Emperor* (1927) AIR Lah 194, p. 195. See also *Dinnah v*

[A]ll these authorities lay down the rule that even if the accused were to cause more harm than is *absolutely* necessary in repelling the attack, it cannot be said that he exceeded the right given to him by law.[21]

Secondly, criticism stems from the wording of the Exception itself. If an accused must have 'with due care and attention' (that is, reasonably) believed the harm inflicted by her or him to be necessary in the circumstances, it seems tautological for the Exception to go on to require that the accused's defensive action must have been done 'without any intention of doing more harm than is necessary for the purpose of such defence'. Simply put, how can a person who reasonably believes the harm inflicted by her or him to be necessary at the same instance intend to do more harm than she or he considers necessary? The same may also be said of the other element of 'without premeditation' required by the Exception. It is difficult to envisage how a person could harbour a precedent malice against her or his assailant and yet be held to have inflicted only that amount of harm which he or she reasonably believed to be necessary by way of self-defence.

Thirdly, requiring the accused to have reasonably believed that her or his defensive action was necessary runs counter to the Code framers' justification for recognizing excessive self-defence. Surely an accused who honestly albeit unreasonably believed in the necessity of the harm caused by her or him in self-defence should be allowed to escape a conviction of the most heinous crime under the Code. Although such a person may have been culpable in applying excessive force, the law should require the culpability to be mitigated by the fact that the force was in response to an unlawful attack by the deceased.

---

*Emperor* (1948) AIR Lah 117; *State v Satish Sangma* (1954) AIR Ass 56; *Jabbar Dar v State*, Cr LJ 1179 (1955); *Raman Raghavan v State* (1968) Cr LJ 255; *Parichatt v State* (1972) AIR SC 535; *Rama Yeshwant Kamat v State* (1978) Cr LJ 1843.

[21] *Ghasi Ram v State* AIR (1952) Bhopal 25, p. 30 per Radke AJC. (Emphasis added.) In this respect, the discussion of the issue by Sornarajah, op. cit. n. 5, pp. 767–8 should be qualified. He had suggested that the Exception was rationalized on the ground that a person who is subjected to physical assault cannot be expected to measure with a degree of precision the extent of violence he or she could use in self-defence. In the light of the above-mentioned authorities this proposition applies with equal force to a situation involving the general plea of self-defence.

## C. Resolving the Difficulty

Possibly with the above criticisms in mind, the courts have largely paid lip-service to the element of 'good faith' contained in the Exception. That is to say, while they continue to link this expression with the infliction of harm, they have gone on to ignore that requirement when it came to applying the law to the facts of a case. The usual pattern in a judgement begins with the holding that the harm inflicted by the accused was objectively excessive. The judge would then recite or paraphrase the wording of the Exception and conclude simply that the accused was not guilty of murder because the Exception succeeded on the facts.[22] Hence, in practice, the courts have effectively taken a subjective stance by refusing to ensure whether the accused had reasonably believed the harm inflicted by her or him to be necessary.

There are a few cases where the courts have actually made the effort to analyse what the expression 'in good faith' means in the Exception. In line with the judicial practice just described, the courts in these cases have resorted to equating 'in good faith' with the purely subjective term of 'honestly'. The following passage from the Rangoon High Court case of *Po Mye v R* bears this out:

> We have been referred to the words of the exception which state that the offender, to benefit by it must act 'in good faith', and then to Section 52 (of the Code) which says 'nothing is said to be done in good faith which is done without due care and attention'. What is due care and attention depends on the position which a man finds himself, and varies in different cases. The question here must be whether the offender acted *honestly*, or whether he used the opportunity to pursue a private grudge and to inflict injuries which he intended to inflict regardless of his right. [Exception 2] punishes a criminal act in excess of the right of private defence, and *it is impossible to regard 'due care and attention' in the sense which is usually ascribed to it as an element in such criminality.*[23]

---

[22]The Indian law reports are replete with examples including Supreme Court decisions. For instance, see *Abdul Aziz v Emperor* AIR 1933 Pat 508; *Emperor v Muzaffar Hussain* AIR 1944 Lah 97; *Ghansham Dass v State*, 1979 Cr LJ 28; *Rafiq v State* AIR 1979 SC 1179; *Mohinder Pal Jolly v State* AIR 1979 SC 577; *Laxman v State* (1989) Cr LJ 1714; *Sundaramurthy v State* (1990) AIR SC 2007.

[23]AIR 1940 Rang 129, p. 132 per Chief Justice Roberts. (Emphasis added.) Compare this with *State v Inush Ali* (1982) Cr LJ 1044, p. 1046 where Justices Lahari and Hansaria equated 'in good faith' appearing in Exception 2 with committing an act without pretence.

Another example is found in the Allahabad High Court case of *In re Whittaker*, where a British soldier had shot dead an Indian and pleaded self-defence to a murder charge. Justice Straight instructed the jury that 'if the prisoner in firing the gun did so ... under the reasonable apprehension that life or limb was in danger, and in the honest belief that it was necessary for the purpose of self-defence, but at the same time his act was in excess of what an ordinary and reasonable man should have resorted to under the circumstances, he is guilty of culpable homicide not amounting to murder'.[24] A third example comes from Sudan, which has an identical provision in its Penal Code to Exception 2. In *Sudan Government v Mohamed Adam Onour*, the Court of Appeal viewed the provision in the following manner:

> [T]his section postulates three requisites: (1) good faith, (2) absence of premeditation, and (3) absence of intention to do unnecessary harm. The cumulative effect of these three exceptions is that the accused was placed in such circumstances that he honestly thought that if he did not kill, he would be killed or suffer serious injury.[25]

While this interpretation of the expression 'in good faith' in Exception 2 is to be commended for bringing the law into line with the Australian doctrine of excessive force, it suffers from a number of defects. One criticism is that it fails to answer the criticism of tautology. If the Exception already requires, by virtue of the expression 'in good faith', the honest belief by the accused that the harm he or she inflicted was necessary, why does it require further that the accused must have done so 'without intention of doing more harm than is necessary' for the purpose of private defence? Furthermore, there is an uneasiness in giving to the expression 'in good faith' a meaning clearly inconsistent with that which the Code framers gave to it. It is one thing to temper an objective standard with subjectivity, as has been done in relation to Section 99(4) by the qualification that the harm inflicted by the accused should not be weighed on golden scales. It is quite another thing to replace an objective measurement such as 'in good faith' with the completely subjective concept of 'honestly'.

Exception 2 could be interpreted in another way which does not strain the meaning of 'in good faith' while at the same time enabling the Exception to succeed when an accused honestly albeit

[24](1882) AWN 172, p. 174.
[25](1963) SLJR 157, p. 158.

unreasonably believed the harm inflicted by her or him was necessary. This can be achieved by giving the word 'exercise' the meaning 'invoke' so that the opening words of the provision will in effect read: 'Culpable homicide is not murder if the offender, in invoking in good faith the right of private defence ....' Viewing the word 'exercise' in this manner avoids connecting to it the question whether the infliction of harm was necessary. Instead, the word comes to be understood in terms of a *summoning* of or relying upon the right of private defence as opposed to an *acting* out of that right. Under this interpretation, the purpose of the expression 'in good faith' is to require the existence of circumstances which avail the accused of the right of private defence. These circumstances are spelt out in the Code provisions of private defence and include whether there existed a situation of danger confronting the accused; where the accused was the initial aggressor; whether the nature of the fight had not so altered as to put the accused in a position of self-defence; whether the accused had reasonable opportunity to take recourse to police protection; and whether the danger confronting the accused was the act of a public servant within Section 99(2) of the Code.

This proposed role of 'in good faith' finds some support in the following comment by the Supreme Court of India in *Munney Khan v State*:

> The right of private defence is codified in sections 96 to 100 (of the Penal Code), which have all to be read together in order to have a proper grasp of the scope and limitations of this right. By enacting these sections the authors of the Code wanted to except from the operation of its penal clauses classes of acts done *in good faith* for the purpose of repelling unlawful aggression.[26]

To like effect is the holding of the Lahore High Court in *Lal v Emperor* that to attract the application of the Exception 'it is

[26]AIR 1971 SC 1491, p. 1494. (Emphasis added.) Admittedly, the court was not dealing with Exception 2 but with the general plea of private defence. However, its use of 'in good faith' is especially significant to this discussion since that expression does not appear in Sections 96 to 100 (apart from Sections 99(2) and (3), which concern a public servant, and not the accused, acting in good faith). One commentator achieves the same result by saying that the Exception 'deals with those situations where a person who is *lawfully* exercising his right of private defence exceeds the limits of his defence and causes the death of his assailant': see Medani, A., 'Some Aspects of the Sudan Law of Homicide', *Journal of African Law* 92, p. 99 (1974). (Emphasis added.)

necessary that the person causing the harm must have done so in the *bona fide* exercise of the right of private defence'.[27] Seen in this light, the opening words of the Exception merely serve to pronounce that this mitigatory plea arises out of the law of private defence. The next part of the Exception, namely, 'exceeds the power given to him by law, and causes the death etc.' spells out the situation where the general plea of private defence has failed so as to bring the Exception into play. The remaining part, namely, 'without premeditation and without any intention of doing more harm than is necessary etc.' specifies the conditions which the accused must satisfy to benefit from the Exception. The rationale for excessive private defence lies in this final part. The defence enables the accused to avoid a murder conviction since, although the killing was objectively excessive and therefore warrants punishment, the accused had acted under an honest belief that it was necessary in the circumstances. The lesser degree of culpability occasioned by this honest mistaken belief is adequately reflected in a conviction of culpable homicide not amounting to murder.

This last interpretation of 'in good faith' is most in accord with the doctrine of excessive self-defence as it was known under Australian common law. It is also likely to have been what the Code framers had intended. To summarize, for the Exception to succeed, the accused need not show that he or she had reasonable grounds to believe that the harm inflicted was necessary. The accused need only show that her or his act of killing was not (1) motivated by any premeditated malice towards the victim nor (2) carried out with any intention of doing more harm than was necessary. These two requirements ensure that the accused's belief as to the force being necessary was honestly held. Doubtless, any evidence of premeditated malice or an intention to do more harm than was necessary would automatically result in a jury's concluding that the accused lacked the honest belief which underpins the doctrine of excessive self-defence.[28]

Regrettably, the illustration accompanying the Exception constitutes a major obstacle to this suggested reading of the

[27](1946) Cr LJ 809, p. 811.
[28]For examples of cases where the Exception failed on account of one or the other of these requirements, see *In re Ponthala Narisi Reddi* (1914) Cr LJ 447; *Ammupujare v Emperor* (1942) Cr LJ 753; *Latchmi Koeri v State* 1960 AIR Pat 62; *Roshdi v PP* [1994] 3 SLR 282.

Exception. It reads:

> Z attempts to horse-whip A, not in such a manner as to cause grievous hurt to A. A draws out a pistol. Z persists in the assault. A, believing in good faith that he can by no other means prevent himself from being horse-whipped, shoots Z dead. A has not committed murder, but only culpable homicide.

Hence, there is an unambiguous application of the expression 'in good faith' to A's infliction of harm upon Z. This automatically compels the same expression appearing in the Exception itself to be treated in like fashion.

In recognizing the important role illustrations serve in interpreting the substantive provisions of the Indian Penal Code, the courts have quite correctly been reluctant to reject them on the ground of repugnancy to the provisions themselves.[29] Yet, they do envisage an illustration being so rejected provided that 'a very special case' existed and rejection of the illustration amounted to 'the very last resort of construction'.[30] It is submitted that the illustration accompanying Exception 2 to Section 300 is just such a special case and should be rejected by courts for being repugnant to the substantive provision. Not to do so will mean that the current state of affairs will continue, with the courts either paying mere lip-service to the requirement of 'in good faith'[31] or interpreting that expression in purely subjective terms.[32] Both the interpretation and practical application of the Exception will be better served by amending the illustration so as to bring it into line with the doctrine of excessive self-defence. A possible revision of the illustration is made in chapter 4 together with a model provision for the defence of excessive self-defence.[33]

In conclusion, it may be said that the Code framers were far in advance of the English and Australian lawmakers of their day in recognizing the doctrine of excessive self-defence. Unfortunately, the framers' inclusion of the expression 'in good faith' in the Exception has given rise to problems. Some Indian courts have risen to the occasion by interpreting the expression in ways which

---

[29] See *Mahomed Syedol Ariffin v Yeoh Ooi Gark* 1916 AIR PC 242, p. 244; *Ram Lal v Emperor* 1928 AIR Oudh 15, p. 17.

[30] *Mahomed Syedol Ariffin v Yeoh Ooi Gark* 1916 AIR PC 242, p. 244.

[31] See the cases listed in n. 22 above and the accompanying main text.

[32] As in *Po Mye v The King* 1940 AIR Rang 129 and in *Sudan Government v Mohamed Adam Onour* (1963) SLJR 157.

[33] See p. 184.

avoid requiring the accused to have reasonably believed the force to be necessary in self-defence. Others have simply not applied the expression to the facts of the case. Whichever approach is taken, it shows that the Indian judges were alive to the underlying principle of the doctrine, namely, that a person who honestly but mistakenly believed that her or his act of killing was necessary in self-defence did not deserve to be convicted of murder.

The Indian experience also shows that the Exception has been successfully invoked in practice without undue problems of comprehension by the triers of fact. This was the finding of the Law Commission of India charged with examining the provisions of the Indian Penal Code with a view to reform.[34] The Commission proposed no changes to the Exception, opining that it 'had been carefully thought out' and had 'stood the test of practical application over the years'.[35] While the Commission may have been broadly correct in its observation, the discussion has shown that both the wording of the Exception and its illustration have created uncertainty in the law. It would have been preferable for the Commission to have taken the opportunity to rectify these defects. Besides revising the illustration, the Commission could have made the meaning of the Exception clearer by deleting any reference to 'in good faith' altogether. In chapter 4, a revised provision is presented which could comprise a model for reform.

## D. Poor Adherence to the Requirements of the Exception

Many Indian judges have, of late, failed to ensure that the requirements of Exception 2 to Section 300 are strictly adhered to in a given case. Unfortunately, the Supreme Court of India is not exempt from this criticism. There are all too many instances when the following sequence of decision-making has appeared in the judgements. In a murder case involving a plea of self-defence, the court begins by considering whether there were circumstances that warranted regarding the accused's killing as an act of defence of person or property. Having decided that such circumstances were present, the court proceeds to determine whether the killing was reasonably necessary. If it was not, the court rules that the accused is prevented from successfully relying on the general plea of self-

[34]42nd Report, Indian Penal Code (1971).
[35]Ibid., para. 16.7.

defence. So far, these steps in decision-making are unexceptional. However, from that last step of deciding that the killing was not reasonably necessary, the court goes on to conclude, without any elaboration whatsoever, that the accused should have the benefit of the Exception and thereby have the charge of murder reduced to culpable homicide not amounting to murder. The reader of judgements of this nature is left with the distinct impression that the court failed to ensure that, before the Exception could succeed, the accused must be shown to have honestly believed that the killing was necessary in the circumstances. As noted under the previous heading, the Exception imposes this element of honest belief by requiring the accused not to have premeditated the killing nor intended to cause more harm than was necessary by way of defence.

A few Supreme Court case examples will bear this out. In *Tara Chand v State*, D had attacked V who had committed criminal trespass by driving a tractor onto a field in D's lawful possession.[36] The court accepted that D was exercising his right of private defence of property under Section 97(2) of the Code. However, that right was subject to the restrictions under Section 99, particularly, that D must not have inflicted more harm than was necessary for the purpose of defence. In the present case, the number and nature of wounds showered by D on V showed that D had applied excessive force. Additionally, the court noted that there was evidence suggesting that even after V had fallen down D had continued to injure him 'in a vindictive and revengeful spirit'.[37] The court was then content to simply conclude that D failed under the general plea of self-defence but could have his charge reduced to culpable homicide not amounting to murder by virtue of Exception 2. Given the finding of the court that the final blows inflicted by D were motivated by revenge, the proper conclusion would appear to be that D intended to do more harm than was necessary by way of defence. As this was an integral requirement of Exception 2, D should not have been allowed to successfully rely on the Exception.

In *Baljit Singh v State*, a party of powerful Rajput zaminders of a village had gone to a field legally possessed by the Ds, who were Kahars, a socially and educationally backward minority group residing in the same village.[38] The zaminders were armed with

[36]AIR 1971 SC 1891.
[37]Ibid., p. 1897.
[38](1976) 4 SCC 590.

sticks and had come onto the field for the purpose of dispossessing the Kahars of it and to uproot their crops. In the course of the ensuing fight, the Ds killed one of the zaminders and were charged with his murder. The court accepted that in the circumstances, the Ds would undoubtedly have a reasonable apprehension of hurt being caused to them and were therefore entitled to defend their person and property in the exercise of their right of private defence. However, the court ruled that the Ds had 'grossly' exceeded their right of private defence due to the very large number of serious injuries on the deceased.[39] In spite of this finding, the court concluded that the case fell within the purview of Exception 2. What the court should have done was to consider whether the number of injuries was consistent with Ds' honest belief that those injuries were necessary to defend themselves against the deceased.

One final case example will suffice.[40] In *Madan Mohan Pandey v State*, two warring parties had met and, in the ensuing fight, D had fired six shots indiscriminately which resulted in the death of a member of the opposing party and injuries to several others.[41] The court noted that D had not received any injuries and that members of his party had suffered only minor injuries. On the basis of this evidence, the court held that while D had a right of private defence he had exceeded that right by firing the shots. It concluded that there was no reason to disturb the trial court's decision to convict D of culpable homicide not amounting to murder. Again, it is submitted that the proper approach would have been for the court to consider whether D had fired the shots with premeditation or with the intention of doing more harm than was necessary for the purpose of defence. If this was the case, the Exception should not have been available and he should have been convicted of murder instead.

The Supreme Court has, however, not always been as recalcitrant in its application of the Exception. For instance, in *Onkarnath Singh v State*, V had confonted D as to why he had slapped V's young cousins.[42] D retorted that he would repeat the

[39]Ibid., p. 600.

[40]For other examples, see *Keshoram Bora v State* (1978) 2 SCC 407; *Sampat Singh v State* 1969 AIR SC 956. See also the Gujarat High Court case of *Memon Yakubbhai Janmohmed v State* 1989 Cr LJ 1843.

[41]AIR 1991 SC 769.

[42](1973) 3 SCC 276. For another example, see *Mohinder Pal Jolly v State* (1979) SCC (Cri) 635.

feat, whereupon V threw and pinned him to the ground. As V was walking away from the spot, D and several other supporters surrounded V and D killed V with a spear. The court held that, in the circumstances, the spearing was out of all proportion to the supposed danger from V so that D was not entitled to successfully plead general self-defence. The court also observed that D's spearing was 'exceedingly vindicative and maliciously excessive' so as to deny D the benefit of Exception 2. This holding stands in stark contrast to the one handed down by the Supreme Court in *Tara Chand* noted above.

It may well be that in those cases where the requirements of the Exception were poorly examined, the court might have been convinced that these requirements were satisfied and had simply omitted to articulate this finding. However, given the carefully structured way in which the Code framers had drawn up the general and partial pleas of private defence and the interplay between them, it should have been incumbent upon the courts to express that finding in some detail in their judgements. There is also much to be said for the maxim that in such cases justice must not only be done but must be seen to be done. Accordingly, it is submitted that the Supreme Court should take the lead at the next available opportunity to present a model judgement which systematically and thoroughly works through the general plea of private defence followed by the partial plea, being careful along the way to account for all the requirements of both these pleas and their application to the facts of the case at hand.

# 3. Excessive Self-Defence under English Law

## A. *Previous Judicial Recognition of the Defence*

As indicated earlier, there are nineteenth century English cases which lend support to the doctrine of excessive self-defence.[43] In *R v Cook,* V had gone to D's house with an arrest warrant and commenced to break down the door. D fired his gun at V and

---

[43]For other discussions of these cases, see Morris, N., and C. Howard, *Studies in Criminal Law,* pp. 127–31 (1964); Smith, P., 'Excessive Defence—A Rejection of an Australian Initiative?', *Criminal Law Review* 524, pp. 528–9 (1972). James Stephen, relying on *Hale's Pleas of the Crown,* also thought that English law recognized the doctrine: see *A History of the Criminal Law of England,* Vol. III, p. 67 (1883).

killed him.[44] The court held that D could not be acquitted altogether since he had seen V and voluntarily shot him. However, he was entitled to a verdict of manslaughter and not murder since V was executing the warrant unlawfully and D had some justification in preventing him from doing so. In the case of *R v Whalley,* D had injured V by throwing stones at him when V, a prosecutor, had confronted D with an illegal warrant to appear.[45] In the course of his judgement, the trial judge said that if death had ensued the offence would have been manslaughter and not murder. The next case is *R v Patience,* where D was acquitted of charges of wounding with intent to murder and to do grievous bodily harm, the injuries having occurred in resisting an illegal arrest.[46] Parke B said that '[i]f a person receives illegal violence and he resists that violence with anything he happens to have in hand and death ensues, that would be manslaughter'.[47]

Admittedly, these decisions were by no means clear and unambiguous pronouncements supporting the doctrine of excessive force in self-defence. On a strict interpretation, they were cases where force was applied to resist an unlawful execution of a warrant or an unlawful arrest and accordingly were not concerned with circumstances involving self-defence against an assault. Furthermore, it is extremely difficult to assess the extent to which provocation might have played a part in soliciting the judicial statements about manslaughter. These may have been among the reasons why the Privy Council in *Palmer v R*[48] rejected *Cook, Whalley* and *Patience* as authority for the doctrine of excessive self-defence.

## B. Current Judicial Rejection of the Defence

*Palmer* was an appeal from Jamaica which provided the Privy Council with its first opportunity to consider the doctrine. The accused, who had stolen a bag of cannabis, was pursued by several people whose intentions to beat him were made abundantly clear. He shot dead one of his pursuers and was charged with murder. His plea that the charge should be reduced to manslaughter on

[44] Cro Car 537 (1639), 79 ER 1063.
[45] 7 C & P 245 (1835), 173 ER 108.
[46] 7 C & P 775 (1837), 173 ER 338.
[47] 7 C & P 775, p. 776 (1837), 173 ER 338, p. 338.
[48] [1971] AC 814.

account of excessive self-defence was rejected by the lower courts and the Privy Council. In the course of its judgement, the Privy Council reviewed the previously mentioned English cases and concluded as follows:

> If in any of the above cases there is a suggestion that a measure of dispensation or tolerance, where a death is intentionally and unnecessarily caused, is to be found in the circumstance that someone is acting on an illegal warrant or is (as in *Cook's* case) executing process unlawfully it is not one that commends itself to their Lordships.[49]

Regrettably, the Privy Council did not expressly state its reasons for this view. By so holding, the court may have been affirming recent English judicial developments which frowned upon the use of excessive force to resist an unlawful arrest.[50] This is evidenced by the court's reference to Lord Goddard's comment in *R v Wilson*[51] that if a person was purporting to arrest another without a lawful warrant, the person arrested may use force to avoid being arrested but 'he must not use more force than necessary'; if more force than necessary was used it is not justified in any way whatsoever.[52] If this was what the Privy Council was doing, it is submitted that the court was remiss in using the analogy with excessive force in unlawful arrest cases to reject the doctrine of excessive force in self-defence. As one commentator has asserted, '[i]t would seem at least arguable that excessive defence, depending as it must upon the principle of inexigibility of alternative conduct, is for that very reason distinguishable from resisting unlawful arrest with its battery of constitutional alternatives'.[53] The contention here then is that the Privy Council in *Palmer* should have evaluated the legal principle underlying the doctrine of excessive self-defence rather than simply rejected the doctrine on the basis of a dubious analogy with excessive force against unlawful arrests. We shall see later that an evaluation of this principle by the Australian courts resulted in their recognition of the doctrine at least for a while until concerns over the lack of jury comprehension of the doctrine were permitted to hold sway.

---

[49]Ibid., p. 825 per Lord Morris, who delivered the judgement of the court.
[50]For example, see *R v Fennell* [1970] 3 WLR 513. See further James, C., 'The Queensbury Rules of Self Defence', 21 *International and Comparative Law Quarterly* 357, p. 358 (1972).
[51][1955] 1 WLR 493.
[52][1971] AC 814, p. 825–6.
[53]James, op. cit., n. 50, p. 358.

To be fair, the Privy Council in *Palmer* did take note of a couple of English cases where the doctrine appears to have been recognized in circumstances of self-defence. One was *R v Weston*, a murder case involving D who had shot and killed V.[54] Chief Justice Cockburn directed the jury that:

> if the prisoner had resorted to the gun in self-defence, against serious violence or in the reasonable dread of it, it would be justifiable, and that even if there was not such violence, or ground for the reasonable apprehension of it, yet ... if an assault, though short of serious injury, was committed on the prisoner, then it would be manslaughter.[55]

For some inexplicable reason, the Privy Council refused to regard *Weston* as a case involving force used in self-defence, preferring instead to regard the case together with *Cook*, *Whalley* and *Patience* and dismissing it in exactly same way as the court had done for these other cases.[56]

The second case was *R v Biggin*, where D had killed V in defending himself against V's violent homosexual attack.[57] At D's trial for murder, the trial judge had directed the jury that if D had used more violence than was really necessary in the circumstances, that would justify a verdict of manslaughter. On appeal, the Court of Criminal Appeal did not take exception to this direction, thereby suggesting its tacit approval. However, the Privy Council in *Palmer* rejected this suggestion, observing that the terms in which the direction was given had not been set out so that the Court of Criminal Appeal had no need to examine it.[58]

Overall, the main criticism of the Privy Council's approach to these earlier cases was its insistence on the need for judicial precedence to support the doctrine of excessive self-defence. This resulted in the court's failure to test the validity of the principle supporting the doctrine. Despite its faults, *Palmer* was subsequently followed by the English Court of Appeal in *R v McInnes* which regarded the Privy Council decision as providing high persuasive authority which it would 'unhesitatingly accept'.[59] It also referred to an earlier decision of its own which had regarded the doctrine

[54](1879)14 Cox CC 346.
[55]Ibid., p. 351.
[56][1971] AC 815, p. 825.
[57][1920] 1 KB 213.
[58][1971] AC 815, p. 826.
[59][1971] 1 WLR 1600, p. 1608. The court did not bother discussing any of the earlier English cases.

of excessive self-defence as 'a novelty in present times'.[60] Unfortunately, as with the Privy Council in *Palmer*, the Court of Appeal rejected the doctrine without giving any thought to the legal principle upon which the doctrine stood. *Palmer* will be revisited when discussing the Australian law, since that decision played a pivotal role in the recent demise of the doctrine of excessive self-defence in that jurisdiction.

The latest airing of the issue to be given by an English court was by the House of Lords in *R v Clegg*.[61] The House was much more circumspect in its approval of *Palmer*. It noted that several recent English law reform bodies had lent their wholehearted support for the defence and acknowledged that their recommendations were 'entitled to great weight'.[62] The House seriously considered whether it was the proper lawmaking body to introduce the doctrine of excessive self-defence into English law.[63] Ultimately, it felt that any law which reduced what would otherwise be murder to manslaughter was essentially a matter for decision by the legislature.

Given that the English common law has refused to recognize the doctrine of excessive self-defence in relation to killings done for the protection of the person, *a fortiori*, the law does not recognize the doctrine in respect of killings done for the protection of property. The English law of defence of property is covered by Section 3 of the *Criminal Law Act* 1967 (UK), which states that '[a] person may use such force as is reasonable in the circumstances in the prevention of crime'.[64] The term 'prevention of crime' is wide enough to embrace acts done in defence of property since defensive action taken against such acts as criminal trespass, criminal damage and larceny will invariably involve the prevention of trespassers, vandals and thieves from committing those property

---

[60] *R v Hassin* [1963] Crim LR 852; *The Times*, October 3, 1963 CCA. The doctrine was also viewed with scepticism by the House of Lords in *Reference under s 48A of the Criminal Appeal (Northern Ireland) Act 1968 (No 1 of 1975)*, [1976] 2 All ER 937, p. 956, 959.

[61] [1995] 2 WLR 80. See further, Harrison, R., 'Excessive use of Force in Self-Defence: R v Clegg' (1995), 50 *Journal of Criminal Law*, 28.

[62] Ibid., pp. 91–2. The law reform bodies are presented below.

[63] Ibid., pp. 91–3.

[64] Section 3(1). The provision also covers the use of reasonable force to effect or assist in lawful arrest of offenders or suspected offenders or of persons unlawfully at large.

offences. The question as to when it is reasonable to kill in order to prevent a property offence is speculative. It cannot be reasonable to do so unless it was needed to prevent the crime and unless the evil which would follow from failure to prevent the crime was so great that a reasonable person might feel justified in killing to avert that evil.[65] Conceivably, these conditions will be more readily satisfied were the property offence defended against to contain an element of violence to the person, for example, robbery. They will be less likely to be satisfied were the property offence in question not to have such an element of personal violence. This speculative nature of the law has led Professors Smith and Hogan to pose the question: 'How much force may be used to prevent the destruction of a great work of art?'[66] Suffice it to note here that the Indian Penal Code, in confining justifiable killings in defence of property to a list of offences (all of which contain violence to the person or a threat thereof) under Section 103 makes the law in that jurisdiction much clearer than the English law.[67]

## C. Law Reform Proposals Favouring the Defence

When discussing the recent House of Lords case of *Clegg*, reference was made to the fact that current English law reform bodies have lent their full support to the recognition of a form of manslaughter based on excessive force in defence of person or property. Thus, the Criminal Law Revision Committee in its report on *Offences Against the Person* recommended the creation of a new defence reducing murder to manslaughter. The Committee proposed that:

> Where a defendant kills in a situation in which it is reasonable for some force to be used in self-defence but he uses excessive force, he should be liable to be convicted of manslaughter and not murder if, at the time of the act, he honestly believed that the force he used was reasonable in the circumstances. Furthermore, where a person has killed using excessive force in the prevention of crime in a situation in which it was reasonable for some force to be used and at the time of the act he honestly believed that the force he used was reasonable in the circumstances, we consider that he should not be convicted of murder but should be liable to be convicted of manslaughter.[68]

[65]Smith, J.C. and B. Hogan, *Criminal Law*, 7th ed., p. 254 (1992).
[66]Ibid.
[67]See above, on pp. 120–1.
[68]14th Report (1980), Cmnd 7844, para. 288.

The Committee was therefore recommending that the defence should cover not only cases where a person killed while defending her or his person or that of another but also cases where the accused killed when defending property. The latter falls within the description found in the quotation of 'prevention of crime'.[69]

Subsequently, the Law Commission charged with drawing up a Criminal Code for England and Wales drafted the following clause to implement the Committee's proposal:

> A person who, but for this section, would be guilty of murder is not guilty of murder if, at the time of his act, he believes the use of the force which causes death to be necessary and reasonable to effect a purpose referred to in section 44 (use of force in public or private defence), but the force exceeds that which is necessary and reasonable in the circumstances which exist or (where there is a difference) in those which he believes to exist.[70]

Again we note that the Commission's proposal was for the defence to cover both cases of killings in defence of the person and of property. This is because the purposes referred to in Section 44 of the Commission's Draft Criminal Code include the protection of oneself or another from unlawful force as well as the protection of property from unlawful appropriation, destruction or damage.[71]

This clause later received the support of the Select Committee of the House of Lords on murder and life imprisonment.[72] Like the Commission, the Committee noted that the High Court of Australia had recently abrogated the defence. However, it had done so 'not because it thought the principle was unsound' but because it was too difficult for juries to understand and apply.[73] Both the Committee and the Commission were confident that the proposed clause, together with those on proof and the use of force in public or private defence contained in the Draft Criminal Code, should

[69]As noted previously when discussing Section 3 of the *Criminal Law Act 1967* (UK). See above, pp. 138–9.

[70]Law Com No. 177, *A Criminal Code for England and Wales* (1989), cl. 59 of its Draft Criminal Code. This clause was taken directly from an earlier report presented to the English Law Commission, namely, Law Com No. 143, *Codification of the Criminal Law* (1985), *Draft Criminal Code Bill*, Section 61.

[71]Clause 44(1)(c) and (e) respectively. This clause is reproduced in the Appendix to this work.

[72]*Report of the Select Committee on Murder and Life Imprisonment* (Session 1988–89, HL Paper 78), paras. 86–9.

[73]Ibid., paras. 88–9; Law Commission, op. cit., n .70, para. 14.19.

enable a trial judge to direct the jury in readily comprehensible terms. The contrast is noted between, on the one hand, the cases of *Palmer* and *McInnes,* where the principle underlying the doctrine was not considered at all and, on the other hand, these law reform bodies which did examine the principle and, upon so doing, recommended that excessive self-defence manslaughter be recognized under English law. As noted earlier, these recommendations were found to be attractive to the House of Lords in *Clegg,* the latest English case to consider the doctrine of excessive self-defence, although the House eventually decided that the proposed change to the law was best left to Parliament.

At this juncture it may be pertinent to mention briefly a nineteenth century English law reform body which considered adopting the provision on excessive self-defence contained in the Indian Penal Code. This was the Criminal Code Bill Commission of 1879. The Commissioners rejected the Indian provision out of hand, saying:

> If we thought that the common law was such as is here supposed, we should without hesitation suggest that it should be altered. But we think that such is not and never was the law of England.[74]

In the Commissioners' view, self-defence and provocation exhausted the possibilities. As with *Palmer* and *McInnes,* the Commissioners' rejection of the doctrine stems from their failure to give proper weight to the legal principle underlying it. The nature of this principle and the arguments for and against recognizing excessive self-defence have been fully examined in recent years under Australian law. To this I now turn.

# 4. Excessive Self-Defence under Australian Law

## A. Previous Judicial Recognition of the Defence

At the outset of this chapter, a passage was quoted from the South Australian Court of Criminal Appeal's judgement in *Howe* which recognized excessive self-defence manslaughter. A majority of the High Court of Australia subsequently agreed in substance with this holding.[75] The defence was applied shortly thereafter in a series

[74]C 2345, English Parliamentary Papers, Vol. 36, p. 201 (1879).
[75](1958) 100 CLR 448, p. 462 per Chief Justice Dixon, with Justices McTiernan and Fullagar concurring at p. 464.

of cases[76] so as to lead one commentator to conclude that the defence 'is here to stay' in the common law jurisdictions of Australia.[77]

The defence applied to cases involving killings both in defence of the person and in defence of property. Indeed, the defence under Australian common law was first recognized in the Victorian Court of Criminal Appeal case of *McKay,* in which the accused had killed a thief in defence of his property and consequently in prevention of the crime of larceny.[78] The facts and holding of this case inspired the following illustration to be given by one of the English law reform bodies recently supporting the defence:

> D, a chicken farmer, has suffered grave losses through nocturnal thefts of his birds. He wakes in the middle of the night to see P running away with a chicken under his arm. Being unable to prevent P's escape in any other way, he shoots at him with a shotgun. He intends to cause serious injury and is aware that he may kill. P is killed. D believes that the thief is the cause of his previous heavy losses but in fact he is a tramp who has never been there before. Assuming that the judge rules that any reasonable jury would find, or the jury finds, that the force used was unreasonable even if P had been the persistent thief, D is guilty of murder unless he may have believed that the force used was reasonable, in which case he is guilty of manslaughter.[79]

Practically speaking, the general plea of self-defence (as opposed to the partial plea of excessive self-defence) will never afford D a complete acquittal in cases where D had killed solely in defence of her or his property. This is due to the ruling expressed by Justice Smith in *McKay* that '[t]he act done must have been necessary, in the sense that the mischief sought to be prevented could not have been prevented by less violent means; and what was done must not have been out of proportion to that mischief'.[80] It is difficult

---

[76]*R v Bufalo* [1958] VR 363; *R v Haley* (1959) 76 WN(NSW) 550; *R v Enright* [1961] VR 663; *R v Tikos (No 1)* [1963] VR 285; and *R v Tikos (No 2)* [1963] VR 306.

[77]Howard, C., 'An Australian Letter—Excessive Defence', *Criminal Law Review* 448, p. 450 [1964].

[78][1957] VR 560. For another Australian case where the defence of excessive force succeeded in respect of a killing in defence of property, see *R v Turner* [1962] VR 30.

[79]Law Com No. 143, *Codification of the Criminal Law*, op. cit., n. 70, p. 234.

[80][1957] VR 560, p. 569. This ruling has been endorsed by the High Court in *Howe* (1958) 100 CLR 448; *Viro* (1978) 141 CLR 88 and *Zecevic v DPP*

to envisage a situation where the death of a criminal is regarded as proportionate to the injury to property which the criminal threatens. Conceivably, it is only when the property offence sought to be prevented contains an element of personal violence, such as robbery, that D might justifiably kill. However, in such a case, D would have been defending both her or his property and person. It would make for neatness and facilitate the expeditious handling of cases were the Australian law on the general plea of self-defence to expressly single out, as falling within its operation, selected types of property offences containing an element of personal violence or threatened violence. This same criticism was earlier made against the English law on defence of property.[81] In this regard, the Indian Code framers' drawing up of a specific list of property offences under Section 103 of the Code against which an accused could justifiably kill in defence is to be preferred. No such list is required in respect of the partial plea of excessive self-defence. This is because Australian law (as instanced in *McKay*), like the law under Exception 2 to Section 300 of the Indian Penal Code, can still operate in cases where D had honestly, albeit unreasonably, believed it to be necessary to kill to prevent a criminal from committing a property offence which did not contain an element of personal violence. The absence of such an element renders the killing objectively excessive but so long as D had honestly believed that it was not excessive, he or she will have the benefit of the partial defence.

As observed in my discussion of the English law, the plea of excessive self-defence did not fare so well before the Privy Council in *Palmer*. The Privy Council refused to recognize the defence, preferring instead to view self-defence as either succeeding so as to result in an acquittal or, failing, in which case the defence was rejected. At this point in time, it was quite understandable for one Australian commentator to regard the defence as having 'received its quietus' in Australia[82] with the decision in *Palmer*, since it was then the law that Privy Council cases, whether originating from Australia or not, were binding on all Australian courts including the High Court. Accordingly, excessive self-defence ceased to be

---

*(Vic)* (1987) 71 ALR 641. See further, Morris, N., 'The Slain Chicken Thief', 2 *Sydney Law Review* 414, p. 429 (1958).

[81] See above, at pp. 138–9.

[82] Elliott, I., 'Excessive Self-Defence in Commonwealth Law: A Comment', 22 *International and Comparative Law Quarterly* 727 (1973).

recognized by the Australian courts[83] until the position changed with the High Court case of *R v Viro*.[84]

In *Viro*, the High Court unanimously held that Privy Council cases, including past decisions, were no longer binding on the High Court. This opened the way for the High Court to decide whether its earlier decision in *Howe* was to be preferred to that of the Privy Council in *Palmer*. Six of the seven judges (some with reservations) concluded that *Howe* should be followed in recognizing excessive self-defence as a partial defence to murder.[85] The aftermath of *Viro* was that, in practice, whenever the issue of defence of person or property arose in a murder case, trial judges would invariably instruct the jury on the law of excessive self-defence as well.[86] Furthermore, the scope of the defence was extended on the initiative of the State courts beyond murder to cover statutory offences having as their mental element the 'intent to murder.'[87] Accordingly, there was every reason to suppose that, having come such a long way since *Howe*, the doctrine of excessive self-defence was now a firmly entrenched component of Australian common law.[88] It is little wonder then that the High Court's subsequent rejection of the defence, and reversion to the ruling in *Palmer*, came as a great shock to the criminal legal fraternity in the common law jurisdictions of Australia.

---

[83]For examples of cases approving of *Palmer*, see the trial judge in *R v Viro* (1978) 141 CLR 88 and *Bennett v Dopke* [1973] VR 239. Cf. *R v Olasiuk* (1973) 6 SASR 255.

[84](1978) 141 CLR 88.

[85]*Viro* will be discussed in detail later in this part.

[86]As we shall see, this was the result of the application by trial judges of certain propositions on the law of self-defence formulated by Justice Mason in *Viro*.

[87]See *R v Bozikis* [1981] VR 587; *R v McManua* (1985) 2 NSWLR 448. An example of such an offence is wounding with intent to murder: see Section 11 of the *Crimes Act* 1958 (Vic) and Section 27 of the *Crimes Act* 1900 (NSW).

[88]It was so regarded by many learned authorities. For example, see Howard, C., *Criminal Law* 4th edn, pp. 89-93 (1982); O'Connor, D. and P. Fairall, *Criminal Defences*, pp. 145-6 (1984); Williams, G., *Textbook of Criminal Law*, 2nd edn, pp. 546-7 (1983); Smith, J.C., and B. Hogan, *Criminal Law*, 5th edn, pp. 331-2 (1983); Criminal Law Revision Committee, op. cit., n. 68, para. 288; Law Reform Commission of Canada, Working Paper 33, *Homicide* (1984), p. 71.

## B. *The Facts of and Decision in* Zecevic

The controversial case was *Zecevic Director v Public Prosecutions (Victoria)*, which was an appeal from the Victorian Full Court[89] to the High Court[90] against a murder conviction. The facts were as follows. The accused and the deceased were neighbours in a block of flats. There was evidence of animosity between them prior to the day of the killing, stemming from the deceased's refusal to shut the security gates to the courtyard of the block. In an unsworn statement, the accused said that on the fatal day the deceased had left the gates open yet again. The accused confronted the deceased about the gates outside the door of the latter's unit. An altercation then occurred during which the deceased stabbed the accused in the chest and said 'I'll blow your head off.' Believing that the deceased might have a shotgun in his car and was going to get it, the accused ran back to his own flat to collect his own gun. From there he went downstairs and saw the deceased approaching his car. In a state of fear and anger, the accused fired a number of shots at the deceased which caused his death.

At his trial for murder, the accused raised the issue of self-defence but the trial judge, Justice Gray, withdrew that issue from the jury. He took this course upon concluding that the only inference open from the evidence was that the accused did not reasonably believe that an unlawful attack which threatened him with death or serious bodily harm was being or was about to be made on him. In so ruling, the trial judge had in mind the first of the six propositions formulated by Justice Mason (as he then was) in *Viro*.[91] These propositions were what Justice Mason, together with Justices Stephen and Aickin, considered to be the issues which arose for determination by the jury according to the earlier High Court case of *Howe*. Ever since these propositions appeared, trial judges found them a convenient way of instructing juries on the law of self-defence. It would be convenient at this juncture, and to facilitate later discussion, to set out these propositions in full:

1. (a) It is for the jury first to consider whether when the accused killed the deceased the accused reasonably believed that an unlawful attack which threatened him with death or serious bodily harm was being or was about to be made upon him.

[89][1986] VR 797.
[90](1987) 71 ALR 641.
[91](1978) 141 CLR 88, p. 146–7.

(b) By the expression 'reasonably believed' is meant, not what a reasonable man would have believed, but what the accused himself might reasonably believe in all the circumstances in which he found himself.

2. If the jury is satisfied beyond reasonable doubt that there was no reasonable belief by the accused of such an attack no question of self-defence arises.

3. If the jury is not satisfied beyond reasonable doubt that there was no such reasonable belief by the accused, it must then consider whether the force in fact used by the accused was reasonably proportionate to the danger which he believed he faced.

4. If the jury is not satisfied beyond reasonable doubt that more force was used than was reasonably proportionate it should acquit.

5. If the jury is satisfied beyond reasonable doubt that more force was used, then its verdict should be either manslaughter or murder depending on the answer to the final question for the jury—did the accused believe that the force which he used was reasonably proportionate to the danger which he believed he faced?

6. If the jury is satisfied beyond reasonable doubt that the accused did not have such a belief the verdict will be murder. If it is not satisfied beyond reasonable doubt that the accused did not have that belief the verdict will be manslaughter.[92]

The first four propositions deal with the full defence of self-defence using reasonable force, which, if successfully pleaded, results in an acquittal. Only the fifth and sixth propositions concern the defence of excessive self-defence. In *Zecevic*, the arguments raised by defence counsel pertaining to self-defence at both the trial and on appeal before the Victorian Full Court were confined to the first proposition and, in particular, to the question whether the accused had reasonable grounds to believe that the deceased was about to shoot him. The Full Court upheld the trial judge's decision not to leave the issue of self-defence to the jury since, in its opinion, there was insufficient evidence to indicate such a reasonable belief on the part of the accused.[93]

On further appeal to the High Court, defence counsel submitted that the propositions in *Viro* were incorrect on two counts. First, he argued that, contrary to the first two propositions, it should no longer be part of the common law of self-defence that an accused must reasonably have believed that he was

[92]Ibid.
[93][1986] VR 797, p. 805  per Justices Kaye and O'Bryan, and at p. 819 per Justice Tadgell.

threatened with death or serious bodily harm.[94] The High Court unanimously rejected this submission and retained the objective requirement of reasonable belief.[95] Secondly, counsel contended that the third and fourth propositions were erroneous in requiring that the force used by the accused had to be reasonably proportionate to the perceived danger. In counsel's opinion, an accused person should be acquitted if he had killed in the honest belief that it was necessary to do so in lawful self-defence.[96] The High Court was again unanimous in rejecting this argument, holding that the law of self-defence required an objective element of reasonable belief by the accused that the force used was reasonably necessary to combat the attack.[97] However, the appeal was eventually allowed and a new trial ordered on the basis that the evidence did raise the issue of self-defence which the accused was entitled to have left to the jury.[98]

Strictly in terms of the grounds of appeal before the High Court in *Zecevic*, there was no need for it to decide whether the doctrine of excessive self-defence should continue to be recognized at common law. Indeed, neither the Crown nor defence counsel had questioned the correctness of the fifth and sixth propositions in *Viro* which encompass the doctrine. However, the High Court saw the case as an opportunity to re-examine all the propositions in *Viro* because trial judges were finding great difficulty in expressing

[94]The High Court did not mention any of the case authorities which might have been cited by defence counsel in support of this submission. These would probably have included *Morgan v Colman* (1981) 27 SASR 334 at pp. 336–7 per Justice Wells, and *McManus* (1985) 2 NSWLR 448, p. 462 per Chief Justice Street. See also the English Court of Criminal Appeal in *R v Gladstone Williams* (1983) 78 Cr App R 276 and *R v Asbury* [1986] Crim LR 258, and most recently the Privy Council decision in *Beckford v R* [1987] 3 WLR 611.

[95](1987) 71 ALR 641, p. 645 per Chief Justice Mason; at pp. 648–50 per Justices Wilson, Dawson and Toohey; at p. 659 per Justice Brennan; at pp. 660–1 per Justice Deane; and at p. 668 per Justice Gaudron.

[96]Authority for this contention may be found in *Viro* (1978)141 CLR 88, pp. 158, 168 per Justices Jacobs and Murphy respectively.

[97](1987) 71 ALR 641, p. 645 per Chief Justice Mason; at p. 652 per Justices Wilson, Dawson and Toohey; at p.655 per Justice Brennan; at p. 661 per Justice Deane; and at p. 668 per Justice Gaudron.

[98]Ibid., p. 646 per Chief Justice Mason; at pp. 654–5 per Justices Wilson, Dawson and Toohey; at p. 659 per Justice Brennan; at pp. 667–8 per Justice Deane; and at p. 668 per Justice Caudron.

them in a way which was comprehensible to the jury. One result of this re-examination was that, by a majority of five to two,[99] excessive self-defence ceased to be a part of the common law of Australia. The current law of self-defence may be summarized in the following extracts from the joint majority judgement of Justices Wilson, Dawson and Toohey:

> The question to be asked in the end is quite simple. It is whether the accused believed upon reasonable grounds that it was necessary in self-defence to do what he did. If he had that belief and there were reasonable grounds for it, or if the jury is left in reasonable doubt about the matter, then he is entitled to an acquittal. Stated in this form, the question is one of general application and is not limited to cases of homicide.[100]

> ... [T]he use of excessive force in the belief that it was necessary in self-defence will not automatically result in a verdict of manslaughter. If the jury concludes that there were no reasonable grounds for a belief that the degree of force used was necessary, the defence of self-defence will fail and the circumstances will fail to be considered by the jury without reference to that plea.[101]

The majority also declared that henceforth the law of self-defence was in conformity with English law on that subject as expounded by the Privy Council in *Palmer* and the English Court of Appeal in *McInnes*.[102]

We can now proceed to examine critically the various reasons given by the majority in *Zecevic* for rejecting the doctrine of excessive self-defence. This will be followed by the reasons why the minority felt that the doctrine should be maintained.

## C. The Case for Abolishing Excessive Self-Defence

A major reason given by Justices Wilson, Dawson and Toohey for refusing to recognize excessive self-defence was that it lacked the

[99]The majority comprised Justices Wilson, Dawson, Toohey and Brennan and Chief Justice Mason. The minority judges were Deane and Gaudron.
[100](1987) 71 ALR 641, p. 652, and approved of by Chief Justice Mason at p. 646 and Justice Brennan at p. 655. It appears that the dissenting judges, Justices Deane and Gaudron, at pp. 667 and 668 respectively, also agreed with this statement of the law.
[101](1987) 71 ALR 641, p. 654 and approved of by Chief Justice Mason at p. 646 and by Justice Brennan at 659. This statement was rejected by Justice Deane at pp. 663–5 and by Justice Gaudron at pp. 669–71.
[102]Ibid.

support of case authority. They first cited Chief Justice Dixon's comment in *Howe* that 'there is no clear and definite judicial decision' favouring the defence[103] and went on to note that it had not been accepted by the Privy Council in *Palmer*.[104] They then questioned the status of *Viro* as authority for the defence on the basis that only three of the seven judges, Justices Mason, Stephen and Aickin, were prepared to recognize the defence as formulated in *Howe*.[105] Of the remaining judges in *Viro*, Justices Gibbs, Jacobs and Murphy presented differing opinions but eventually agreed that the law should recognize the defence only in order to achieve a measure of certainty; Chief Justice Barwick was in dissent.[106] Regarding the law as uncertain, Justices Wilson, Dawson and Toohey thought it desirable to restate the law of self-defence with the result that *Palmer* was followed in preference to *Howe*.

With respect, the High Court decisions of *Howe* and *Viro* are much stronger authorities in support of excessive self-defence than Justices Wilson, Dawson and Toohey regarded them. In their reference to *Howe*, they mentioned only Chief Justice Dixon, and Justices McTiernan and Fullagar as favouring recognition of the defence.[107] They appear to have overlooked Justice Menzies, who was also clearly in support of the defence.[108] The remaining judge, Justice Taylor, was likewise prepared to have the charge of murder reduced to manslaughter but on a much broader basis than the accused's honest though unreasonable belief.[109] Turning next to *Viro*, a closer analysis of the judgement of Justice Jacobs reveals that he would have given his full support to the defence if he was incorrect in his view that the law of self-defence did not possess

---

[103](1958) 100 CLR 448, p. 461.

[104](1987) 71 ALR 641, p. 651. Justice Brennan must be regarded as having fully endorsed all that was said in the joint judgement of Justices Wilson, Dawson and Toohey on the doctrine of excessive self-defence: see ibid. at p. 659. The judgement of the other majority judge, Chief Justice Mason, contains a number of comments which stand apart from the joint judgment and these will be highlighted either in the main text or by way of a footnote.

[105]Ibid.

[106](1978) 141 CLR 88, p. 128  per Justice Gibbs; at p. 158 per Justice Jacobs; at p. 171 per Justice Murphy; and at p. 102 per Chief Justice Barwick.

[107](1987) 71 ALR 641, p. 651.

[108](1958) 100 CLR 448, pp. 476–7.

[109]Ibid. at p. 468. The broader basis suggested by Justice Taylor was whether 'what the accused did was done primarily for the purpose of defending himself'.

an objective element.[110] A clear majority in *Viro* and a unanimous decision in *Zecevic* confirm that self-defence has such an objective component. Accordingly, Justice Jacobs' judgement should be added to those of Justices Mason, Stephen and Aickin to form a majority decision in *Viro* supporting the doctrine of excessive self-defence.[111] In the final analysis then, '*Viro* was a considered decision of a majority of the whole court confirming a previous considered decision of a majority of the court on the same point.'[112]

Another reason given by the majority in *Zecevic* for rejecting the doctrine of excessive self-defence was that it was creating problems for trial judges and juries. As Justices Wilson, Dawson and Toohey noted, 'it is apparent that difficulties have been experienced in instructing juries in accordance with the fifth and sixth propositions in *Viro* which, being based upon *Howe*, necessarily contain refinements which cannot be expressed in a way which makes them readily understandable'.[113] The Privy Council in *Palmer* had made just such an observation when it criticized *Howe* as presenting too fine a distinction for juries to draw between what a reasonable person placed in the accused's situation would consider to be necessary force and what the accused honestly believed to be necessary force.[114] As the majority in *Zecevic* saw it, the solution was to remove the doctrine of excessive self-defence altogether and to restate the law of self-defence in terms readily understandable to a jury. In his judgement, Chief Justice Mason said that, with the benefit of hindsight, he should not have incorporated the issue of onus of proof into his propositions in *Viro*.[115] Even so, he did not think that a reformulation of his propositions could make the trial judge's task of explaining the law of self-defence much simpler. Accordingly, he felt that there was a serious risk of the doctrine not operating in the way it was intended.[116]

---

[110](1978) 141 CLR 88, p. 153. This was so observed in *Zecevic* (1987) 71 ALR 641 by Chief Justice Mason at p. 645 and by Justice Deane at p. 662.
[111]Ibid., per Justice Deane.
[112](1987) 71 ALR 641, p. 663 per Justice Deane.
[113]Ibid., p. 651.
[114][1971] 2 WLR 831, p. 843 per Lord Morris. See also *McInnes* [1971] 1 WLR 1600, p. 1610 per Edmund-Davies LJ.
[115](1987) 71 ALR 641, p. 646.
[116]Ibid.

It cannot be denied that the retention of the doctrine of excessive self-defence would make the law significantly more complicated for juries to comprehend. However, one wonders whether the majority judges in *Zecevic* were being over-zealous in throwing out the doctrine in their attempt to simplify the general law of self-defence.Owing to the difficulties encountered by juries in comprehending the *Viro* propositions, various efforts have been made by the State courts to reformulate the propositions in less technical language.[117] These reformulations deal with the first four propositions but leave virtually intact the fifth and sixth propositions. This suggests that, contrary to Chief Justice Mason's opinion, the difficulties encountered by juries predominantly stem from the particular way in which his propositions are framed. Apart from the matter of onus of proof, his propositions require juries to consider in step-by-step form three different elements of reasonableness,[118] thereby making the law of self-defence unduly technical and complicated. While these elements of reasonableness are a necessary part of the law as pronounced in *Howe*, they could be presented to the jury in a much looser fashion. As we shall see later, the minority judges in *Zecevic* have suggested some ways of doing so. It is also pertinent to note that during the twelve-year period between the decisions of *Howe* and *Palmer*, there do not seem to have been any of the problems confronting juries which the *Viro* propositions have created.[119] In the same vein, ever since the Irish Supreme Court approved *Howe* twenty-six years ago in *People v Dwyer,* the doctrine of excessive self-defence has operated in that jurisdiction with no apparent difficulties of comprehension by juries.[120]

---

[117]For example, see *McManus* (1985) 2 NSWLR 448, pp. 461–2 per Chief Justice Street and approved in *R v Lawson and Forsythe* [1986] VR 515, p. 548 [1986]; and *Morgan v Colman* (1981) 27 SASR 334, pp. 336–7 per Justice Wells and approved in *R v Kincaid* (1983) 33 SASR 552, pp. 556–7.

[118]Namely, a reasonable belief as to the threat, the use of reasonably proportionate force to counter the threat and the belief that the force used was reasonably proportionate. These are elaborated upon by Justice Deane in *Zecevic* (1987) 71 ALR 641, p. 660.

[119]The cases which followed *Howe*, see op. cit., n. 76, do not indicate that the juries were experiencing any such difficulties. See also the empirical evidence gathered by the Law Reform Commission of Victoria, Report No. 40, *Homicide* (1991), para. 219.

[120][1972] IR 416. See further this work at pp.165–7 below.

A third reason given by Justices Wilson, Dawson and Toohey for removing the doctrine of excessive self-defence was that it 'restores consistency to the law relating to self-defence whether raised in a case of homicide or otherwise.'[121] They regarded this reason as 'compelling'[122] but unfortunately failed to clarify what precisely it was that the doctrine caused to be inconsistent in the law of self-defence. It might have been their opinion that, as far as possible, the plea of self-defence should operate uniformly across the whole spectrum of offences so that the doctrine of excessive self-defence, being applicable only to select types of offences,[123] was out of keeping with this felt need for uniformity. If this was their view, the doctrine has the support of both legal principle and standard perceptions of justice which override their desire for consistency in the law. The legal and justificatory bases for excessive self-defence will be explored in the next section and it should suffice to state here that they had the effect of compelling the minority judges in *Zecevic* to come down on the side of the defence. Or perhaps, Justices Wilson, Dawson and Toohey were referring to consistency in terms not of the law itself but its application. If this was what they meant, they were making the point that the doctrine of excessive self-defence, with its 'half-way house' verdict of manslaughter for murder cases, encouraged arbitrary and compromise verdicts to be given by juries. This was because the verdict they gave would depend on their level of capacity to understand the law and the degree of sympathy they felt towards the accused.[124] In reply, it is reiterated that the instructions to the jury on the law of self-defence could be stated in much simpler terms than the *Viro* propositions. Furthermore, although the provision for a verdict of manslaughter may occasionally work to the prejudice of either the accused or the Crown, it does allow both jury and sentencing judge a desirable amount of flexibility to ensure that the charge and punishment accurately reflect the

---

[121](1987) 71 ALR 641, p. 654.

[122]Ibid.

[123]Apart from murder, excessive self-defence is applicable to statutory offences which have, as part of their definition, the 'intent to murder': see above, n. 87 and accompanying main text.

[124]This view was taken by Justice Dickson, speaking on behalf of the Supreme Court of Canada in *R v Faid* (1983) 2 CCC (3d) 513, p. 518. That court unanimously rejected the doctrine of excessive self-defence.

accused's moral culpability.[125]

Having given their reasons for abolishing the doctrine of excessive self-defence, the majority in *Zecevic* concluded their judgements by suggesting that any harshness to the accused caused by the change in the law was alleviated by a number of factors. On their part, Justices Wilson, Dawson and Toohey[126] cited the passage in *McInnes* that:

> it is important to stress that the facts upon which the plea of self-defence is unsuccessfully sought to be based may nevertheless serve the accused in good stead. They may, for example, go to show that he may have acted under provocation or that, although acting unlawfully, he may have lacked the intent to kill or cause seriously bodily harm, and in that way render the proper verdict one of manslaughter.[127]

In his judgement, Chief Justice Mason observed that it was for the Crown to establish that there was an absence of reasonable grounds for the accused's belief that the force used was necessary for his self-defence. In his view, a jury would be slow to accept the Crown's submission if it failed to satisfy them that the accused did not honestly believe the force used to be necessary.[128] Finally, the majority judges pointed to the fact that a jury would return a verdict of murder only if the Crown satisfied them beyond a reasonable doubt that the accused had an intention to kill or inflict grievous bodily harm.[129]

The above factors do assist in reducing the risk of a murder conviction for an accused person who honestly (although unreasonably) believed that the force he or she used was necessary. Nevertheless, there will still be some instances where such a conviction can be avoided only by resort to the plea of excessive self-defence. For instance, not every case where self-defence has failed can be salvaged by the defence of provocation. The obvious example would be where the accused had resorted to excessive force when in total control of themselves. Indeed, there might be some inconsistency between an honest belief that the force used was

[125]See the comment by Lord Simon in *Attorney-General for Northern Ireland's Reference (No 1 of 1975)* [1977] AC 105, p. 152.
[126](1987) 71 ALR 641, p. 652.
[127][1971] 1 WLR 1600, p. 1608. This is reminiscent of the view held by the Criminal Code Bill Commission of 1879 discussed in this work at p. 141.
[128](1987) 71 ALR 641, p. 646.
[129]Ibid., p. 654 per Justices Wilson, Dawson and Toohey; and at p. 646 per Chief Justice Mason.

necessary and the loss of self-control which forms the core of the defence of provocation.[130] As for Chief Justice Mason's proposition that juries would be slow to find that an accused's belief lacked reasonable grounds if they thought he or she held an honest belief, there will be cases where the jury would nonetheless have no option but to reject the plea of self-defence. For example, the jury might be prepared to conclude that the accused genuinely believed the force used was necessary but that was only because he or she was of low mental intelligence or had led an unusually sheltered life; otherwise, the accused's belief could not be supported on reasonable grounds.

Having critically examined the main reasons for the majority's decision to reject the doctrine of excessive self-defence, I shall now consider the opposing reasons which led the minority judges, Justices Deane and Gaudron, to rule strongly in favour of its retention.

## D. *The Case for Maintaining Excessive Self-Defence*

In *Zecevic*, Justices Deane and Gaudron differed from the majority view by regarding *Viro* as having 'unambiguously settled' the existence of the doctrine of excessive self-defence under Australian common law.[131] In their opinion, the conflicting Privy Council decision in *Palmer* had been carefully considered by the Full Bench of the High Court in *Viro* and rejected by a clear majority. Furthermore, there was no public perception that the previous High Court case of *Howe*, upon which the majority in *Viro* had based their decision, had been mistaken in its pronouncement of the law. While accepting that the High Court was entitled to overrule a previous decision of its own, the minority felt that this should be done only in exceptional circumstances such as where the previous decision had been an unconsidered or isolated one or had presented the law in ambiguous terms, or where the law had since undergone material alteration.[132] Since none of these circumstances

---

[130](1987) 71 ALR 641, pp. 664–5 per Justice Deane; *Faid* (1983) 2 CCC (3d) 513, pp. 524–5 per Justice Dickson. Cf. *Van Den Hoek v R* (1986) 161 CLR 158, pp. 167–9 per Chief Justice Mason.

[131](1987) 71 ALR 641, p. 664 per Justice Deane; pp. 668–9 per Justice Gaudron.

[132]Ibid., p. 663 per Justice Deane; p. 669 per Justice Gaudron.

existed, the doctrine of excessive self-defence should be left undisturbed. Justice Deane pursued this issue further by saying that to abolish so established a defence would reduce the administration of criminal law to 'a macabre lottery' whereby an accused was adjudged guilty or innocent of murder according to whether his trial is completed before or after the date of abolition.[133]

The minority judges also observed that the doctrine found strong support from considerations of legal principle. The principle regards an accused person who uses excessive force to kill an assailant but who genuinely believes his action to be necessary in self-defence as lacking the requisite *mens rea* for murder.[134] The following passage from Justice Mason's judgement in *Viro*, which was cited by Justice Gaudron in *Zecevic*, succinctly outlines the development of this principle as applied first to the defence of provocation and then to excessive self-defence:

> In earlier times the element of malice aforethought was supplied by the mere existence of an intent to kill or inflict grievous bodily harm except in those cases in which the formation of the intention was held to be excusable or justifiable, e.g. self-defence. At one time it was thought that the existence of provocation negatived the formation of an intention to kill or inflict such harm: see *Holmes v Director of Public Prosecutions* [1946] AC 588, per Viscount Simon at 598. Now it is accepted that 'The defence of provocation may arise where a person does intend to kill or inflict grievous bodily harm but his intention to do so arises from sudden passion involving loss of self-control by reason of provocation' (*Attorney-General (Ceylon) v Perera* [1953] AC 200 at 206; *Lee Chun-Chuen v R* [1963] AC 220 at 228). Consequently, in the case of provocation, the intention to kill or inflict grievous bodily harm which, but for the extenuating circumstances in which it originates would have the quality of malice aforethought, lacks that quality, and the offence sinks to the level of manslaughter. Now that it has been acknowledged that provocation does not deny the existence of such an intention, no insurmountable barrier remains in the way of reaching the conclusion that circumstances giving rise to an occasion of self-defence also deprive an intention to kill or inflict grievous bodily harm formed in consequence thereof of the quality of malice aforethought. Then, if the response is not excessive, the accused commits no offence; if it is excessive, he is guilty of manslaughter.[135]

[133](1987) 71 ALR 641, p. 664.
[134]Ibid., p. 663 per Justice Deane; pp. 669–71 per Justice Gaudron.
[135](1978) 141 CLR 88, pp. 145–6. See also *Howe* (1958) 100 CLR 448, pp. 467–8 per JusticeTaylor.

The majority in *Zecevic*, including Chief Justice Mason, steered clear of discussing this legal principle and, in their failure to rebut it, may be taken to have tacitly acknowledged its soundness. Likewise, in the majority's zeal to follow the ruling in *Palmer* and *McInnes*, they neglected to answer the criticism against those decisions of being based on the perceived lack of judicial precedent favouring the doctrine of excessive self-defence rather than upon any firm legal principle.[136]

Yet another reason for the minority's decision to support the doctrine was their view that the moral culpability of a person who kills another while defending herself or himself, and who honestly believes the force was reasonable when it was not, falls short of the moral culpability normally associated with murder.[137] As Justice Aickin in *Viro* put it, there is:

> a real distinction in the degree of culpability of an accused who has killed having formed the requisite intention without any mitigating circumstance, and an accused who, in response to a real or a reasonably apprehended attack, strikes a blow in order to defend himself, but uses force beyond that required by the occasion and thereby kills the attacker.[138]

It is pertinent to note that the majority in *Zecevic* expressly conceded the strength of this reason for retaining the defence, with Chief Justice Mason going so far as to say that he still believed 'that the doctrine ... expresses a concept of self-defence which best accords with acceptable standards of culpability'.[139] Elsewhere it has also been stated that the recognition of excessive self-defence avoids the anomaly of allowing a concession to a killer who acts on provocation in anger but denying it to persons who have the right

---

[136]See pp. 137–8 above. See also Glazebrook, P.R., 'The Categories of Manslaughter are Never Closed', 35 *Cambridge Law Journal* 14 (1975); James, op. cit. n. 50, p. 358; Smith, op. cit., n. 43, at 528–33.

[137](1987) 71 ALR 641, pp. 662–3 per Justice Deane; p.669 per Justice Gaudron.

[138](1978) 141 CLR 88, p. 180, and cited by Justice Gaudron in *Zecevic* (1987) 71 ALR 641, p. 669. See also Justice Mason in *Viro* (1978) 141 CLR 88, p. 139 and cited by Justice Deane in *Zecevic* (1987) 71 ALR 641, p. 663.

[139](1987) 71 ALR 641, p. 646 per Chief Justice Mason. See also p. 654 per Justices Wilson, Dawson and Toohey.

to use some force to defend themselves in circumstances which make the precise measuring of their blows extremely difficult.[140]

Implicit in the judgements of the minority was their disagreement with the Privy Council's view in *Palmer* that the boundaries of self-defence could simply be left to the good sense of the jury.[141] Neither were they prepared to accept the suggestion of a distinguished commentator that a direction to the jury along the lines of *Palmer* would cause them rarely to conclude that a person acting in good faith nevertheless used excessive force.[142] In this connection, Justice Deane issued the following stern remark:

> Nor is it any answer ... to say that a jury, encouraged by sympathetic directions by a trial judge on the question of reasonableness, is unlikely to disregard commonly accepted notions of justice and completely acquit any accused who has acted genuinely in self-defence if excessive self-defence is not available as a defence which reduces murder to manslaughter. It is an indictment, rather than a vindication, of a proposition of criminal law to say that its harshness is such that it will be avoided by a perception, on the part of judge and jury, that the avoidance of injustice to an accused requires that what was unreasonable should be rationalised as reasonable so that, given the choice between murder and complete acquittal in a case where the only remaining defence was self-defence, a person who had intentionally killed in unreasonable or excessive defence of himself or another can be found not guilty of any crime at all.[143]

The minority judges were therefore adamant in maintaining that, so long as there was a possibility of a case arising where a person applied force which he or she honestly but unreasonably believed to be necessary, the doctrine of excessive self-defence should be available to enable the offender to avoid the stigma of a murder conviction and to allow for a more lenient sentence for manslaughter.

Having stated their reasons for supporting the doctrine of

[140]Law Reform Commission of Canada, op. cit., n. 88, p. 71; O'Brien, N., 'Excessive Self-Defence: A Need for Legislation', 25 *Criminal Law Quarterly* 441, p. 451 (1982-83); Williams, op. cit., n. 88, p. 547.

[141][1971] 2 WLR 831, pp. 843–4. For similiar disagreement with *Palmer* on this point, see Smith, op. cit., n. 43, p. 531; Leigh, P.H., 'Manslaughter and the Limits of Self-Defence', 34 *Modern Law Review* 685, pp. 689–90 (1971).

[142]See Professor John Smith's case comment on *Palmer, Criminal Law Review* 648, p. 650 (1971).

[143](1987) 71 ALR 641, p. 665.

excessive self-defence, the minority judges then applied their minds to overcoming the problem confronting juries in understanding the law of self-defence as formulated in the *Viro* propositions. Justice Gaudron opined that, while those propositions correctly pronounced the law, 'their specificity tends to detract attention from the basic question which falls for answer when self-defence is raised as an issue in answer to homicide'.[144] She also thought that the isolation of the issue of proportionate force in the *Viro* formulation led to unnecessary complexity for juries, and preferred to relegate that issue to one of many factors by reference to which the jury would decide upon the nature of the belief held by the accused.[145] As for a formulation of the general law of self-defence, Justice Gaudron agreed with Justices Wilson, Dawson and Toohey that it should be framed simply in terms of whether the accused believed on reasonable grounds that it was necessary in self-defence to do what he did.[146] She then dealt with how the jury should be instructed on the doctrine of excessive self-defence:

> It is neither necessary nor desirable to set forth a formula for the instruction of juries as to the distinction between murder and manslaughter when self-defence is an issue. Provided the matters of onus and standard of proof are properly explained it is sufficient that a jury be instructed in the context of the relevant facts, that a person, although not entitled to the full benefit of self-defence, is guilty of manslaughter and not murder, if he or she believed on reasonable grounds, that it was necessary to resort to force in self-defence, and otherwise believed, although unreasonably, that his or her actions were necessary in self-defence.[147]

Justice Deane's approach to simplifying the law of self-defence for the benefit of juries was to see if the different elements of reasonableness contained in the *Viro* propositions could be merged together.[148] He identified the first type of reasonableness as being that the accused's belief as to the existence of an unlawful attack must have been reasonable not in the completely objective sense of what a reasonable man would have believed but what the accused himself might reasonably believe taking into account all the circumstances in which he found himself. The second type of reasonableness in the *Viro* formulation pertained to the accused's

---

[144]Ibid., p. 668.
[145](1987) 71 ALR 641, p. 671.
[146]Ibid., p. 668.
[147](1987) 71 ALR 641, pp. 671–2.
[148]Ibid., pp. 660–1.

belief that the force used was proportionate to the perceived attack. In his view, this belief had to be a reasonable one, not in the sense of what a reasonable person would have considered to be proportionate force but what the accused himself might reasonably believe to be proportionate force. His analysis of the first two types of reasonableness led him to conclude that there was no difference in nature between them since each consisted of a requirement that the subjective perception of the accused should be reasonable in the circumstances in which he was placed. This being the case, the only obstacle which prevented these two types of reasonableness from being merged together was that judicial decisions had thus far confined the doctrine of excessive self-defence to the second type of reasonableness, namely, the use of disproportionate force. Justice Deane could not see why the doctrine should not operate equally in respect of the first type of reasonableness. He began by noting that the majority in *Viro* had not addressed itself to that question. He then stressed that the common law defence of self-defence requires an element of reasonableness before it can be a complete answer to a charge of homicide.[149] He continued:

> If the defence failed as a complete defence only by reason of the absence of the element of reasonableness of the accused's belief, there is no real basis in principle or justice for the drawing of general distinctions in terms of moral culpability or subjective malice according to whether the reason for the failure was that the accused's perception of an occasion of self-defence was unreasonable or that his belief that the amount of force used was reasonably proportionate to the danger was unreasonable.[150]

Since there was no longer any need to separate the first and second types of reasonableness under the *Viro* formulation, Justice Deane's advice to trial judges was as follows:

> The criminal onus of disproof which rests on the Crown in relation to self-defence would, of course, need to be carefully explained. Otherwise, the jury could be instructed to the effect that self-defence constitutes a complete defence if, when the accused killed the deceased, he was acting in reasonable self-defence and that he had been so acting if he had reasonably believed that what he was doing was reasonable and necessary in his own defence against an unjustified attack which threatened him with death or serious bodily harm. Those elements of the defence would,

[149](1987) 71 ALR 641, p. 666.
[150]Ibid.

of course, need to be adjusted according to the circumstances of particular cases.... The members of the jury could thereafter be told that, even though they were satisfied that the belief of the accused was not reasonable, it sufficed to reduce what would otherwise be murder to manslaughter if, when the accused killed the deceased, he believed what he was doing was reasonable and necessary in his own defence against an unjustified attack of the relevant kind.[151]

Justice Deane's application of the doctrine of excessive self-defence to cases where a person had honestly albeit unreasonably believed that there existed an occasion of self-defence does appear to be a logical extension of the law as pronounced in *Viro*.[152] If this view were to be accepted as a correct statement of the law, there would be a considerable increase in the use of the doctrine, since it has until now been thought that an absence of reasonable belief concerning a threatened attack prevents the issue of self-defence from proceeding any further.[153] However, Justice Deane stands very much alone in his analysis of this aspect of the law, not being supported even by Justice Gaudron, the other member of the minority in *Zecevic*.

## E. Legislation and Law Reform Proposals Favouring the Defence

Dissatisfied with the demise of excessive self-defence under Australian common law, the South Australian legislature enacted in 1991 a version of the defence.[154] That version was subsequently found to be unworkable[155] and revisions were made to it in 1997.[156]

---

[151](1987) 71 ALR 641, p. 667.

[152]For the suggestion that Justice Deane's approach should be incorporated into Irish law, see Charleton, op. cit., n. 19, pp. 160–1.

[153]For example, see the second proposition in *Viro* reproduced in main text accompanying n. 92 above.

[154]*Criminal Law Consolidation Act* 1936 (SA), Section 15, which came into force in December 1991.

[155]It was so regarded by the Court of Criminal Appeal of South Australia in *R v Gillman* (1995) 76 A Crim R 553. Cf. Grant, M., Case and Comment: *Gillman*, 19 *Criminal Law Journal* 38 (1995); Grant, M., 'Self Defence in South Australia: A Subjective Dilemma', 16 *Adelaide Law Review* 309 (1994).

[156]By virtue of the *Criminal Law Consolidation (Self Defence) Amendment Act* 1997 (SA). The relevant provisions are Sections 15 and 15A and they are reproduced in the Appendix to this work.

The South Australian model comprises two sections, the first on the defence of the person and the second on the defence of property. Defence of the person is covered under Section 15, subsection (1) (entitled 'Acts directed at the defence of life, bodily integrity or liberty'), which provides that:

It is a defence to a charge of an offence if—

(a) the defendant genuinely believed the conduct to which the charge relates to be necessary and reasonable for a defensive purpose; and

(b) the conduct was, in the circumstances as the defendant genuinely believed them to be, reasonably proportionate to the threat that the defendant genuinely believed to exist.

Subsection (2) then prescribes the partial defence of excessive force in the following terms:

It is a partial defence to a charge of murder (reducing the offence to manslaughter) if—

(a) the defendant genuinely believed the conduct to which the charge relates to be necessary and reasonable for a defensive purpose; but

(b) the conduct was not, in the circumstances as the defendant genuinely believed them to be, reasonably proportionate to the threat that the defendant genuinely believed to exist.

Defence of property is covered under Section 15A of the South Australian legislation. Subsection (1) specifies the general defence, the relevant parts of which read:

It is a defence to a charge of an offence if—

(a) the defendant genuinely believed the conduct to which the charge relates to be necessary and reasonable—

(i) to protect property from unlawful appropriation, destruction, damage or interference; or

(ii) to prevent criminal trespass to land or premises, or to remove from land or premises a person who is committing a criminal trespass;...

(b) if the conduct resulted in death—the defendant did not intend to cause death nor did the defendant act recklessly realising that the conduct could result in death; and

(c) the conduct was, in the circumstances as the defendant genuinely believed them to be, reasonably proportionate to the threat that the defendant genuinely believed to exist.

Subsection (2) then provides for the partial defence of excessive force in the following terms:

> It is a partial defence to a charge of murder (reducing the offence to manslaughter) if—
>
> (a)  the defendant genuinely believed the conduct to which the charge relates to be necessary and reasonable—
>
>   (i)  to protect from unlawful appropriation, destruction, damage or interference; or
>
>   (ii)  to prevent criminal trespass to land or premises, or to remove from land or premises a person who is committing a criminal trespass;...
>
> (b)  the defendant did not intend to cause death; but
>
> (c)  the conduct was not, in the circumstances as the defendant genuinely believed them to be, reasonably proportionate to the threat that the defendant genuinely believed to exist.

Some of the special features of this South Australian model need to be highlighted. First, in every case where D claims to have acted in defence, whether of person or property, the law only requires for D to have genuinely (or honestly) perceived the threat to be of a certain nature.[157] This element, comprising as it does a purely subjective belief, also represents the English common law.[158] However, under the Australian common law[159] and the Indian Penal Code,[160] an objective element is prescribed whereby D's perception of the threat must be based on reasonable grounds. Since this work is concerned primarily with excessive self-defence rather than the general plea of self-defence, the arguments for and against a purely subjective belief as to the nature of the threat need not concern us here.[161] Of significance, however, to the present discussion is that for the general plea of self-defence, the South Australian model

[157] Sections 15(1)(a), 15(2)(a), 15A(1)(a) and 15A(2)(a). But see Section15(4), reproduced in the Appendix, which requires the belief as to the unlawfulness of the threat to be reasonable in cases of resisting arrest or resisting a response to an unlawful act.

[158] See *R v Gladstone Williams* (1983) 78 Cr App R 276; *R v Asbury* [1986] Crim LR 258; *Beckford v R* [1988] AC 130.

[159] *Zecevic* (1987) 71 ALR 641. Under Justice Deanes approach in *Zecevic*, noted on pp. 158–60 above, the plea of excessive self-defence would be available to the accused.

[160] Indian Penal Code, Sections 102 and 105.

[161] For a detailed discussion of this issue, see Yeo, S., *Compulsion in the Criminal Law*, pp. 200–19 (1990) and the authorities cited there.

prescribes partly subjective and partly objective components to the issue of the force used in defence.[162] This also represents the English[163] and Australian[164] common laws and the position taken under the Indian Penal Code.[165] With this requirement in place, the South Australian model then provides for the partial plea of excessive self-defence in murder cases where D genuinely but unreasonably believed that the force applied in defence was necessary. This represents the law under Exception 2 to Section 300 of the Indian Penal Code and the Australian common law prior to *Zecevic*.

Another feature of the South Australian model worth highlighting is the specification of property offences in Section 15A against which a person may defend herself or himself. Unlike Section 103 of the Indian Penal Code, these offences do not contain an element of personal violence or threat thereof. This probably explains why Section 15A prescribes a restriction based on the intent to murder in cases where D has killed in defence of property. To be completely acquitted by virtue of the general plea of self-defence under Section 15A(1), D must not have intended to cause death nor acted recklessly realising that her or his conduct could result in death.[166] As might be expected, this restriction is lessened where the partial defence is pleaded under Section15A(2), in which case D must not have intended to cause death alone.[167] This is an innovative approach to the application of both the general and partial pleas in cases of causing death in defence of property. Given that the South Australian model does not impose similar restrictions in respect of cases of causing death in defence of the person, the underlying rationale for these restrictions must be that the legislature took the view that no interest in property is so valuable as to warrant protection by conduct performed with the intention of causing death or, in the case of the general plea of self-defence, of

---

[162]Sections 15(1)(b) and 15A(1)(c), with the subjective component in the form of the accused's genuine belief as to the threatening circumstances and the objective component comprising the accused's conduct having to be reasonably proportionate to those perceived threatening circumstances.
[163]*R v Shannon* (1980) 71 Cr App R 192. See also Williams, op. cit., n. 88, p. 507.
[164]*Zecevic* (1987) 71 ALR 641.
[165]Indian Penal Code, Section 99(4).
[166]Section 15A(1)(b).
[167]Section 15A(2)(b).

recklessly causing death. Yet, as the framers of the Indian Penal Code pointed out, there may be some circumstances where property may be so valuable (at least in the eyes of its possessor) that he or she may have genuinely believed that it was necessary to kill the person threatening it.[168] In such cases, for the law to deny any leniency whatsoever to an accused charged with murder is to ignore the fact that he or she had killed while acting in defence, albeit of property. Accordingly, it is submitted that in this important respect the approach taken in Exception 2 to Section 300 of the Indian Penal Code is to be preferred to the South Australian model. Under the Exception, the accused will have the charge of murder reduced to culpable homicide not amounting to murder so long as he or she did not intend to do more harm than was necessary for the purpose of defending property. This result may occur even though the accused had intended to kill the person threatening her or his property.

Besides the South Australian legislation, mention should be made of the views of the Law Reform Commission of Victoria on the doctrine of excessive force in self-defence. The Commission recommended in its report on *Homicide* that the doctrine should not be reintroduced.[169] However, this decision was taken only because the Commission had recommended the abolition of all objective requirements presently contained in the general plea of self-defence.[170] Under this scheme, the general plea of self-defence (as opposed to the partial defence of excessive self-defence) would acquit a person of murder who honestly but unreasonably believed that deadly force was necessary and proportionate to the threatened danger. However, the Commission felt that such a person should not be entitled to a complete acquittal given her or his grossly unreasonable mistake. Its solution was to create a new offence of 'culpable homicide' which was less serious than negligent manslaughter.[171] This was because a person who mistook the

[168]Macaulay, Macleod, Anderson and Millett, op. cit., n. 2, Note M, Reprint, pp. 147–8 and quoted above on p.123.

[169]Law Reform Commission of Victoria, op. cit., n. 119, recommendation 26.

[170]Ibid., recommendation 28.

[171]Law Reform Commission of Victoria, op. cit., n. 119, paras 222–3, and recommendation 27. The new offence reads: 'A person who kills another in self-defence on the basis of a belief that was grossly unreasonable either in relation to the need for force or in relation to the degree of force that was necessary should be guilty of the offence of culpable homicide'. The

necessity of her or his response to a crisis was not in the same category as one who put others at risk by gross negligence. This is an attractive arrangement. However, since it hinges on certain radical changes being made to the law governing the general plea of self-defence, a critical evaluation of it is beyond the scope of this work. What is significant to the present discussion is the Commission's wholehearted acknowledgement of the need for the law to draw a moral distinction between cases of murder and a killing done in excessive self-defence.[172] The Commission's response stands in stark contrast to the one taken by another Australian law reform body which had also considered the matter. This was the Committee set up to review Australian Commonwealth criminal law.[173] The Committee was content to simply endorse the majority decision in *Zecevic* without any consideration of the legal principle and other cogent reasons for recognizing the doctrine of excessive self-defence.[174]

## F. Recognition of Excessive Self-Defence under Irish Law

It would be useful here to briefly present the law of Eire on excessive self-defence since it has adopted the Australian common law defence prior to its demise in *Zecevic*.[175] The leading case is *The People (A-G) v Dwyer*, a decision of the Supreme Court of Eire.[176] D had stabbed V to death in the course of a fight. D claimed that he believed V or his cohorts had some weapon with which he had been hit on the head. D also claimed to be in fear of his life. There was a dearth of evidence to suggest that D's stabbing was reasonably necessary by way of self-defence. The trial judge directed the jury in terms of self-defence which required the force applied

---

Commission proposed a maximum penalty of seven years' imprisonment which accorded with the one for the offence of culpable driving causing death under Section 318 of the *Crimes Act* 1958 (Vic).

[172]Ibid., paras 213–4.

[173]Review of Commonwealth Law, Interim Report, *Principles of Criminal Responsibility and Other Matters* (1990).

[174]Ibid., para. 13.25.

[175]For a detailed discussion, see McAuley, F., 'Excessive Defence in Irish Law' in S. Yeo (ed.), *Partial Excuses to Murder*, p. 194 (1990). Cf. Canadian law has refused to adopt the defence: See O' Brien, N., Excessive Self-defence: A Need for Legislation (1982–83) 25 *Criminal Law Quarterly* 441.

[176][1972] IR 416.

by D to have been objectively proportionate to the threat occasion. D's subjective belief, if accepted by the jury in raising a reasonable doubt, was therefore irrelevant. D was convicted of murder and he appealed to the Supreme Court. The court held the trial judge to be in error and gave two reasons for its decision. First, D's honest belief negated the *mens rea* for murder. As Justice Walsh explained:

> When the evidence discloses a question of self-defence and where it is sought by the prosecution to show that the accused used excessive force, that is to say more than would be regarded as objectively reasonable, the prosecution must establish that the accused knew that he was using more force than was reasonably necessary. Therefore, it follows that if the accused honestly believed that the force that he did use was necessary, then he is not guilty of murder. The onus, of course, is upon the prosecution to prove beyond reasonable doubt that he knew that the force was excessive or that he did not believe that it was necessary. If the prosecution does not do so, it has failed to establish the necessary malice.[177]

The second reason given by the court was that a person who uses excessive force in self-defence and kills her or his assailant lacks the full degree of moral culpability associated with murder.[178] I have noted earlier that both these reasons were relied on by the minority in the Australian High Court case of *Zecevic* in support of their view that the doctrine of excessive self-defence should continue to operate in that jurisdiction.[179]

The defence has apparently not caused confusion in its application in Eire.[180] This is because the Irish Supreme Court in *Dwyer* had cast the defence in terms which could readily be understood by juries.[181] Neither has the defence been treated as an easy option by juries, who have been shown to avail accused persons of the defence only when the evidence clearly supported it. Should the defence be abolished, there is every danger that juries would acquit a person who had honestly used excessive force to repel a deadly attack, since they would be reluctant to classify such a person

---

[177]Ibid., p. 424.

[178]Ibid., p. 429.

[179]See pp. 155–7 above.

[180]Charleton, op. cit., n. 19, p. 159.

[181]For the suggestion that the simple formulation in *Dwyer* satisfactorily answers the concern expressed in *Palmer* and *McInnes* that juries would have difficulty in understanding the law, see Glazebrook, op. cit., n. 136.

as a murderer. Justice would be better served if the jury was given the option of convicting such a person of manslaughter.

# 5. The Place of Excessive Self-Defence in the Law of Self-Defence and in the Criminal Justice Process

Although there are strong moves in England and Australia to recognize the doctrine of excessive self-defence in their criminal laws, the debate continues over whether this is the right stance and, if so, the form such recognition should take. The Indian Penal Code and the Australian common law prior to *Zecevic* gave the doctrine the role of a partial defence to murder rather than a complete defence or a sentencing consideration. It will be argued here that the Code framers and Australian judges were right to have done so. This will, in the main, be borne out by applying the criminal law theory of justifications and excuses to both the pleas of general self-defence and of excessive self-defence.

## A. Justification, Excuse and Self-Defence

The legal recognition and development of defences does not come about in a vacuum. As with every other aspect of the criminal law, moral evaluations play a dominant role in formulating the law, with judges and legislators striving towards creating legal rules which adequately reflect moral values, demands and expectations. Such compatibility between the law and moral values and expectations is crucial for gaining the community's respect for the law and for the law's smooth operation. It is submitted that the doctrine of excessive self-defence is crucial in reflecting the moral values and expectations in cases involving fatal defensive action.

There exists in criminal jurisprudence a theory which enables criminal defences to accord closely with moral values and expectations.[182] The theory categorizes defences into justifications and excuses. A person claiming a justification acknowledges her or his responsibility for the harmful conduct but contends that it was

---

[182]Professor George Fletcher is accredited with being the chief proponent of the theory in recent years: see his treatise entitled *Rethinking Criminal Law* (1978).

done in circumstances which made the conduct rightful in the eyes of society. Since society approves or at least tolerates the conduct, the actor deserves praise rather than blame. The focus then is on the person's act or conduct rather than the person as an individual. A person claiming an excuse likewise acknowledges the harm done by her or his conduct. Unlike justifications, however, the person concedes that her or his conduct is disapproved by society. What is being pleaded is that while the conduct was wrong, there were particular circumstances which made it just that society should render the actor blameless for the harm committed. The focus then is on the person of the actor rather than the conduct performed.

Self-defence is traditionally recognized as a justification because society regards the conduct of the defender as preferable to the conduct of her or his aggressor.[183] This may be because society regards the aggressor's wrongful conduct as rendering her or his life less valuable than the defender's. Or it may be that society views the defender as protecting the general peace of the community as well as her or his own person. Before society is prepared to praise or condone the defender's action, several requirements must be satisfied. Some of these requirements concern the nature of the threatened attack confronting the defender such as the need for the impending attack to be of a particular kind and for the attack to have been imminent.[184] Other requirements concern the degree of force applied by the defender to counter the threatened attack. They include the requirement that the force used by way of self-defence was reasonably necessary and proportionate to the

[183]See generally, Omichinski, N., 'Applying the Theories of Justifiable Homicide to Conflicts in the Doctrine of Self-Defence', 33 *Wayne Law Review* 1447 (1997); Dressler, J., 'New Thoughts about the Concept of Justification in the Criminal Law: A Critique of Fletcher's Thinking and Rethinking', 32 *University of California at Los Angeles Law Review* 61 (1984); Kadish, S., 'Respect for Life and Regard for Rights in the Criminal Law', 64 *California Law Review* 871 (1976).

[184]Under Australian and Indian laws, the accused must have honestly and reasonably believed that the attack was of this nature: see *Zecevic* (1987) 71 ALR 641; Section 100 of the Indian Penal Code. A different position has been taken under English law where an accused's honest belief alone will suffice: see *Beckford v R* [1988] 1 AC 130; *R v Williams (Gladstone)* (1983) 78 Cr App R 276. See generally, Yeo, S., *Compulsion in the Criminal Law*, chapter 6 (1990).

threatened danger.[185] All these requirements have the purpose of ensuring that the defender's actions resulted in less harm (sometimes described in terms of 'a lesser evil' or conversely 'a greater good') than what would have transpired from the threatened attack.[186]

The doctrine of excessive self-defence, as its name suggests, is concerned with the requirement of degree of force applied by way of self-defence. A person relying on the doctrine has an initial right to take defensive action in that there were reasonable grounds for thinking that he or she was being confronted with an imminent and life-threatening or otherwise seriously injurious attack upon the person.[187] The defender fails to successfully plead self defence because the force applied to counter the attack was not reasonably necessary and proportionate to the attack. In these circumstances, society cannot approve the defender's conduct because the harm he or she inflicted was in fact greater than that which was sought to be avoided. In other words, in such a case, the defender's actions are not justifiable and he or she cannot be acquitted on account of a plea of self-defence. However, the defender is not altogether blameworthy because he or she honestly believed that the force applied was reasonably necessary and proportionate to the threatened attack. The doctrine of excessive self-defence highlights such an honest belief plus the fact that the defender had an initial right of self-defence. Circumstances therefore exist warranting the defender to be exculpated for applying excessive force. Hence, the doctrine is excusatory in nature and functions by salvaging those aspects of an unsuccessful justificatory plea which

[185]English, Australian and Indian laws leave this to be objectively assessed by the triers of fact. This is to be contrasted with Sections 15 and 15A of the *Criminal Law Consolidation Act* 1936 (SA), which has changed the test to one of whether the accused honestly believed the force to be reasonably necessary and proportionate to the threatened attack: see pp. 160–3 above. A similar change has been proposed by the Law Reform Commission of Victoria, op. cit., n. 119: see pp. 164–5 above. As noted previously, such a change would cause the general plea of self-defence to be widened to cover cases which currently attract the plea of excessive self-defence.

[186]See Fletcher, op. cit., n. 182, pp. 788–98; Kadish, op. cit., n. 183, p. 882; Eser, A., 'Justification and Excuse', 24 *Amercian Journal of Comparative Law* 621. p. 632 (1976).

[187]This echoes my earlier discussion of how the expression 'in good faith' appearing in Exception 2 to Section 300 of the Indian Penal Code should be interpreted: see pp. 127–8 above.

have the effect of rendering the accused less blameworthy than one who kills without recourse to self-defence.

## B. A Partial and Not a Full Defence

The doctrine of excessive self-defence exculpates an accused of the charge of murder because he or she lacks the malice aforethought required for that offence. Although the accused may have caused the death of another with intent to kill so as to have technically possessed the requisite *mens rea* for murder, this is negated because the accused had killed under an honest belief that it was necessary in self-defence.[188]

Accepting that murder has not been made out, it may be asked why the accused should be convicted of manslaughter (or of culpable homicide not amounting to murder in India) instead of being acquitted altogether of any charge. The answer is simply that absence of malice aforethought does not have such a far-reaching effect in cases involving excessive self-defence. The accused's act of killing is still construed as an act of unlawful homicide because he or she had applied force beyond that reasonably permitted by the circumstances.

Support for regarding excessive self-defence as a partial plea may also be found in the distinction between general self-defence, which is justificatory in nature, and excessive self-defence, which is an excuse. In respect of justificatory self-defence, society will require the defender's conduct to have been objectively reasonably necessary and proportionate to the threatened danger before approving of such conduct. A person who has taken objectively excessive defensive action cannot rely on such a justification. Should that person have honestly albeit unreasonably believed that the action was reasonably necessary, the doctrine of excessive self-defence is available to her or him. But with what result? If the doctrine operates as a full defence to entirely exculpate the defender, the result is exactly the same as reliance upon the justificatory plea of self-defence and, consequently, the moral message conveyed by the law is blurred.[189]

---

[188]See pp. 155–6 above.
[189]See Dressler, J., 'Justifications and Excuses: A Brief Review of the Concept and the Literature', 33 *Wayne Law Review* 1155, pp. 1169–71 (1987); Horowitz, D., 'Justification and Excuse in the Program of the Criminal Law', 49 *Law and Contemporary Problems* 109, pp.110–112 (1986).

By acquitting completely a person who has exercised the right of self-defence in a reasonably necessary and proportionate manner, the law declares its approval of the conduct. What is the community to think if a person who has taken unnecessary and disproportionate defensive action is likewise acquitted altogether of any crime? Maintaining excessive self-defence as a partial defence ensures that the theoretical distinctions between justificatory self-defence and excusatory excessive self-defence are proclaimed through respectively separate verdicts.[190]

It may be asked at this juncture why excessive self-defence should not be described as a partial justification rather than a partial excuse. This looks appealing at first sight since it seems logical to say that since excessive self-defence has some although not all the requirements of justificatory self-defence, it could be described as a partial justification. However, this proposition fails to square with the balancing of harms rationale underlying justifications. A person who has applied excessive force has, by that very fact, done more harm than that which was sought to be avoided. The conduct is therefore wrongful, and society is not prepared to tolerate, let alone approve it. The doctrine cannot therefore be described as a partial justification and fits most snugly as a partial excuse.

## C. A Partial Defence and Not a Sentencing Factor

If the doctrine of excessive self-defence has only a partially exculpating effect, what reasons are there for not recognizing it at the sentencing stage? Of course, such a suggestion is conditioned upon the replacement of a fixed penalty for murder with some flexibility in sentencing. This is already the case in the Australian jurisdictions of New South Wales[191] and Victoria[192] and has been strongly advocated in England by the House of Lords Select Committee on murder and life imprisonment.[193] The Indian Penal Code also gives a limited discretion to judges when sentencing

---

[190]For a detailed analysis of this issue but in relation to the defence of provocation, see Dressler, J., 'Provocation: Partial Justification or Partial Excuse?', 51 *Modern Law Review* 467 (1988).

[191]*Crimes Act* 1900 (NSW), Section 19A.

[192]*Crimes Act* 1958 (Vic) Section 3.

[193]Op. cit., n. 72, paras. 118–19.

murderers.[194] Supporters of this approach might contend that partial defences to murder such as provocation, diminished responsibility[195] and excessive self-defence owe much of their origin to circumventing the fixed penalty for murder.[196] Once that is removed, they see no reason why these partial defences cannot be transformed into pleas for mitigation of sentence.

It is submitted that the fixed penalty should not be accredited with such significance in the development of partial defences to murder.[197] The preceding discussion on the doctrine of excessive self-defence should have amply shown how other more influential considerations were at work in bringing about its inception into Indian law and, for a time, Australian law. One of these considerations was that the partial defence was being applied to the crime of murder, not because of its fixed penalty, but because of the expression of the name of the crime itself.[198] As an Australian legislator has put it: 'In our culture, to describe someone as a "murderer" is to employ the most bitterly and effectively stigmatising epithets available in the language'.[199] That being the case, it would be most inappropriate, indeed unjust, to label a person who has acted in excessive self-defence a 'murderer' and to then temper her or his sentence. Besides this injustice to the offender, there are societal demands and expectations to consider.

[194]See Section 302, which provides the choice of imposing the death penalty or life imprisonment.

[195]This is a statutory creation which is recognized under the laws of England and New South Wales but not by any of the other jurisdictions studied.

[196]For example, see Gordon, G.H., *Criminal Law of Scotland* 2nd edn, p. 764 (1978); Thomas, D.A., 'Form and Function in Criminal Law' in P.R. Glazebrook (ed.), *Reshaping the Criminal Law*, pp. 28–9 (1978); Review of Commonwealth Law, op. cit., n. 173, para. 13.56; Law Reform Commission of Canada, op. cit., n. 88, pp. 71, 73.

[197]See Wasik, M., 'Partial Excuses in the Criminal Law', 45 *Modern Law Review* 516, pp. 520–1 (1982).

[198]See the House of Lords, *Report of the Select Committee on Murder and Life Imprisonment*, op. cit., n. 72, paras 81–3.

[199]The NSW Attorney-General, Mr Frank Walker, when introducing amending legislation to the homicide provisions in the *Crimes Act* 1900 (NSW) and justifying why the label 'murder' should be retained in the law. The comment is cited and discussed in Woods, G., 'The Sanctity of Murder, Reforming the Homicide Penalty in New South Wales', 57 *Australian Law Journal* 161, p. 162 (1983). See also the Law Reform Commission of Victoria, op. cit., n. 119, para. 216.

The assertion here is that society will want 'to reserve its major condemnation for the cold-blooded killer, and to have the mistaken victim of an attack convicted of the same crime tends to weaken this condemnation'.[200]

Another reason for maintaining excessive self-defence as an exculpatory plea rather than a sentencing factor lies in the functioning of the criminal process itself. Relegating the doctrine to the sentencing stage will mean that the evidence supporting it will not be subject to the same exposure and scrutiny as if it were introduced at the trial proceedings. Consequently, there might be insufficient evidence of excessive self-defence for sentencing purposes.[201] A related matter is that the sentencing judge will not know whether the jury had convicted the defendant of murder because it had rejected the plea of self-defence outright or had found the defendant to have killed in self-defence but with excessive force.[202] Such a determination would be crucial to the judge when deciding on the specific sentence to be imposed on the particular defendant.

Two other reasons could be briefly mentioned, both derived from the nature of the doctrine of excessive self-defence itself. The first has already been covered in some detail, namely, that the element of malice aforethought, which is crucial for the crime of murder, is absent in a case involving excessive self-defence.[203] If the defendant lacks such malice it would be unjust to bring down a conviction of murder. Second, the claim of having acted in excessive self-defence differs from the mitigating factors normally taken into account in sentencing. The difference is that the defender claims to have exercised an initial right of self-defence and this is a matter which has more to do with exculpation than with the form of sentence.

For these reasons, the framers of the Indian Penal Code were correct in insisting on regarding excessive self-defence as a matter

---

[200]Smith, op. cit., n. 43, p. 534. See also the Criminal Law Revision Committee, op. cit., n. 68, para. 288; Smith and Hogan, op. cit., n. 65, p. 261.
[201]Cf. the Law Reform Commission of Canada, op. cit., n. 88, p. 74, which proposed that new rules of procedure and evidence could be implemented to meet this problem.
[202]See the Law Reform Commission of Victoria, op. cit., n. 119, para. 216. Of course, this is not a problem in India, where jury trials have been abolished.
[203]See pp. 155–6, 166 above.

going to exculpation rather than to sentencing. By the same token, the judges in cases like *Palmer* and *McInnes* and the majority in *Zecevic* were wrong in rejecting the doctrine as a defence for this would invariably have consigned it to consideration at the sentencing stage.

## 6. Conclusion

The evaluation of the doctrine of excessive self-defence undertaken in this chapter finds it to be sound in principle, criminal legal theory and practice. The Indian contribution has been that the doctrine has generally stood the test of practical application over the years with Exception 2 to Section 300 of the Indian Penal Code being frequently used by the courts to dispense justice in appropriate cases. With regard to England, the recent proposals by law reform bodies have made up for the lacklustre response to the doctrine by the English courts. The Australian law, prior to the abrogation of the doctrine by the High Court in *Zecevic*, has played a crucial role in persuading these law reform bodies to support the doctrine. These bodies could likewise have drawn support from the Indian experience, which, insofar as it was the product of some of the finest nineteenth century English legal minds, has a stronger claim to recognition by these bodies than does the Australian law. A further Australian contribution to this area of the law has been the airing of the arguments for and against recognition of the doctrine and the form which such recognition should take.

Among the common law jurisdictions of England and Australia and the codified criminal law of India, India alone recognizes the doctrine of excessive self-defence.[204] Besides its claim of antiquity, there is another aspect of the Indian Penal Code which argues for the revival of the doctrine by the Australian courts and its introduction into English law. It will be recalled how the Code permits an accused to kill in self-defence only in order to repel one of a list of specific threat occasions.[205] Apparently, residents of India quickly embraced the Code and became well-versed in its provisions, including those pertaining to self-defence. As James Stephen somewhat earnestly observed, 'pocket editions of these

---

[204]This work did note, however, that the doctrine is recognized under Irish common law and by legislation in South Australia.
[205]That is, Section 100, which is reproduced in n. 9 above.

codes are published, which may be carried about as easily as a pocket Bible; and I doubt whether, even in Scotland, you would find many people who know their Bibles as Indian civilians know their codes'.[206] Despite such a clear legal declaration and its appreciation by the Indian community, the Code framers nevertheless felt it necessary to provide for the case of a defender who overstepped the boundaries imposed by the law. As a commentator on the Code has said:

> The provisions relating to the right of private defence invites people to do acts which border on homicide, and the boundary between attacks which may legally be repelled by causing death and those which may not is to some extent arbitrary and may very well be outside the knowledge of the offender. [Exception 2] is intended to cover cases in which the offender's act is outside the scope of the provisions governing the right of private defence but is done for the reason for which the right of private defence is recognised.[207]

By contrast, the English and Australian common law is still far from clear as to the categories of threat occasions which will permit killings in self-defence.[208] Furthermore, unlike the case of a Code, common law pronouncements on self-defence are not readily accessible (and accordingly not as well known) to the inhabitants of England and Australia. The vagueness of the common law on this matter calls for justice to be done by giving a person who, when killing her or his assailant, has exceeded the permissible limits of self-defence, the benefit of the doctrine of excessive self-defence.

For all the many reasons canvassed in this chapter, a strong case can be made for recognizing excessive self-defence manslaughter in England and Australia as has been the position in India for the past 136 years. Accordingly, in the final chapter of this work, a couple of model provisions of the defence will be presented which could be adopted by those jurisdictions.

---

[206]As cited in Trevelyan, G.O., *The Life and Letters of Lord Macaulay,* Vol. 1, p. 367 (1920). Stephen was referring to both the Penal Code and the Criminal Procedure Code.

[207]Gledhill, A., *The Penal Codes of Northern Nigeria and the Sudan,* p. 480 (1963).

[208]Recognition of threat occasions giving rise to the right of self-defence has been on a piecemeal basis: see Smith and Hogan, op. cit., n. 65, p. 258; Yeo, op. cit., n. 184, pp. 64–7. The view expressed here is in reply to the opposing view taken by Elliott, op. cit., n. 82 pp. 739–40.

# Chapter 4

# Improving the Law

Having completed the comparative study of provocation and excessive self-defence, it would greatly assist lawmakers desirous of improving the laws if model provisions were drafted which incorporated all the best features of the defence formulations from the jurisdictions that have been examined in this work. Each defence will be considered in turn.

## 1. Provocation

In chapter 2, I concluded that, while there are some aspects of the defence of provocation that could be improved upon, the laws in the three jurisdictions studied are in a reasonably satisfactory state. Much of the impetus for improvement has come from legislative enactment of the defence. Thus, in England, Section 3 of the *Homicide Act* 1957 (UK) brought about significant clarifications and changes to the existing common law. For example, the provision made it clear that words alone could amount to provocation in law and enabled the courts to attribute certain of the accused's personal characteristics to the ordinary person. Section 23 of the New South Wales *Crimes Act* 1900 (NSW), as amended in 1982, made the same improvements to the existing law. However, the New South Wales provision went further and laid to rest several other contentious issues that had arisen in both the Australian and English common law. For instance, it stipulated that provocation could be cumulative, that the act of killing need not immediately precede the provocation, and that there was no legal rule that the act of the accused causing death should be reasonably proportionate to the provocation.

The main part of Exception 1 to Section 300 of the Indian Penal Code which describes the nature and effect of the defence of provocation is outmoded and ambiguous on several matters by comparison to the English and New South Wales provisions. However, the same cannot be said of the provisos to the Exception which deal with issues that are not, but should be, covered by the English and New South Wales provisions. These provisos exclude three types of provocative conduct: provocation that was sought by the accused as an excuse to harm a person, provocation comprising lawful acts done pursuant to the exercise of a public legal duty or in obedience to law, and lawful acts done in the exercise of private defence. Besides, the wording of the Exception has lent itself to interpretation by the Indian courts with the result that the Indian law on provocation is at least as progressive as the New South Wales law in some respects, and more progressive in others. Hence, besides also having all the positive features of the New South Wales provision mentioned previously, the Indian law recognizes hearsay provocation in limited circumstances and requires the mode of killing to be evaluated objectively.

In the light of this state of affairs, it is suggested that a model provision on the defence of provocation could be formulated, using the New South Wales provision as the basic structure. The various positive features of the Indian law which are not found therein could be added to the provision. Also worthy of inclusion in the model provision are the various suggestions made in chapter 2 for improving the operation of the defence which are presently not part of the laws of any of the jurisdictions examined. The model provision could read as follows:

(1) Where, on the trial of a person for murder, it appears that the act or omission causing death was an act done or omitted under provocation and, but for this subsection and the provocation, the trier of fact would have found the accused guilty, the trier of fact shall acquit the accused of murder and find the accused guilty of culpable homicide not amounting to murder.[1]

(2) For the purposes of subsection (1), an act or omission causing death is an act done or omitted under provocation where—

[1] Under English and Australian laws, the expression 'culpable homicide not amounting to murder' should be replaced with 'manslaughter'.

    (a)   the act or omission is the result of a loss of self-control on the part of the accused to such an extent that the accused formed an intent to kill, an intent to cause bodily injury which is sufficient in the ordinary course of nature to cause death or an intent to cause such bodily injury as the offender knows to be likely to cause the death of the person to whom the harm is caused;[2]

    (b)   the act or omission was induced by any conduct of the deceased (including grossly insulting words or gestures) towards or affecting the accused; and

    (c)   that conduct of the deceased was such as could have induced an ordinary person in the position of the accused to have become enraged[3] and to have performed the same or similar act or omission as the accused did;

whether that conduct of the deceased occurred immediately before the act or omission causing death or at any previous time.

(3) For the purposes of subsection (2)(c),[4] when assessing whether such an ordinary person might have become enraged, the ordinary person may be invested with—

    (a)   any of the accused's characteristics which affect the gravity of the provocation; and

    (b)   the accused's age, ethnic, cultural and social background.

(4) For the purpose of determining whether an act or omission causing death was an act done or omitted under provocation as provided by subsection (2), there is no rule of law that provocation is negatived if—

    (a)   there was not a reasonable proportion between the

---

[2]These are the forms of murderous intention specified in the first three clauses of Section 300 of the Indian Penal Code. In England and Australia, the provision should be modified to read 'such an extent that the accused formed an intent to kill or to do grievous bodily harm' as these are the forms of murderous intention recognized by those two jurisdictions.

[3]Should my proposal for rage to replace loss of self-control prove unacceptable, this subclause could quite easily be couched in terms of loss of self-control and so too might subclause (3)(b), and illustration (b) proposed below.

[4]Under English and Australian laws, only the accused's age will be taken into account.

act or omission causing death and the conduct of the
deceased that induced the act or omission;

(b) the act or omission causing death was not an act done
or omitted suddenly;

(c) the provocation constituted a report on the conduct
of the deceased to the accused provided that the report
engendered a reasonable belief that such conduct had
occurred.

(5) For the purpose of subsection (1), any conduct of the
deceased which induced the accused to lose self-control
cannot be taken into account if —

(a) such conduct was sought by the accused as an excuse
to kill or cause harm to the deceased or any other
person;

(b) such conduct was a reasonably predictable result of
the accused's own conduct;

(c) such conduct was performed in the lawful exercise of
a public duty or in obedience to law;

(d) such conduct was performed in the lawful exercise of
defence of person or property.

Additionally, at least insofar as the Indian Penal Code is
concerned, the model provision could have the following new
illustrations added to the existing ones accompanying Exception 1
to Section 300:

### Illustrations

(a) Z provokes A into losing his self-control and inflicting
multiple stab-wounds on Z resulting in Z's death. A may
successfully rely on the defence of provocation even though
there was no reasonable proportion between his acts causing
death and Z's provocation. However, should A have cut
off Z's testicles and left him to bleed to death, A will be
denied the defence on the ground that an ordinary person
could not have performed the same or a similar act as A
did.

(b) Z provokes A, an eighteen-year-old woman belonging to a
hill tribe, into losing her self-control and killing Z. A's
age, sex, ethnic, cultural and social background may be
attributed to the ordinary person when assessing the gravity
of the provocation. However, only A's age, ethnic, cultural

and social background, but not her sex, may be attributed to the ordinary person when assessing whether such a person might have become enraged.

(c) A, while under loss of self-control induced by Z's provocation, intentionally kills Z a short time after the provocation was given. Although the provocation was trivial when seen in isolation, it was the last of a series of provocative incidents by Z towards A. Here, A has not committed murder but merely culpable homicide not amounting to murder.[5]

(d) A hears from Y, a reliable witness, that Z has sexually assaulted A's young child. A, while in a state of lost self-control induced by the report, finds Z and kills him. Here, A has not committed murder but merely culpable homicide not amounting to murder.[6]

Rather than commenting on each aspect of the model provision, it will suffice here to highlight the more salient features. All references to illustrations in the ensuing discussion are to the new ones described above.[7] Subsection (2)(a) describes the degree of lost self-control required for the defence in terms of the formation of a murderous intent.[8] This is an improvement on the present laws of all the three jurisdictions studied which have tended to rely on metaphors to describe the required degree of lost self-control. Subsection (2)(c) contains another improvement of the law by stipulating that the provocation could have induced the ordinary person to have become enraged. This differs from the present laws in all three jurisdictions which require the ordinary person to have lost self-control. It has been suggested in this work that this test of enragement is a more comprehensible, practicable and just test to apply than the one based on lost self-control.[9]

Subsection (2)(c) contains another improvement to the present laws in that it requires the mode of killing selected by the accused

---

[5]Under English and Australian laws, the expression 'culpable homicide not amounting to murder' should be replaced with 'manslaughter'.

[6]Under English and Australian laws, the expression 'culpable homicide not amounting to murder' should be replaced with 'manslaughter'.

[7]There are presently six illustrations marked (a) to (f) accompanying Exception 1 to Section 300.

[8]See this work at pp. 48–9.

[9]See this work at pp. 99–101.

to have been one which could have been performed by an ordinary person placed in the same circumstances as the accused. This is the modal rule,[10] distinguishable from the reasonable relationship rule, the latter of which is not a requirement of the defence, as is clearly indicated in subsection (4)(a).[11] Illustration (a) contains factual examples of the difference between these two rules. While on the subject of the accused's reaction to the provocation, it is observed that subsection (4)(b) declares that it is unnecessary for the accused to have killed the provoker immediately after the provocative incident.[12] Both illustrations (c) and (d) show that the defence is available even though a time interval had transpired between the provocation and the killing so long as the accused was still deprived of self-control when the offence was committed.

The nature of the ordinary person test is elaborated upon in subsection (3), where the division is made between the accused's personal characteristics affecting the gravity of the provocation and those causing enragement to the ordinary person.[13] Illustration (b) provides a factual example of the operation of the subsection. In England and Australia, where practical problems of proof are likely to prevent the accused's ethnic, cultural or social background to be taken into account in an intelligible way, it has been suggested in this work that these characteristics should not be attributed to the ordinary person.[14] Accordingly, the accused's age alone may be attributed to the ordinary person when assessing whether such a person might become enraged. Subsection (3) and illustration (b) will need to be modified to reflect this position in those two jurisdictions.

As for what may constitute provocation in law, subsection (2)(b) makes it clear that 'grossly insulting words' alone might suffice[15]

---

[10]See this work at pp. 106–7.

[11]See this work at pp. 101–2.

[12]See this work at pp. 51–6.

[13]See this work at pp. 59–60 where the discussion is in terms of an ordinary person losing self-control rather than becoming enraged. The discussion on characteristics attributable to the ordinary person is unaffected by whether the law opts to retain the loss of self-control test or to replace it with the enraged test.

[14]See this work at pp. 92. However, an exception could be made in respect of Australian Aboriginal accused persons residing in geographically isolated Aboriginal communities.

[15]See this work at pp. 15–21.

and the concluding words of subsection (2) state that the provocative conduct may be cumulative.[16] Illustration (c) affords a factual example of cumulative provocation. There is also subsection (4)(c) which permits hearsay provocation to support the defence provided that the report could be reasonably believed.[17] A case example of this is given in illustration (d). Finally, subsection (5) specifies four types of provocative conduct which will not be permitted to support the defence. These are provocation sought by the accused as an excuse to harm a person,[18] provocation which was a predictable result of the accused's own conduct,[19] provocation comprising lawful acts done in discharge of a public legal duty or in obedience to law, and provocation constituting lawful acts performed in private defence.[20]

## 2. Excessive Self-Defence

In chapter 3, I noted that the English common law has refused to recognize a defence of excessive self-defence which reduces a charge of murder to manslaughter.[21] However, recent English law reform bodies have been persuaded by the Australian common law development instanced in cases like *Howe* and *Viro* to propose recognition of such a defence.[22] Unfortunately for the Australian law, a majority of the High Court of Australia in the recent case of *Zecevic* chose to abrogate the defence. They did so primarily out of concern over the jury's inability to comprehend the distinction between excessive self-defence and the general plea of self-defence. This work has examined this and the other reasons of the majority and found them wanting.[23] Much more persuasive were the arguments based on legal principle and notions of justice which the minority judges in *Zecevic* relied on in support of the defence.[24] The role of excessive self-defence in the law of homicide

---

[16]See this work at pp. 21–7.
[17]See this work at pp. 27–32.
[18]See this work at pp. 32–40.
[19]See this work at pp. 34–40.
[20]See this work at pp. 40–6.
[21]See this work at pp. 135–9.
[22]See this work at pp. 139–141.
[23]See this work at pp. 149–154.
[24]See this work at pp. 154–7.

was reaffirmed when we examined the interrelationship between excessive self-defence and the general plea of self-defence and the different functions that each served.[25] Further support for recognizing the defence came from the strong arguments in favour of treating excessive self-defence as an exculpatory plea rather than merely a mitigating factor in sentencing.[26]

As for selecting an existing formulation upon which to base a model provision, the Australian common law formulation has proven unduly complicated in practice. Certainly, the various suggestions for improvement by the minority judges in *Zecevic* are a possibility although they are more expositional of the law than propositional in nature.[27] A more functional formulation may be the one found in Irish law as expressed by the Irish Supreme Court decision in *People (A-G) v Dwyer*:

> A person is entitled to protect himself from unlawful attack. If, in doing so, he uses no more force than is reasonably necessary, he is acting lawfully and commits no crime even though he kills his assailant. If he uses more force than may objectively be considered necessary, his act is unlawful and, if he kills, the killing is unlawful.... [H]owever, if his intention in doing the unlawful act was primarily to defend himself [that is, if he exercises no more force than he honestly believes to be necessary in the circumstances], the killing, though unlawful, would be manslaughter only.[28]

Besides these judicial models, there are those contained in legislation or proposed by law reform bodies. One of these is the recent South Australian legislation recognizing the doctrine of excessive self-defence, although that model contains features which are contentious or morally disputable in certain respects.[29] However, the same cannot be said of the proposal by the English Law Commission codifying the criminal law. The proposal, with some minor embellishments, reads:

> A person who would be guilty of murder is guilty only of manslaughter if, at the time of his act, he honestly believes the use of force which causes death to be necessary and reasonable in the circumstances, but

---

[25]See this work at pp. 169–71.

[26]See this work at pp. 171–3

[27]See this work at pp. 158–60.

[28]This direction is derived from the certified question before the court [1972] IR 416, p. 419, which it unanimously approved of, and from Justice Butler's ruling, pp. 429–30.

[29]See this work at pp. 160–4.

the force exceeds that which is necessary and reasonable in the circumstances which exist or (where there is a difference) in those which he believes to exist.[30]

Alternatively, Exception 2 to Section 300 of the Indian Penal Code might constitute a viable model. The provision appears to have worked reasonably well in practice except for the troubling inclusion of the expression 'in good faith' in both the Exception and the illustration accompanying it.[31] This work has suggested amending the Exception and illustration to exclude all references to 'in good faith'. The revised provision and illustration could then read as follows:

Culpable homicide is not murder if the offender, in the exercise of the right of private defence of person or property, exceeds the power given to him by law, and causes the death of the person against whom he is exercising such a right of defence, without premeditation and without any intention of doing more harm than is necessary for the purpose of such defence.[32]

*Illustration*

Z attempts to horse-whip A, not in such a manner as to cause grievous hurt to A. A, in the exercise of the right of private defence, draws out a pistol. Z persists in the assault. A, honestly believing that he can by no other means prevent himself from being horse-whipped, shoots Z dead. A has not committed murder but only culpable homicide not amounting to murder.[33]

Either the English law reform proposal or the slightly modified Indian provision could be a workable model provision for adoption by English and Australian lawmakers.

A closing observation may be made. This study has covered only a small area of the criminal law. It would, however, have been obvious to the reader that the comparative analysis of the laws of India, England and Australia has permitted the strengths

---

[30]For the original unaltered version, see this work at p. 140. Under the Indian law, the expression 'manslaughter' should be replaced with 'culpable homicide not amounting to murder'.

[31]See this work at pp. 123–5, 129–30.

[32]For the original unaltered version, see this work at p. 119.

[33]For the original unaltered version, see this work at p. 130. Under English and Australian laws, the expression 'culpable homicide not amounting to murder' should be replaced by 'manslaughter'.

and weaknesses of the present laws on provocation and excessive self-defence to be clearly identified. This has in turn promoted ways of improving the laws. The general lesson then for law reformers and judges is that they should make every possible effort to engage in similar comparative exercises when dealing with all spheres of the criminal law.

## Postscript

In October 1997, the New South Wales Law Reform Commission delivered its report on *Partial Defences to Murder: Provocation and Infanticide* (Report 83). Unfortunately, it was too late for a detailed discussion of this report to be included in the main body of this work. However, it may be said that many of the Commission's recommendations are identical to those suggested in the model provision presented in this chapter. The Commission proposed retaining much of section 23 of the *Crimes Act* (NSW) at the same time making several proposals for improvement. One was the inclusion of a clause stating that provocative conduct could occur outside of the accused's presence provided the accused believed on reasonable grounds that the deceased had offered the provocation. This is covered in subsection (4) (c) of my model provision. Another was the inclusion of a clause which clearly states that the defence is unavailable in a case where the accused had provoked the deceased with a premeditated intention to kill or to inflict grievous bodily harm. This is covered by subsection (5) (a) of my model provision. Yet another proposal was a clause which made clear that the defence is not excluded on the basis that the provocation was lawful. This is covered with greater specificity in subsections (5) (c) and (d) of my model provision.

A major proposal of the Commission which differs from my model provision is the abolition of the ordinary person test. In its place, the Commission suggested that the trier of fact be left to decide whether 'the accused, taking into account all of his or her characteristics and circumstances, should be excused for having so far lost self-control as to have formed an intent to kill or to inflict grievous bodily harm ...as to warrant the reduction of murder to manslaughter'. It is observed that this proposal is closely similar to the one suggested by the Victorian Law Reform Commission and English Criminal Law Revision Committee (discussed on pages 84 and 85 of this work). The same criticism made in that discussion of the unacceptable vagueness of this formula applies with equal force to the New South Wales Law Reform Commission's recommendation.

# Appendices

# Indian Provisions on Private Defence

## Indian Penal Code

### Right of Private Defence

96. Nothing is an offence which is done in the exercise of the right of private defence.
97. Every person has a right, subject to the restrictions contained in Section 99, to defend—
    (1) his own body, and the body of any other person, against any offence affecting the human body;
    (2) the property, whether movable or immovable, of himself or of any other person, against any act which is an offence falling under the definition of theft, robbery, mischief, or criminal trespass, or which is an attempt to commit theft, robbery, mischief, or criminal trespass.
98. When an act, which would otherwise be a certain offence, is not that offence, by reason of the youth, the want of maturity of understanding, the unsoundness of mind, or the intoxication of the person doing that act, or by reason of any misconception on the part of that person, every person has the same right of private defence against that act which he would have if the act were that offence.

### Illustrations
(a) Z, under the influence of madness, attempts to kill A. Z is guilty of no offence. But A has the same right of private defence which he would have if Z were sane.

(b) A enters, by night, a house which he is legally entitled to enter. Z, in good faith, taking A for a housebreaker, attacks A. Here Z, by attacking A under this misconception, commits no offence. But A has the same right of private defence against Z, which he would have if Z were not acting under that misconception.

99. (1) There is no right of private defence against an act which does not reasonably cause the apprehension of death or of grievous hurt, if done, or attempted to be done, by a public servant acting in good faith under colour of his office, though that act may not be strictly justifiable by law.

(2) There is no right of private defence against an act which does not reasonably cause the apprehension of death or of grievous hurt, if done, or attempted to be done, by the direction of a public servant acting in good faith under colour of his office, though that direction may not be strictly justifiable by law.

(3) There is no right of private defence in cases in which there is time to have recourse to the protection of the public authorities.

(4) The right of private defence in no case extends to the infliction of more harm than it is necessary to inflict for the purpose of defence.

*Explanation 1.* — A person is not deprived of the right of private defence against an act done, or attempted to be done, by a public servant, as such, unless he knows, or has reason to believe, that the person doing the act is such public servant.

*Explanation 2.* — A person is not deprived of the right of private defence against an act done, or attempted to be done, by the direction of a public servant, unless he knows, or has reason to believe, that the person doing the act is acting by such direction; or unless such person states the authority under which he acts, or, if he has authority in writing unless he produces such authority, if demanded.

100. The right of private defence of the body extends, under the restrictions mentioned in Section 99, to the voluntary causing of death or of any other harm to the assailant, if the offence which occasions the exercise of the right is of any of the following descriptions:

(1) such an assault as may reasonably cause the apprehension that death will otherwise be the consequence of such assault;

(2) such an assault as may reasonably cause the apprehension that grievous hurt will otherwise be the consequence of such assault;

(3) an assault with the intention of committing rape;

(4) an assault with the intention of gratifying unnatural lust;

(5) an assault with the intention of kidnapping or abducting;

(6) an assault with the intention of wrongfully confining a person, under circumstances which may reasonably cause him to apprehend that he will be unable to have recourse to the public authorities for his release.

101. If the offence is not of any of the descriptions enumerated in Section 100, the right of private defence of the body does not extend to the voluntary causing of death to the assailant, but does extend, under the restrictions mentioned in Section 99, to the voluntary causing to the assailant of any harm other than death.

102. The right of private defence of the body commences as soon as a reasonable apprehension of danger to the body arises from an attempt or threat to commit the offence, though the offence may not have been committed; and it continues as long as such apprehension of danger to the body continues.

103. The right of private defence of property extends, under the restrictions mentioned in Section 99, to the voluntary causing of death or of any other harm to the wrongdoer, if the offence, the committing of which, or the attempting to commit which, occasions the exercise of the right, is an offence of any of the following descriptions:

(1) robbery;

(2) housebreaking by night;

(3) mischief by fire committed on any building, tent, or vessel, which building, tent, or vessel is used as a human dwelling, or as a place for the custody of property;

(4) theft, mischief, or house-trespass, under such circumstances as may reasonably cause apprehension that death or grievous hurt will be the consequence, if such right of private defence is not exercised.

104. If the offence, the committing of which, or the attempting to

commit which, occasions the exercise of the right of private defence, is theft, mischief, or criminal trespass, not of any of the descriptions enumerated in Section 103, that right does not extend to the voluntary causing of death, but does extend, subject to the restrictions mentioned in Section 99, to the voluntary causing to the wrongdoer of any harm other than death.

105. (1) The right of private defence of property commences when a reasonable apprehension of danger to the property commences.

(2) The right of private defence of property against theft continues till the offender has effected his retreat with the property, or till the assistance of the public authorities is obtained, or till the property has been recovered.

(3) The right of private defence of property against robbery continues as long as the offender causes or attempts to cause to any person death, or hurt, or wrongful restraint, or as long as the fear of instant death, or of instant hurt, or of instant personal restraint continues.

(4) The right of private defence of property against criminal trespass or mischief, continues as long as the offender continues in the commission of criminal trespass or mischief.

(5) The right of private defence of property against housebreaking by night continues as long as house-trespass which has been begun by such housebreaking.

106. If, in the exercise of the right of private defence against an assault which reasonably causes the apprehension of death, the defender is so situated that he cannot effectually exercise that right without risk of harm to an innocent person, his right of private defence extends to the running of that risk.

### *Illustration*

A is attacked by a mob who attempt to murder him. He cannot effectually exercise his right of private defence without firing on the mob, and he cannot fire without risk of harming young children who are mingled with the mob. A commits no offence if by so firing he harms any of the children.

# Appendix II

# South Australian Provisions of Defence of Person and Property

## Criminal Law Consolidation Act 1936 (SA), as amended by the Criminal Law Consolidation (Self Defence) Amendment Act 1997 (SA)

## Acts directed at the defence of life, bodily integrity or liberty

15. (1) It is a defence to a charge of an offence if—
    (a) the defendant genuinely believed the conduct to which the charge relates to be necessary and reasonable for a defensive purpose; and
    (b) the conduct was, in the circumstances as the defendant genuinely believed them to be, reasonably proportionate to the threat that the defendant genuinely believed to exist.

    (2) It is a partial defence to a charge of murder (reducing the offence to manslaughter) if—
    (a) the defendant genuinely believed the conduct to which the charge relates to be necessary and reasonable for a defensive purpose; but
    (b) the conduct was not, in the circumstances as the defendant genuinely believed them to be, reasonably proportionate to the threat that the defendant genuinely believed to exist.

    (3) For the purposes of this section, a person acts for a defensive purpose if the person acts—
    (a) in self defence or in defence of another; or

(b) to prevent or terminate the unlawful imprisonment of himself, herself or another.

(4) However, if a person —

    (a) resists another who is purporting to exercise a power of arrest or some other power of law enforcement; or

    (b) resists another who is acting in response to an unlawful act against person or property committed by the person or to which the person is a party,

the person will not be taken to be acting for a defensive purpose unless the person genuinely believes, on reasonable grounds, that the other person is acting unlawfully.

(5) If a defendant raises a defence under this section, the defence is taken to have been established unless the prosecution establishes beyond reasonable doubt that the defendant is not entitled to the defence.

## Defence of Property, etc.

**15A.** (1) It is a defence to a charge of an offence if—

    (a) the defendant genuinely believed the conduct to which the charge relates to be necessary and reasonable—

        (i) to protect property from unlawful appropriation, destruction, damage or interference; or

        (ii) to prevent criminal trespass to land or premises, or to remove from land or premises a person who is committing a criminal trespass; or

        (iii) to make or assist in the lawful arrest of an offender or alleged offender or a person who is unlawfully at large; and

    (b) if the conduct resulted in death—the defendant did not intend to cause death nor did the defendant act recklessly realizing that the conduct could result in death; and

    (c) the conduct was, in the circumstances as the defendant genuinely believed them to be, reasonably proportionate to the threat that the defendant genuinely believed to exist.

(2) It is a partial defence to a charge of murder (reducing the offence to manslaughter) if—

   (a) the defendant genuinely believed the conduct to which the charge relates to be necessary and reasonable—

      (i) to protect property from unlawful appropriation, destruction, damage or interference; or

      (ii) to prevent criminal trespass to land or premises, or to remove from land or premises a person who is committing a criminal trespass; or

      (iii) to make or assist in the lawful arrest of an offender or alleged offender a person who is unlawfully at large; and

   (b) the defendant did not intend to cause death; but

   (c) the conduct was not, in the circumstances as the defendant genuinely believed them to be, reasonably proportionate to the threat that the defendant genuinely believed to exist.

(3) For the purposes of this section, a person commits a criminal trespass if the person trespasses on land or premises—

   (a) with the intention of committing an offence against a person or property (or both); or

   (b) in circumstances where the trespass itself constitutes an offence.

(4) If a defendant raises a defence under this section, the defence is taken to have been established unless the prosecution establishes beyond reasonable doubt that the defendant is not entitled to the defence.

# Appendix III

# English Law Commission Provisions on Public and Private Defence

## Law Commission No 177, A Criminal Code for England and Wales (1989), Draft Criminal Code

### Use of Force in Public or Private Defence

44. (1) A person does not commit an offence by using such force as, in the circumstances which exist or which he believes to exist, is immediately necessary and reasonable—

    (a) to prevent or terminate crime, or to effect or assist in the lawful arrest of an offender or suspected offender or of a person unlawfully at large;

    (b) to prevent or terminate a breach of the peace;

    (c) to protect himself or another from unlawful force or unlawful personal harm;

    (d) to prevent or terminate the unlawful detention of himself or another;

    (e) to protect property (whether belonging to himself or another) from unlawful appropriation, destruction or damage; or

    (f) to prevent or terminate a trespass to his person or property.

    (2) In this section, except where the context otherwise requires, 'force' includes, in addition to force against a person—

    (a) force against property;

    (b) a threat of force against person or property; and

    (c) the detention of a person without the use of force.

(3) For the purposes of this section, an act is 'unlawful' although a person charged with an offence in respect of it would be acquitted on the ground only that —

    (a) he was under ten years of age; or

    (b) he lacked the fault required for the offence or believed that an exempting circumstance existed; or

    (c) he acted in pursuance of a reasonable suspicion; or

    (d) he acted under duress, whether by threats of circumstances; or

    (e) he was in a state of automatism or suffering from severe mental illness or severe mental handicap.

(4) Notwithstanding subsection (1), a person who believes circumstances to exist which would justify or excuse the use of force under that subsection has no defence if —

    (a) he knows that the force is used against a constable or a person assisting a constable; and

    (b) the constable is acting in the execution of his duty, unless he believes the force to be immediately necessary to prevent personal harm to himself or another.

(5) A person does not commit an offence by doing an act immediately preparatory to the use of such force as is referred to in subsection (1).

(6) Subsection (1) does not apply where a person causes unlawful conduct or an unlawful state of affairs with a view to using force to resist or terminate it; but subsection (1) may apply although the occasion for the use of force arises only because he does anything he may lawfully do, knowing that such an occasion may arise.

(7) The fact that a person had an opportunity to retreat before using force shall be taken into account, in conjunction with other relevant evidence, in determining whether the use of force was immediately necessary and reasonable.

(8) A threat of force may be reasonable although the use of force would not be.

(9) This section is without prejudice to the generality of section 185 (criminal damage: protection of person or property) or any other defence.

## Use of Excessive Force

59.　A person who, but for this section, would be guilty of murder
is not guilty of murder if, at any time of his act, he believes
the use of the force which causes death to be necessary and
reasonable to effect a purpose referred to in Section 44 (use
of force in public or private defence), but the force exceeds
that which is necessary and reasonable in the circumstances
which exist or (where there is a difference) in those which he
believes to exist.

# Bibliography

Ashworth, A., 'Self-Induced Provocation and the Homicide Act', *Criminal Law Review* 483 (1973).

——————'The Doctrine of Provocation', 35 *Cambridge Law Journal* 292 (1973).

Bose, V., 'The Migration of the Common Law: India'. 76 *Law Quarterly Review* 59 (1960).

Brett, P., 'The Physiology of Provocation', *Criminal Law Review* 634 (1970).

Brown, B., 'The "Ordinary Man" in Provocation: Anglo-Saxon Attitudes and "Unreasonable Non-Englishmen"', 13 *International and Comparative Law Quarterly* 203 (1964).

Cameron, C.H. and D. Eliott, *The First and Second Reports on the Indian Penal Code as Originally Framed in 1837*, Madras: Higginbotham and Co. (1888).

Chan, W., 'A Feminist Critique of Self-Defense and Provocation in Battered Women's Cases in England and Wales', 6 *Women and Criminal Justice* 39 (1994).

Charleton, P., *Offences Against the Person*, Dublin: The Round Hall Press (1992).

Criminal Law and Penal Methods Reform Committee of South Australia, Fourth Report, *The Substantive Criminal Law*, Adelaide (1977).

Criminal Law Revision Committee, 14th Report, *Offences Against the Person*, Cmnd 7844, London: HMSO (1980).

Dressler, J., 'New Thoughts about the Concept of Justification in the Criminal Law: A Critique of Fletcher's Thinking and Rethinking', 32 *UCLA Law Review* 6i (1984).

——————'Justifications and Excuses: A Brief Review of the Concept and the Literature', 33 *Wayne Law Review* 1155 (1987).

——————'Provocation: Partial Justification or Partial Excuse?', 51 *Modern Law Review* 467 (1988).

East, E.H., *A Treatise of the Pleas of the Crown*, Vol. I, London:

Macmillan (1803).

Editorial Note, 'The Cultural Defense in the Criminal Law', 99 *Harvard Law Review* 1293 (1986).

Edwards, S., 'Battered Women Who Kill', *New Law Journal* 1380 (1990).

Elliott, I., 'Excessive Self-defence in Commonwealth Law: A Comment', 22 *International and Comparative Law Quarterly* 727 (1973).

Eser, A., 'Justification and Excuse', 24 *American Journal of Comparative Law* 621(1976).

Fisse, B., *Howard's Criminal Law*, 5th edn, Sydney: Law Book Co. (1990).

——————, (ed.), *The Laws of Australia. Criminal Law: Homicide*, Sydney: LBC Information Services (1992).

Fisse, B., and P. Fairall, *The Laws of Australia. Criminal Offences: Homicide*, Vol. 10.1, Sydney: LBC Information Services (1996).

Foster, M., *Crown Law, Discourse II on Homicide* 2nd edn (1776), Abingdon, Oxfordshire: Professional Books (1982).

Glazebrook, P.R., 'The Categories of Manslaughter are Never Closed', 34 *Cambridge Law Journal* 14 (1975).

Gledhill, A., *The Penal Codes of Northern Nigeria and the Sudan*, London: Sweet and Maxwell (1963).

Goode, M., 'On Subjectivity and Objectivity in Denial of Criminal Responsibility: Reflections on Reading *Radford*', 11 *Criminal Law Journal* 131 (1987).

Gordon, G.H., *The Criminal Law of Scotland*, 2nd edn, Edinburgh: Green (1978).

Gour, H.S., *Gour's Penal Code of India*, Vol. III, 10th edn, Allahabad: Law Publishers (1983).

Grant, M., 'Self Defence in South Australia: A Subjective Dilemma', 16 *Adelaide Law Review* 309 (1994).

Hale, M., *The History of the Pleas of the Crown*, Vol. I (1736), London: Professional Books Ltd (1972).

Harrison, R., 'Excessive Use of Force in Self-Defence: *R v Clegg*', 59 *Journal Criminal Law* 281 (1995).

Hawkins, W., *A Treatise of the Pleas of the Crown*, Vol. I, 8th edn, London: Macmillan (1795).

Horder, J., 'The Duel and the English Law of Homicide', 12 *Oxford Journal of Legal Studies* 420 (1992).

——————*Provocation and Responsibility*, Oxford: Oxford University Press (1992).

——————, 'Provocation's Reasonable Man Reassessed', 112 *Law Quarterly Review* 49 (1996)

Horowitz, D., 'Justification and Excuse in the Program of the Criminal Law', 49 *Law and Contemporary Problems* 109 (1986).

Howard, C., 'An Australian Letter—Excessive Defence', *Criminal Law Review* 448 (1964).

——————, *Criminal Law* (4th edn, 1982), Sydney: Law Book Company

James, C., 'The Queensbury Rules of Self-Defence', 21 *International and Comparative Law Quarterly* 357 (1972).

Kadish, S., 'Respect for Life and Regard for Rights in the Criminal Law', 64 *California Law Review* 871 (1976).

Kaye, J.M., 'Early History of Murder and Manslaughter', 83 *Law Quarterly Review* 569 (1967).

Kelkar, R., 'Provocation as a Defence in the Indian Penal Code', 5 *Journal of the Indian Law Institute* 319 (1963).

Koh, K.L., C. Clarkson, and N. Morgan, *Criminal Law in Singapore and Malaysia: Text and Materials,* Singapore: Malayan Law Journal (1989).

Lanham, D., 'Provocation and the Requirement of Presence', 13 *Criminal Law Journal* 133 (1989).

Law Commission of India, 42nd Report, *Indian Penal Code,* New Delhi: Government Printers (1971).

Law Commission, No. 177, *A Criminal Code for England and Wales,* Vol. 2, London: HMSO (1989).

Law Reform Commission of Canada, Working Paper 33, *Homicide,* Ottawa (1984).

Law Reform Commission of Victoria, Report No. 40, *Homicide,* Melbourne (1991).

Law Reform Commissioner of Victoria, Report No. 12, *Provocation and Diminished Responsibility as Defences to Murder,* Melbourne (1982).

Leader-Elliott, I., 'Sex, Race and Provocation: In Defence of *Stingel*', 20 *Criminal Law Journal* 72 (1996).

Leigh, L.H., 'Manslaughter and the Limits of Self-Defence', 34 *Modern Law Review* 648 (1971).

Macaulay, T.B., J.M. Macleod, G.W. Anderson and F. Millett, *The Indian Penal Code as Originally Framed in 1837 with Notes,* Madras: Higginbotham and Co. (1888).

McAuley, F., 'Provocation: Partial Justification, Not Partial Excuse', in Yeo, S. (ed.), *Partial Excuses to Murder,* Sydney: Federation

Press (1991).

McColgan, A., 'In Defence of Battered Women Who Kill', *Oxford Journal of Legal Studies* 508 (1993).

Medani, A., 'Some Aspects of the Sudan Law Homicide', *Journal of African Law* 92 (1974).

Morgan, W. and A. MacPherson, *The Indian Penal Code with Notes,* London: G.C. Hay and Co. (1861).

Morris, N., 'The Slain Chicken Thief', *Sydney Law Review* 414 (1958).

Morris, N. and C. Howard, *Studies in Criminal Law,* Oxford: Clarendon Press (1964).

*Nelson's Indian Penal Code*, Vol. II, 7th edn, revised by Mulla S.N., and L.G. Gupta, Allahabad: Law Book Co. (1983).

Nicolson, D., 'Telling Tales: Gender Discrimination, Gender Construction and Battered Women Who Kill', 3 *Feminist Legal Studies* 185 (1995).

Nicolson, D. and R. Sanghvi, 'Battered Women and Provocation: The Implications of *R v Ahluwalia*', *Criminal Law Review* 728 (1993).

O'Brien, N., 'Excessive Self-defence: A Need for Legislation', 25 *Criminal Law Quarterly* 441 (1982-83).

O'Connor, D. and P. Fairall, *Criminal Defences,* 1st edn, Sydney: Law Book Company (1984).

Odgers, S., 'Contemporary Provocation Law—Is Substantially Impaired Self-Control Enough?', in Yeo, S. (ed.), *Partial Excuses to Murder,* Sydney: Federation Press (1991).

Omichinski, N., 'Applying the Theories of Justifiable Homicide to Conflicts in the Doctrine of Self-Defence', 33 *Wayne Law Review* 1446 (1987).

Patra, A.C., 'An Historical Introduction to the Indian Penal Code', 3 *Journal of the Indian Law Institute* 351 (1961).

Review of Commonwealth Law, Interim Report, *Principles of Criminal Responsibility and Other Matters,* Canberra: AGPS (1990).

Samuels, A., 'Excusable Loss of Self-Control in Homicide', 34 *Modern Law Review* 163 (1971).

Smith, J.C., 'Case Comment on *Palmer*', *Criminal Law Review.*

Smith, J.C. and B. Hogan, *Criminal Law,* 4th edn, London: Butterworths (1978).

————*Criminal Law,* 7th edn, London: Butterworths (1992).

Smith, P., 'Excessive Defence--A Rejection of an Australian

Initiative?', *Criminal Law Review* 524 (1972).

Sornarajah, M., 'Excessive Self-defence in Commonwealth Law', 21 *International and Comparative Law Quarterly* 758 (1972).

Stephen, J.F., *A History of the Criminal Law of England*, Vol. III, London: Macmillan (1883).

—, *Digest of the Criminal Law* 3rd edn, London: Macmillan (1883).

Taylor, L., 'Provoked Reason in Men and Women: Heat-Passion Manslaughter and Imperfect Self-Defense, 33 *UCLA Law Review* 1679 (1986).

Thomas, D.A. 'Form and Function in Criminal Law', in P.R. Glazebrook (ed.), *Reshaping the Criminal Law*, 21, London: Stevens (1978).

Trevalyan, G.O. *The Life and Letters of Lord Macaulay*, Vol. I, London: Longmans, Green and Co. (1920).

Wasik, M., 'Cumulative Provocation and Domestic Killing', *Criminal Law Review* 932 (1982).

———, 'Partial Excuses in the Criminal Law', 45 *Modern Law Review* 516 (1982).

Weisbrot, D., 'Homicide Law Reform in New South Wales', 6 *Criminal Law Journal* 248 (1982).

Williams, G., *Textbook of Criminal Law*, 2nd edn, London: Stevens (1983).

Woods, G., 'The Sanctity of Murder, Reforming the Homicide Penalty in New South Wales', 57 *Australian Law Journal* 161(1983).

Yeo, S., 'Ethnicity and the Objective Test in Provocation', 16 *Melbourne University Law Review* 67 (1987).

———, *Compulsion in the Criminal Law*, Sydney: Law Book Co. (1990).

———, 'Power of Self-Control in Provocation and Automatism', 14 *Sydney Law Review* 3 (1992).

———, Case Comment on *Peisley* 16 *Criminal Law Journal* 197 (1992).

——— 'Recent Australian Pronouncements on the Ordinary Person Test in Provocation and Automatism', 33 *Criminal Law Quarterly* 280 (1992).

———, 'Rethinking 'Good Faith' in Excessive Private Defence', 30 *Journal of the Indian Law Institute* 443 (1988).

———, 'Sex, Ethnicity, Power of Self-Control and Provocation Revisited', *18 Sydney Law Review* 304 (1996).

————, 'The Role of Gender in the Law of Provocation', 26 *Anglo-American Law Review* 431 (1997).
Zweigert, K. and H. Kotz, *Introduction to Comparative Law*, Vol. 1, 2nd edn, Oxford: Clarendon Press (1987).

# Index

Aboriginal enclaves 83, 84
adultery, as provocation 15–17, 20,
    41, 42, 43
age
    as personal characteristic 68–9,
        9n.233, 70, 72, 77–9, 81,
        82, 89, 181
    and self-control, *See* self-control
Aickin, Justice 145
anger
    in battered women 50–1
    and self-control, loss of 49–51
Australia
    courts of 7
    judges of 7
    law of. *See* Australian law *below*
Australian law
    defence of person under. *See*
        excessive self-defence
    defence of property under. *See*
        excessive self-defence
    ethnicity as personal characteristic
        under 79–81
    excessive self-defence under. *See*
        excessive self-defence
    influence of English law on 3, 5,
        7, 9
    influence of Indian law on 7
    Modal rule under 109–11
    ordinary person test under 56, 84–
        5
    provocation under
        cumulative 24–5

defence of 1, 9, 10, 114–15
    definition of 11–12
    in defendant's presence 28–31
    gravity of, characteristics
        affecting 75–7
    lawful acts, not amounting to
        42–4, 103–4, 109
    self-induced 36–9
    words as 16–17
reasonable relation rule under
    103–4, 109
self-control under
    age affecting 70, 77, 79
    characteristics affecting 77–84
    and ethnicity, effect of 79–81,
        92
    in men 70, 79
    in women 70, 79
self-defence under 190–1. *See also*
    excessive self-defence
Australian Commonwealth Criminal
    Law, Review 165, 167n.173
automatism, state of 48

Barwick, Chief Justice 103, 110
battered women 12n.7, 50,
    50n.163, 51, 52n.171, 53–
    4, 54n.179, 55, 144
Beg, Justice 19, 88, 91n.319
Bertram, Justice 26n.65
blackmail, as provocation 34–5

Cockburn, Chief Justice 137

Code, Indian Penal. *See* Indian Penal Code
Code framer's test of grave provocation 95, 96-7, 98-101, 111
  criticism of 99n.338
  vs. ordinary person test 98-9
Commission
  Criminal Code Bill (1879) 141
    Engish law, on codification of criminal law 73-4, 183
  Law
    of England 140
    of India 131
    Reform, of Victoria 84, 116, 164, 164n.171, 165
Committee, Criminal Law Revision, 73, 74, 84, 102-3, 104, 115 139-40
Comparative law, aim of 2
Coss, Graeme 38
Court of Criminal Appeal of Ceylon 96
Criminal Code Bill Commission 141
*Criminal Law* 63
Criminal Law Commissioners, report of 34, 34n.92
Criminal Law Revision Committee 73, 74, 84, 102-3, 139-40
culpable homicide not amounting to murder 1, 10, 13, 119, 121-2, 127, 129, 164, 164n.171, 170, 177n.1
cultural
  enclaves 79, 92. *See also* Aboriginal enclaves
  subgroups, violent 67-8, 76, 88, 93
  cumulative provocation. *See* provocation

Dawson, Justice 148, 149, 150

Dean, Justice 154, 155, 157, 158-60
defence of provocation. *See* provocation
defendant's presence and provocation. *See* provocation
Delvin, Justice 21, 47, 52
Digest of the Law of Offences against the Person 34
diminished responsibility 172, 172n.195
Diplock, Lord 48, 59, 63, 68, 69, 72, 78, 102, 109
Dixon, Chief Justice 149
domestic violence, Task Force on 25n.58
drunkenness as defence, rejection of 33n.89
duelling, institution of 68, 77

*East's Pleas of the Crown 107*
enclaves
  cultural 79, 92
  Aboriginal 83, 84
English Court of Appeal 11, 36
English Criminal Law Revision Committee 73, 74, 84 104, 115, 139-40
English judges 6
Engish law
  defence of person under. *See* excessive self-defence
  defence of property. *See* excessive self-defence
  excessive self-defence under. *See* excessive self-defence
  influence on Australian law 3, 5, 7, 9
  influence on Indian law 4, 5
  modal rule under 108-9
  ordinary person test under 56, 73 5
  provocation under
    adultery as 15, 17

cumulative 21–3
defence of 1–9, 10, 68
in defendants presence 27–8
definition of 11
gravity of, characteristics affecting 63–8
lawful acts, not mounting to 40–2
self-induced 33–6
words as 15–16, 16n.19, 17
reasonable relationship rule under 102–3
self-control under
age affecting 68–9, 69n.233, 72
characteristics affecting 63–4, 65, 68–73
ethnicity and 72–3, 92
in men 69–71, 72
in women 70, 79
English Law Commission, on criminal law 73–4, 183
ethnic communities 71–2
self-control in 89–93
ethnicity
and equality 81–2
as personal characteristic 71, 72, 79, 80–1, 82–3, 89–92, 115, 181
and self-control 99–100
under Australian law 79–82, 92
under English law 72–3, 92
under Indian law 89–91
excessive killing. *See* excessive self defence *below*
excessive self-defence, doctrine of 6, 117, 144, 167, 169, 170, 174–5
Australian law under 117–18, 141–8, 174, 175
as partial defence 144
reform proposals 160–5
rejection of 148–54

defence of 154–60
degree of force in 168, 169
English law under 3, 118, 134 41, 143, 174, 175
recognition under 134–5
reforms favouring 139–41
rejection under 135–9, 141
exculpatory plea as 171–3
full defence as 170–1
honest belief in 153–4, 157, 169, 170
under Indian law 6, 119–35, 174–5
'in good faith' 119, 123–4, 157, 169, 184
criticism of 124–5
interpretations of 126–31
Irish law under 151, 165–7
malice aforethought in 155, 170, 173
model provisions for 182–5
partial defence as 167, 170, 171–2
moral values and 167–8
reasonable belief and 146, 147, 148, 151, 157, 158–9. *See also Viro* propositions
rejection of 148–54
sentencing factor in 171–4
excusatory self-defence 167–70

fear
in battered women 50–1
and self-defence 49–50
fixed penalty, for murder 171–2
force, in self-defence 168, 169

Gaudron, Justice 154, 155
gestures as provocation 14, 42, 43, 86, 86n.296
Gleeson, Chief Justice 48
Goddard, Lord 136
Goff, Lord 66, 69

grave provocation 25–6
    Aboriginality and 83–4
    Code framers' test for 95, 96–7,
        98–101, 115
        criticism of 99n.338
        characteristics affecting 59–60
            61, 63, 66, 67, 68, 93
        under Australian law 75–7
        under English law 63–8
        under Indian law 86–8, 106
    definition of 96–7, 98
Gray, Justice 145

hearsay provocation 27, 28, 29–32
homicide, culpable. *See* culpable
    homicide
honest belief, in excessive self-defence
        153–4, 157, 169, 170
    under Indian law 127, 132, 133
human fraility, concession to
        35n.100, 42, 107

illustrations
    in Indian law 129–30
    in model provision 179–80
Indian judges 7–8, 9
Indian law
    defence of person under. *See*
        private defence of person
    defence of person under. *See*
        private defence of property
    English law, influence on 4, 5
    ethnicity as personal characteristic
        89–92
    illustrations in 129–30
    influence on Australian judges 7
    lawful acts, not amounting to 45–6
    modal rule under 111–13, 114
    ordinary person test under 57,
        45–6
    provocation under 18, 45–6
        cumulative 25–6, 26n.65, 27,
        113

defence of 1, 9, 10, 113–14,
    115
defendant's presence in 31–2
definition of 13–14
gravity, characteristics affecting
    86–8, 106
hearsay 31–2
reasonable relationship rule under
    104–6
self-control under
    characteristics affecting 88–92
    ethnicity and 98–91
    sudden loss of 54, 55
self-defence under 6, 119–35, 174,
    175
self-induced 39–40
words as 17–21
induced provocation. *See* provocation
Indian Penal Code 3, 4, 7, 9, 18, 20,
    25, 45, 46, 51, 85, 97, 98,
    113, 114, 117–34, 167,
    173–5, 186–9. *See also
    individual* entries on Indian
    law
'in good faith'. *See under* excessive
    self-defence
Irish law, excessive self-defence under
    151, 165–7

Jacobs, Justice 149, 150
jury, role of 36, 41
justificatory self-defence 167–70, 171

King, Chief Justice 11

Law Commission
    of England, proposals of 140
    of India, recommendations on the
        Exception 92–3, 131
Law Commissioners' Digest of 1839
    41
law
    of Australia. *See* Australian
        law

of Eire. *See* Irish law
of England. *See* English law
of India. *See* Indian law
and moral evaluation 167
of provocation. *See* provocation
of self-defence. *See* self-defence
Law Reform Commission of Victoria
report on Homicide 84, 116, 164 16n.171, 165
lawful self-defence 42, 42n.134, 44, 46

malice aforethought 155, 170, 173
Mason, Chief Justice 145, 150, 151, 156
*McGregor* test 87
in Australian law 75–6
in English law 65, 65n.217, 65n.221
McHugh, Justice 82
Menzies, Justice 149
migrants, self-control in 79, 80, 92
modal reasonable relationship rule 106n.361, 109

under Australian law 109–11
under English law 108–9
under Indian law 111–13, 114
and reasonable relationship rule, difference between 106–7
mode
of killing. *See* Modal rule
of retaliation 104. *See* also Modal rule
multicultural societies 9. *See also* ethnicity

New South Wales Task Force on domestic violence 25n.58
New South Wales Law reform commission on provocation 185

North, Justice 64–5

O'Brien, Justice 48
*Offences Against the person*, report on 73
ordinary person test 56–8, 58n.197, 59, 67, 74–5, 78, 95, 181
in Australian law 56
reform proposals 84–5
vs. Code framers' test 98–9
criticism of 60–1, 61n.206, 62
under English law 56
reform proposals 73–5
under Indian law 57, 85–93. *See also* Code framer's test
under New South Wales Crimes Act 57
previous provocation and 49
rationale behind 62
subjective evaluation of 59–60

Park, Justice 28
partial defence to murder. *See* provocation; excessive self-defence
Pearson, Lord 34, 35
personal
characteristics 57, 58, 59–63, 64–5, 66, 67, 93
age as 68–9, 69n.233, 70, 72, 77–9, 81, 82, 89, 181
ethnicity as 71, 72, 79, 80–1, 82–3, 89–92, 115, 181
meaning of 80
predictability, test of 34–5, 35n.100
private defence
law of 122, 128, 128n, 26, 129
of person, right of 119, 120, 120n.9, 121–3, 138, 140, 186–9
South Australian reform proposals regarding 161, 162

208 • *Index*

of property, right of 119, 120,
120n.10, 121, 122, 123,
139, 140, 142–3, 186–9,
191–2
South Australian reform proposals
on 161–2, 163
*See also* excessive self
defence
provocation 11–14
adultery as 41, 42, 43
anger and 49–50
blackmail as 34–5
contrived. *See* self-induced *below*
cumulative
under Australian law 24–5
under English law 21–3
under Indian law 25–6,
26n.65, 27, 113
defence of 1, 9, 10
in Australia 1, 9, 10, 114–15
in England 1, 9, 10, 68
in India 1, 9, 10, 113–14, 115
defendant's presence, in
under Australian law 28–31
under English law 27–8
under Indian law 31–2
definition of 11–12, 13–14, 47,
74
dual test of 10, 10n.3, 11, 13
gender-specific response to 51–6
gestures as 14, 42, 43, 86,
86n.296
gravity of. *See* grave provocation
hearsay 27, 28, 29–32
Indian law under. *See also* Indian
law
insulting words as 41, 42, 43, 181
last triggering incident as 24
law of 4, 9. *See also* individual
entries
lawful acts, not amounting to
under Australian law 42–4
under English law 40–2

under Indian law 45–6
lawful blows as 41
loss of self-control and. *See* self
control
model provisions on 6, 176–82
ordinary person test of. *See*
ordinary person test
previous 21, 22, 23, 24, 26n.65,
49. *See also* cumulative
provocation
reasonable belief and 31
reasonableness of 73
reasonable relationship rule of *See*
reasonable relationship rule
response to 93–4
retaliation and. *See* reasonable
relationship rule
risking of 35, 37, 38, 40. *See also*
self-induced below
self-induced 32–3, 37, 39
under Australian law 36–9
under English law 33–6
under Indian law 39–40
predicatability, test of 34–5,
35n.100
sudden 25, 26, 51, 55
suspicion based on 28
unlawful arrest as 42n.133
words as. *See under* words

rage vs. loss of self control 95–6, 97
reasonable belief, elements of 31,
145–6, 151
in excessive self-defence. *See*
excessive self-defence
person 57–8, 59, 85, 63–4
characteristics of 66, 69, 72
reasonable relationship rule 94,
101–2, 106, 109, 111,
112–3, 114
under Australian law 103–4,
109
under English law 102–3

under Indian law 104–6
and modal rule, difference between 106–7
retaliation and provocation. *See* reasonable relationship rule

self control
age factor in
under Australian law 70, 77–9
under English law 68–9, 69n.233, 72
average power of 100n.339
characteristics affecting 59–60, 61, 63, 68–73, 87, 89, 93
under Australian law 77–84
under English law 63–4, 65, 68–73
under Indian law 88–92
*McGregor* test for. See *McGregor* test
and ethinicity, effect on 60, 99n. 339
under Australian law 79–82m 92
under English law 72–3, 92
under Indian law 89–91
loss of 10, 10n.3
anger and 49–51
emotions underlying 49–51
extent of 48–9
induced 37. *See also* provocation, induced
mental element in 49
rage and 95, 95n.329, 96, 97. *See also* Code framers' test for grave provocation.
subjective nature of 46–7, 48
sudden 47, 51, 52, 54–5
men in
under Australian law 70 79
under English law 69–71, 72
senility affecting 78, 78n.267, 79n.268

migrants of 79, 80, 92
role of contemporary conditions in 77
women in
under Australian law 70, 79
under English law 69–71, 72
youthful immaturity affecting. *See* age factor *above*
self defence 1
body, right of. *See* private defence of person
excessive. *See* excessive self-defence
excessive force in 104n.335, 136
exculpating effect of 170, 171, 173
excusatory 167–70
fear and 49–50
general vs. excessive 170, 183
honest belief in 170
justification for 167–70
lawful 42, 42n.134, 44, 46
as partial plea 121–2, 142, 143, 170–1
of property, right of. *See* private defence of property
rejection of 148–54
self-induced provocation. *See* provocation
senility and loss of self-control 78, 78n.267, 79n.268
sentencing, for murder 171–4
Simon, Lord 69, 72
Simon, Viscount 101, 102, 103, 108
slow burn reaction. *See* battered women
Smith, Justice 24, 142
Stephen James Fitzjames 3, 4
Stephen, Justice 145
suspicion and provocation 28

Task Force on domestic violence 54
Tindal, Chief Justice 47
Toohey, Justice 148, 149, 150

unlawful arrest
  and excessive force 136
  as provocation 42n.133

violent subgroups 67–8, 76, 88, 93
*Viro.* propositions 145–7, 151, 152,
  158–9

Walsh, Justice 166
Wilson, Justice 148, 149, 150

women homicides 70–1. *See also*
  battered women
words, as provocation 14–15, 86,
  86n.296, 96n.332
  under Australian law 16–17
  under English law 15–16, 16n.19,
  17
  under Indian law 17–21
  violent, unaccompanied by
  conduct 18, 19

5